Discovering Radical Contingency

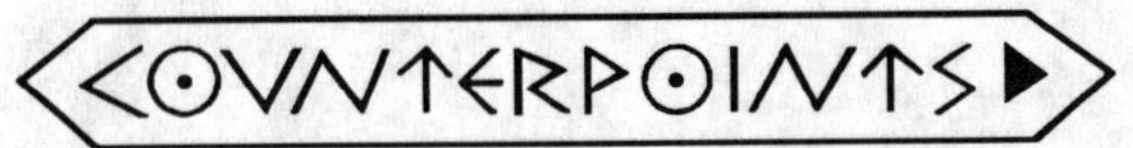

Studies in the Postmodern Theory of Education

Joe L. Kincheloe and Shirley R. Steinberg
General Editors

Vol. 81

PETER LANG
New York • Washington, D.C./Baltimore • Boston
Bern • Frankfurt am Main • Berlin • Vienna • Paris

Richard G. Bagnall

Discovering Radical Contingency

Building a Postmodern Agenda in Adult Education

PETER LANG
New York • Washington, D.C./Baltimore • Boston
Bern • Frankfurt am Main • Berlin • Vienna • Paris

Library of Congress Cataloging-in-Publication Data

Bagnall, R. G. (Richard Gordon).
Discovering radical contingency: building a postmodern agenda
in adult education / Richard G. Bagnall.
p. cm. — (Counterpoints; vol. 81)
Includes bibliographical references (p.) and index.
1. Adult education—Social aspects. 2. Postmodernism and education. I. Title.
II. Series: Counterpoints (New York, N.Y.); vol. 81.
LC5225.S64B34 374—dc21 97-48800
ISBN 0-8204-4001-9
ISSN 1058-1634

Die Deutsche Bibliothek-CIP-Einheitsaufnahme

Bagnall, Richard G.:
Discovering radical contingency: building a postmodern agenda in adult education /
Richard G. Bagnall. –New York; Washington, D.C./Baltimore; Boston;
Bern; Frankfurt am Main; Berlin; Vienna; Paris: Lang.
(Counterpoints; Vol. 81)
ISBN 0-8204-4001-9

Cover design by Andy Ruggirello.

The paper in this book meets the guidelines for permanence and durability
of the Committee on Production Guidelines for Book Longevity
of the Council of Library Resources.

Printed in the United States of America.

Contents

Preface

This work is, and is about, a search for meaning. It is, like its author, singular, yet it is also, like him, inextricably embedded in the contemporary cultural context. That context is grounded in the values, the verities, the questions, the ideologies, the certainties, the visions, and the actions of modernity. Its emergent superstructure, in contrast, is the increasingly postmodern world of anomie, uncertainty, difference, ambiguity, fragmentation, change, superficiality, and ephemerality: a world that not only seems to lack a sense of both history and a vision of the future, but which also seeps down and corrodes the modernist foundations upon which it has arisen.

As with the context, so with the author. My early scholarly work in adult education was firmly grounded in that modernist, indeed the positivist, clarity of purpose and process which still suffused all mainstream discourse in the 1970s—seemingly so naturally, properly, and triumphantly. That work encompassed: investigations of teaching the natural sciences through the engagement of learners as members of original research teams (1975, 1976, 1978a);[1] elucidatory attempts to transfer the adult education experiences of one country to the cultural development of another (1978b); the articulation of universal principles of adult education practice (1978c); and the advocacy of natural science educational programs for adults (1979).

It was also that epistemic framework which underpinned my early evaluation of classification systems of adult education events, and my initial search for the optimal taxonomic approach to the formulation of such systems (1983a, 1983b). That search, however, quickly revealed the problematic nature of the task (1980, 1983c). Given the artificial and potentially infinite heterogeneity of adult education events, it became increasingly clear that no classification system—and therefore no taxonomic theory and methodology—could be used in this field unless there was some generalizable basis upon which we could determine which of that heterogeneity was more properly adult educational and which was less. My search for such a basis—such a foundation—was fruitless: in retrospect an obvious outcome, but profoundly unsettling at the time. I had been enculturated into a world where the role of the academic was paramountly that of elucidating, articulating, and communicating the nature of reality: most notably of best practice in the case of adult education scholarship. I then saw the very concept of best practice disappear before my gaze—fragment into a potential infinity of different and possibly incommensurable best practices. How, then, was I to see my role as an academic? How was I to contribute scholarship of value to practice in the field of adult education? What, indeed, had become of the meaning of "adult education," now that its practice was to be seen as infinitely pluriform? In what might scholarly work now consist?

My initial intellectual response to these questions was one of uncertainty and despondency. I attempted to provide some more open-ended frameworks for the guidance of practice (1982, 1983d) and to reflect on the state of scholarship in the field (1983e), but such ventures were not sufficiently responsive to the newly perceived epistemic realities. Further cogitation led me to explore some of the traditional adult education verities from the perspective of an adult learner (1987a-c, 1988a, 1989a, 1989b). This work evolved into more confident and thoroughgoing critiques of traditional modernist ways of conceptualizing the field, in particular: the ideology of comprehensive surveys of provision and engagement (1988b); research into participation in adult education (1988c, 1989c, 1989d); conceptions of voluntary engagement in the field (1989e); the concept of "lifelong education" (1990a); the intrinsic nature of educational goals (1990b, 1991a); modernistic futures modeling (1990c); the modernistic emphasis on objectivity and its denial of cultural relativism (1991b); traditional perceptions of classification systems in the field (1990d); and the contemporary fetishes for skills training of adult educators (1990e), a contractualist approach to adult education programming (1992a, 1992b), and outcomes-driven, including competency-based, education (1994a).

Emergent from this work was a perception of the possible value of a liberal adult education framework—one refined to focus on freedom from constraint and restraint, and hence supportive of and conducive to the sort of educational heterogeneity in activities, goals, and outcomes that was indicated in my earlier analyses. That perception resulted in some early exploratory work (1989f, 1990f), but has yet to be properly developed.

Also emergent from those critiques of modernist frameworks was a concern to explore the possibilities of extending a traditional humanistic adult educational ethic into one that more broadly values our extrahuman environment. The work motivated by this concern, similarly, is continuing (but see 1992c).

The third concern to emerge from the critiques was for the development of a sounder understanding of the epistemic and normative underpinnings of contemporary culture. From such an understanding, it was hoped that a more appropriate practical framework for the guidance of adult education practice could be developed. That concern has taken the direction of exploring the nature of what is here termed "postmodernity" and its implications for adult education practice, research, and the formation and professional development of adult educators. In the course of that exploration, snippets of the work have been teased out for publication as scholarly papers (1994b-e, 1995a) and have become the starting points of retrospective, reflective reviews and reconstructions of the meanings and passages of the various engagements leading up to them (1994f, 1995b). Like the above-mentioned strands, it continues as an ongoing exploration—one in which the perception of the scenery and the route itself are constantly changing, and of which the destination remains both indeterminate and illusory.

Nevertheless, the perceptions are of such topicality (however momentarily) that other workers in the field may wish to share more fully in them than has been possible to date, with the limited and scattered nature of the published work. That is my excuse for this volume. I invite you to read it only in a critical frame of mind, from which engagement you may, I hope, generate some understandings and meanings that will valuably inform your involvement in the field of adult education.

The work is avowedly modernist in its origins, and perhaps also in its vision, its critique, and its portrayal. It strives, nevertheless, to be both sensitive and sympathetic to those postmodern realities with which it is concerned. Of those realities it seeks to paint a picture, or rather a number of pictures: images which are unavoidably both partial and contestable. You are invited to be a part of the contestation.

The work presented here was begun in earnest during my time in 1992 at the University of Oxford, as the Kellogg Visiting Fellow in Continuing Education, and at the University of Warwick as Visiting Fellow in the Continuing Education Research Centre later in the same year. It has been continued since then with the support of grants from the Australian Research Council.

I should like to acknowledge with gratitude the contributions of Dr. Allan Gardiner and Hilary Rofeta, both of whom have assisted so importantly in seeking out and reviewing the key works that have informed this project. Allan's contribution in particular has been not only facilitative but also formative. I am indebted also to Doreen Dickinson and Christine Webber for their patience and skill in interpreting and formating the manuscript. Most crucially, this volume owes its existence to the constructively critical reviewing of the work by my wife, Kate Bagnall. Without her influence, the project is unlikely to have got to this point, and would certainly be less comprehensible than it is.

Introduction

There is a rapidly accumulating and already extensive body of literature devoted to characterizations of the postmodern condition. The general drift of that scholarship is to suggest that Western culture has, since the early 1960s, been experiencing a shift from modernity to postmodernity, and from modernism to postmodernism: aesthetically, intellectually, epistemically, politically, and socially. Consistent with its nature, this shift is contextually variable in its expression, its profundity, its self-awareness, and its acceptance. While we may not, or not yet, be living in an entirely postmodern world, we are certainly experiencing, as Bauman (1992) has so eloquently observed, "intimations" of its coming.

Postmodernity has its apologists, as well as its detractors and its skeptics. It is variously perceived and evaluated by its commentators and its analysts. Nevertheless, for those with whom it is a reality, it is a cultural development so radical that it may not be ignored by any group of scholars whose work is concerned with contemporary society and culture. This applies no less to adult education than it does to other fields of scholarship and practice.

In accepting here the reality of postmodernity (albeit a contingent reality), and in characterizing it as a cultural condition that is profoundly different and in opposition to the condition of modernity, I do not thereby wish to deny the meaningfulness of seeing it alternatively, but similarly, as the breaking down of modernity and its reformulation in a radically new form (Docherty, 1990; Lyotard, 1984a), or as modernity's latest and most radical form of expression, and not, therefore, sensibly separable from modernity itself, except as "late" or "high" modernity (Giddens, 1990). Such perspectives are broadly consistent with that taken here, wherein what is termed "postmodernity" is seen as a contemporary cultural condition characterized by the radical problematization of the traditional dominant verities of modernity—a process that takes human understanding and action importantly outside or beyond those verities. It is the nature of that problematizing, of that moving beyond, and of its implications for adult education, that are here seen as being the important issues.

Across the field of education as a whole, there has been considerable analysis and debate about the nature of the postmodern condition and its relationships to education.[1] Within the more particular field of *adult* education, there has been very little.[2] The author of the present work has been among those adult educationalists who have sought to redress this lack, through the publication of papers exploring the nature of postmodernity and its implications for adult education practice, scholarship, and the formation and professional development of adult educators (Bagnall, 1994b-g, 1995a). It is that work which the present volume is directed to integrating, extending, sharpening, and elaborating.

The purpose is not therein to provide adult educators with a prescription for working within postmodernity. Neither is it to provide a definitive account of adult education in a postmodern cultural context. The contextuality of postmodern realities denies the validity of any such programs. The purpose is rather to locate, identify, articulate, and explore the opportunities and threats presented by postmodernity to adult education—not just to adult education as a field of practice and engagement, but also as a field that embraces both scholarly endeavor directed to illuminating and informing it, and activity that is directed to the development of persons *as* adult educators, whatever their particular engagements: as facilitators of learning, coordinators of programs, developers of policy, or whatever. The work does, however, seek to build modestly and provisionally on that exploration, in offering some thoughts on the dimensions of an educationally constructive response to the postmodern condition.

The account that is presented here is therefore both personal and partial. As such, the extent to which it may be meaningful and valuable to persons other than its author is a matter which only they can decide. Nevertheless, the account is intended to be a scholarly one. While it is not a review *of* the literature, it is firmly located *in* the literature of postmodern discourse. It is intended to be informed by and sensitive to that discourse, while not seeking to portray its multifarious currents, eddies, backwaters, and black holes. It is written from within a self-conscious postmodernity; nevertheless, in the formality and the abstractness of its analysis, it may be seen as more modernist than postmodern.

The pictures so painted are intended to be sufficiently general to illuminate and inform a diversity of adult education events. They have, accordingly, been framed deliberately in terms of suggested patterns, tendencies, convergences, differences, contradictions, textures, anticipations, hues, aromas, and flavors. Still-life paintings have largely been avoided, for they provide too particular a focus: risking a degree of closure and certainty that I seek to deny. The higher levels of abstraction that are mostly used here, while sitting uneasily in postmodern discourse itself, are meant to leave open the particular to the contingencies of each event. The exceptions to this avoidance of the specific will be found in chapters 6 and 7, where I seek to articulate in brief a selection of exchanges and events that are illustrative of the sort of tendencies arising within postmodern adult education. These exemplifications, it must be stressed, should not be seen as exemplary, but only as an opportunistic selection of available fragments from a potential infinity of alternatives.

The series of pictures here presented both are and are about *realities*, particularly those of adult education: not just concrete, physical realities but also (and more importantly) those imagined, perceived, envisaged, avoided, sought after, or denied. In other words, the concern is with alternative possible worlds or alternative possible states of affairs. The physical world—both within us (as our bodies) and beyond us (as the physical environment or context within which we act) is not denied. Postmodernity, as it is here presented, is not a contemporary form of absolute idealism—such a position is clearly nonsensical.[3] Physical realities are, however, seen as only one set of realities and, moreover, realities which have neither any meaning in themselves, nor any necessary or self-determining ways in which they are to be perceived and understood. In other words, our physical realities can only become a part of our knowledge and can only acquire meaning and significance through the frameworks of perception, understanding, and significance that we take to them.

Through those frameworks, and those frameworks alone, do we have the values necessary to judge whether one picture of our physical realities—our physical world—is better than another. The conception of what is "better," in itself, depends upon those frameworks: at the broadest level, whether it is, for example, a truth function, a function of immediate control, a function of spiritual satisfaction, of self-gratification, or whatever. Similarly and relatedly, the relative privileging of particular senses and ways of knowing is necessarily only brought by us *to* our perception and understanding of our physical realities. The physical world serves, in Vattimo's (1992, p. 25) terms, to provide the context for a "multiplicity of 'fablings'."

The work presented here is essentially philosophical or metatheoretical in approach, in that the nature of adult education in a postmodern world is drawn speculatively, exploratively, and analytically from a particular articulated conception of such a world. That particular conception is itself based on an analysis of scholarly work which variously characterizes, illuminates, and evaluates the postmodern condition or aspects of it. The picture of postmodernity, and hence of postmodern adult education, thus articulated is necessarily selective. As such, it may be assented to by some but not by others, and to varying degrees and in different ways.

In exploring the opportunities and threats presented by postmodern adult education, the work seeks to be both sympathetic to and critical of its subject matter. It is an attempt to identify what any field of adult education may be like in its broad features if it were postmodern. It is not in any way a sociological study of the extent to which contemporary adult education *is* of that nature. The features identified may variously be seen as ramblings to be ignored, speculations to be challenged, postulates to be tested, or standards to be celebrated and attained. It is to be hoped that in all cases they excite at least some criticism and some passion, and that in doing so they make a difference.

The field of adult education—as the substantive focus of this study—is certainly a field of social practice about which its proponents are inclined to be passionate. The tendency to criticism has been less in evidence, but then, from a modernist perspective, education by its nature is a good in itself and, to that extent, is beyond criticism by the sane and the sage. No such conception of adult education is assumed here. Adult education is, rather, perceived broadly and procedurally as embracing activities that are intended to enhance worthwhile adult learning, in ethically appropriate ways. The value of the learning (the extent to which it is worthwhile), and the evaluation of activities by which its enhancement is sought (the ethical propriety of its conduct), are matters to be derived not from its essential nature but from the particular cultural context in which it is embedded or from which it is viewed. Learning, then, may be seen as any process of enhancing individual situational sensitivity, responsiveness, and responsibility. So perceived, education is concerned with facilitating that learning which contributes to individual development or identity formation, whatever values are brought to the demarcation of that learning and the activities of educational engagement, and whatever the distribution of legitimizing power in determinations of those values. "Education" in this sense, therefore includes "training." When a distinction is made between "education" and "training" it is to identify the former with engagement for the purpose of contributing to the development of new or critical perspectives (i.e., with the enhancement of situational sensitivity), and the latter with the development or refinement of modes of behavior, including skills (i.e., with the enhancement of situational responsiveness and responsibility). The focus here is on *adult* education, in the sense of nonformal programs of education developed specifically for adults—rather than on formal schooling or tertiary education. However, the analysis, in its conclusions and in its educational applications, may probably be extended to other, more formal, sectors of the education institution without significant adjustment.

Let me say at the outset, and by way of summative introduction, that "postmodernity" is seen here as culture that is self-consciously and sympathetically informed by an understanding of: (1) the interpretative nature of human perception; (2) the indeterminate, contextualized, and fragmented nature of knowing and being; and (3) the dedifferentiated and generalized nature of contemporary communication.

The conception of "culture" used here is broadly encompassing of the constructed, lived realities of a people: their beliefs, traditions, mores, meanings, symbols, myths, values, and artifacts. The term is used to identify either that whole or any specified part of it—any given set of constructed realities, either perceived or postulated. In this way, contemporary adult education may be seen as constituting a realm of cultural realities. This anthropological or sociological conception of culture (Ferraro, 1994; R. Williams, 1988) is to be distinguished from the much narrower use of the term to denote the traditional products and frames of artistic and intellectual endeavor. The latter, while included as a part of culture, are only a part: artistic or intellectual culture. Culture has—and is recognized as having—significance, meaning, and coherence through its constitutive and formative *traditions:* its communities of shared meanings.

While the meaning of the foregoing articulation of postmodernity will be unpacked in the course of the first four chapters, it may be noted here that the contemporary efflorescence of postmodernity is seen as a transformative cultural change from a modernist epoch to a postmodern one. It incorporates but problematizes modernity: the scientific, industrial, and social programs, institutions, actions, and artifacts generated by the humanistic and enlightenment search for the universal foundations of truth, morality, and aesthetics, in the pursuit of human emancipation. It is seen as constituting a cultural force from the 1960s. In its contemporaneity, it may be seen as an historically periodizing epoch following modernity. However, that contemporaneity is a contingent matter, except to the extent that postmodernity's incorporation and problematization of modernity, and its communicative foundations, render it quite distinct from historically prior periods of radical contingency, with which it may otherwise be compared—such as that of Renaissance humanism in sixteenth century Europe.[4] Nevertheless, it does contain important echoes of those periods.

The postmodern condition is necessary or inevitable only to the extent that the historico-cultural and technological foundations on which it is assembled have come together only in recent decades. As a cultural condition that is informed by a general worldview, it stands in opposition to continuing and emergent currents and elements of the modern (and of the premodern). Those currents and elements may, conceivably, recombine and reform to overwhelm postmodernity as the dominant influence in cultural formation. Alternatively, postmodernity itself may give way to cultural influences not yet envisaged. In other words, while postmodernity may be seen *as* contemporary, it is not *the* contemporary, and it may well lose its contemporaneity. In that sense we may speak of the postmodern "moment," as others—such as Usher and Edwards (1994)—have done. However, that terminology is not followed here, since it privileges the temporality of postmodernity, at the cost of an apprehension of its being also and importantly a coming together of different cultural realities to create the postmodern condition.

Postmodernity therein includes, but goes beyond "postmodernism": that contemporary aesthetic and intellectual movement against modernism in the arts, including literature, architecture, painting, film, and drama. *Modernism,* then, refers to the largely twentieth century movement of autonomous experimentation and criticism (and its products) in these fields: the movement that arose in opposition to classicism. While adhering to the classical autonomy and elitism of art, and the dualism of the perceiving subject and the object of its perception, it sought to reveal the inner, formal truth behind the superficial appearances, through the triumph of the will over rationality, to the end of establishing an aesthetic justification of life. It was a search for eternal, permanent truth in and through art. *Postmodernism* may thus be seen as a rejection of modernism—not a reversion to classicism, since postmodernism denies the meaningfulness of the classical search for truth, the dualism between subject and object, and the apolitical autonomy and elitism of the enterprise. Postmodernism is, rather, the shifting diversity of aesthetic styles, approaches and products that is associated with the decentered, culturally embedded (and hence political), nonprogressive (and in that sense ahistorical), reactive, ironic, cynical, and populist world of art, literature and literary criticism.[5]

The substantive chapters of the book are clustered into three sections or parts. Part One (chapters 1 and 2) introduces the modernist underpinnings of postmodernity: both generally and more particularly with respect to adult education practice. Part Two (chapters 3 to 5) focuses on the nature of postmodernity: contrasting it with the qualities of modernity introduced in the previous section, and drawing those qualities out in a framework of tensions. Part Three, then (chapters 6 to 11), is devoted to what may be seen as the essence of the book: to a range of explorations of various aspects of postmodernity in adult education practice, research, and the professional development of adult educators.

In Chapter 1, a thumbnail sketch of modernity is attempted, by way of outlining what it is that postmodernity is seen as incorporating but problematizing. Modernity is presented here as a cultural condition, rapidly waxing in Western civilization from the late sixteenth century to a position of dominance, until its even more rapid waning from the 1960s. It was a fundamentally secular, humanist, elitist, unilinear, Western, and male cultural tradition, characterized by a representational view of human perception. The modernist individual was seen as being autonomous and self-interested, but solidly integrated into a realm of rule-governed social and institutional connectedness, through which individual freedom and responsibility were exercised. Knowledge was seen as an instrumental commodity, objectively grounded in the material reality which it pictured and over which it gave control. The advancement of knowledge was for the purpose of liberating humanity from privation, fear, myth, superstition, irrational convention, pestilence, ignorance, and want: a project of ordering in which there was the development of progressively more accurate and more powerful knowledge through the application of disciplined reason. In this task, the academic disciplines and the professions were the instruments of knowledge legitimation, through their criteria and procedures by which truth and falsity were assessed. The academic disciplines and the professions were also the central instruments in the tight control exercised over communications. Modernity, centrally, was a cultural tradition committed to progressive change, to the triumph of instrumental human reason over ignorance, for the good of humankind.

Chapter 2 narrows the focus to examine modernist education, particularly adult education. Modernist education was concerned with the molding of pre-adults, according to their inherited intelligence and aptitudes, into appropriate functional roles within the project of modernity. It focused on the education of the intellect—the refinement of cognitive powers of theoretical and practical intelligence—according to knowledge generated through the academic disciplines and honorable professions. Other forms of learning, most notably the training of the body and senses, were of lesser value. Social hierarchies and dichotomies within the system were seen as proper and natural, with an emphasis on schooling, testing, grading, streaming, and pigeonholing. The sociopolitical focus was on the creation of educational opportunity, defined in terms of what each individual's natural intelligence required to reach its full (predetermined) potential. Adult education was a marginal and unimportant component of the modernist educational institution, although it rose rapidly in importance in the late modernity of the twentieth century. It is examined here from two defining perspectives: as the poor cousin of the educational institution, and as its social conscience. From both perspectives, it embodied its own denial. It denied the centrality and importance of adult learning to the nature of individual and social being, and it denied the potential of realities beyond the narrow range of its own Enlightenment vision. Nevertheless, important parts of modernist adult education rendered it much more like its postmodern successor than was more formal modernist education.

With the opening of Part Two in Chapters 3 and 4, attention is shifted to postmodernity, with the sketching of a picture contrasting with the view of modernity presented in Chapter 1. Postmodernity is presented as the problematization of the certainties, presumptions, and commitments that underpinned and constituted the project of modernity. Postmodernity embraces a recognition of perception as being interpretative in nature, wherein what we perceive is an irreducible function of the frameworks of belief and subconscious figuration that we bring to any act of perception. Those frameworks themselves are importantly normative and emotive, as well as descriptive, infusing perception with value and emotion, and denying perceptual objectivity. Belief (including knowledge) in postmodernity is seen as being grounded in particular cultural contexts. Truth and value are both contingent on those contexts and fragmented among them. Belief is always, then, both intersubjective and indeterminate, with competing claims to truth being potentially of equal veracity in their own terms, and lacking any objective terms of foundational arbitration. Individual identity in postmodernity is fragmented, contextualized, and indeterminate, undermining the coherent, autonomous, and determinate identity of the rational humanist of modernity. Each individual is seen as having, or as constituting, an open portfolio of shifting, partial, and provisional identities.

Chapter 4 continues this articulation of postmodernity, firstly through an examination of communication. Postmodern communication is importantly dedifferentiated, with the erosion of our ability to distinguish images from objects, or representations from meanings with any degree of reliability. Communication becomes culturally diffused and democratized, under the combined influences of the postmodern epistemology of contextualized knowledge, its interpretative conception of perception, and contemporary communications technology. In the postmodern frame of mind—to which attention is then shifted—is seen an erosion of the supreme self-confidence and self-righteousness of modernity. Conversely, there emerges an enhanced tolerance of difference and a sympathetic awareness of the postmodern condition, with a tendency to irony, contradiction, skepticism, and cynicism. Overall, postmodern culture is characterized by an erosion of the distinctiveness, power, and standing of the modernist realms of discourse (the theoretical, the ethical, the aesthetic, and so on), of the modernist institutions (education, health, politics, and so forth) and of the modernist organizations serving those institutions.

Chapter 5 is a reconfiguration of the ideas in the preceding two chapters—into a simpler framework that may be used to guide the analyses of adult education that constitute the remainder of the book. A tensional framework is used, in which postmodernity is seen as characterized by tensions in three broad domains of reality: those of belief, identity, and sociality. The notion of tension here is that of two opposing or contrary inclinations, such that for each there are good reasons for inclining toward it, but that to do so—and to the extent that one does so—is to limit, compromise or threaten the possibility of satisfying the contrary inclination. Within each of the three domains, two generic tensions are presented as being of particular importance. Each tension is given both a descriptive label and terms to characterize the two poles of the tension itself. The two tensions in the domain of belief are those of *situatedness* (defined by the tension between transcendence and particularization) and *ambiguity* (defined by the tension between singularity and plurality). The two tensions in the domain of individual identity are those of *determination* (defined by the tension between holism and fragmentation) and *control* (defined by the tension between autonomy and embeddedness). In the domain of sociality, the two identified tensions are those of *homogeneity* (the tension being between differentiation and dedifferentiation) and *temporality* (the tension being between developmentalism and presentism).

Chapter 6 begins the exploration of postmodern adult education. It does so by using each of the six tensions articulated in the previous chapter to frame a dialogue. The dialogues are all composite reconstructions of exchanges between me, in my work in the professional education of adult educators, and students of practice in the field. Each dialogue focuses on a different feature of adult education practice or educational preparation for such practice. The features are selected and presented in such a way as to focus attention on the tension itself. The result is six vignettes—practical implications of postmodernity for adult education practice.

The exploration of postmodern adult education continues in Chapter 7. The focus, though, is shifted, both substantively and methodologically. Substantively, it is shifted from issues arising in the formation and professional development of adult educators, to the actual *practice* of adult educators. Methodologically, it is shifted from the examination of particular dialogues between me and students of the field, to an examination of *case studies* of adult education practice. For each of the tensions articulated in Chapter 5, a case study is presented in which realities defined by the tension are of paramount concern. The case studies cover a diversity of adult educator roles: program planning, policy formulation, needs assessment and marketing, the management of learning situations, the recognition of prior learning, instructional design, and the assessment of prior learning. They also range over a variety of adult education providers and educational situations: university, community, and private providers, workplace education, technical and further education, and self-directed learning. The case studies also include distance and resource-based programs, continuing professional education, and a number of face-to-face engagements.

In Chapter 8 there is a more radical shift in perspective: one which focuses singularly on the postmodern poles of the tensions introduced in Chapter 5. It incorporates an earlier attempt to identify and articulate a limited number of general qualities of postmodern adult education engagement (Bagnall, 1994d). Those qualities—seen as "tendencies" in the nature of adult education engagement—are derived analytically from, and are grounded descriptively in, the earlier articulated nature of the postmodern condition (Chapters 3 and 4), but are illustrated with reference to the dialogues and case studies of the immediately preceding two chapters. They are tendencies for adult education engagement to be: heterodox, expressive, reflexively contextualized, revisionist, indeterminate, privatized, phenomenalist, and dedifferentiated.

In Chapter 9, attention is focused on how agencies that provide adult education may best respond programmatically to the postmodern cultural context. Two broad types of programmatic response—*contractualism* and *open marketeering*—are described, grounded in the earlier articulated case studies, and evaluated. Contractualism involves providing agencies in working directly with the learners in negotiating the nature of program realities. Open marketeering involves providers in publicly marketing programs or program components for subscription and engagement. In contractualism, decision-making authority over the form of the program is shared between the providing agency and the learner, although the provider assumes responsibility for the preparation and conduct of the agreed program. In open marketeering, both authority and responsibility for program development are located with the educationists. The focus here on programmatic activity leads to the identification of four additional, more strongly evaluative, features of postmodern adult education: its cognitively diminished, nonselfsustaining, conceptually situational, and procedurally indefinable nature.

The last two chapters focus attention on the implications of postmodernity for the conduct and nature of *research* in adult education and for the *formation and professional development* of adult education practitioners. Chapter 10 examines the implications for research in the field. Research is seen there as action directed to the generation and dissemination of public knowledge that either illuminates or informs a category of phenomena or actions—in this case, practice in the field of adult education. Three broad qualities of that research in postmodernity are drawn out, articulated, and grounded in the educational literature: its authorial, interpretive, and project-based nature. By "authorial" is meant the situating of research *within* particular discourses or intersubjective frameworks of language and meaning. By "interpretive" is meant the directing of research to interpreting or explaining and critically reflecting upon patterns of belief and action in adult education practice and to articulating those patterns in the public domain. By "project-based" is meant the construction of research into discrete entities (projects) in all of its qualities: the policy that governs it, the funding that supports it, the purposes to which it is directed, the methods by which it is undertaken, its impact, and its evaluation. The chapter finishes with an excursion into the nature of postmodern adult education research as a profession. Such professional engagement is seen as being strongly dedifferentiated: integrated with both adult education practice and other areas of research, relatively open, and pluriform.

Chapter 11—the final chapter—is an exploration of the professional qualities of the adult educator within a postmodern cultural context. It is argued that the sort of person most suited to such a context is the "situationally sensitive wayfarer"—one whose professional engagements are characterized by: reflexive awareness; individual and organizational responsibility; tolerance of and respect for difference; sympathetic understanding of and responsiveness to the particularities of lived events, drawing eclectically upon a wide range of knowledge; respect for persons and their cultural realities; and the capability, understanding, and disposition to negotiate the recognition of discriminative realities and the alleviation of discriminative injustice. This is a sensitivity which facilitates the practitioner's passage into radically unknown events. It embraces ideology, yet it eschews ideological characterization; it works contextually, yet it is essentially transcontextual; it is grounded in human capabilities, yet it transcends skill. Those capabilities are seen as being underpinned and informed by a wide-ranging understanding of the nature and complexity of the human condition, generated through the experience of literature, art, drama, music, the sciences, and diverse religious and ethnic perspectives—experiences both direct and simulated or vicarious. Such a practitioner may be seen as an intercultural wayfarer or a roving diplomat of the human condition. Individual formation and professional development for such a role calls for a curriculum of wide-ranging engagement with the complexities of the human condition.

Finally, in a brief postscript, I reflect back on the journey of exploration that constituted the writing of this book, commenting also on how I hope the content of the book will and will not be used, and on the task of looking beyond it, in search of indications of future directions.

Part One

Modernity and Modernist Adult Education

The two chapters in this section sketch the modernist underpinnings of postmodernity. Chapter 1 presents a picture of modernist culture in general. Chapter 2 focuses more particularly on modernist adult education. Chapter 1 may be seen as informing the analysis in Part Two (postmodernity); Chapter 2, that of Part Three (adult education in postmodernity).

Chapter 1

The Modernist Inheritance 1: Thinking and Being in a Straitjacket

The agenda in this chapter (and in the next) is a perilous one: to characterize modernity (and then modernist adult education) as both paradigmatic and epochal: as a profoundly and importantly distinctive ("paradigmatic") cultural condition that was dominant over an identifiable (epochal) period in the history of Western civilization. Such an agenda requires that the condition (and hence the epoch) be characterized by certain features and not others, and that it be coherent and distinctive in those features, regardless of its undoubted epistemic, normative, and situational differences. The agenda also requires that one generalize, and that one do so selectively: putting aside many realities as not characteristic, seeing and presenting (creating) commonalities among others as being so, and portraying those new realities as meaningful descriptive concepts of the condition and the epoch. It thus requires that we draw a boundary, not only around the cultural condition, but also around the period: recognizing not only some sort of cultural borders, but also some sort of a beginning and some sort of an end. All such decisions are highly problematic, uncertain, and open to counter-argument. Making them will, inevitably, do violence to many realities: not only those judged not to be characteristic and therefore excluded entirely, but also those represented in simplified, more general, or different forms to the ways in which they were conceived by the persons who have lived them and identified with them.

Nevertheless, the characterization of modernity is necessary here not just as a backdrop to the postmodernity which is seen as following it, but because it is seen as importantly leading *to* that postmodernity and as being incorporated *within* it. The features of modernity upon which I am here focusing have been selected as contrasting with those of postmodernity—as a way of directing attention to the differences. In so doing, attention is diverted from the similarities and, most importantly, from the presence throughout modernity, in various combinations, of individual features here presented as characterizing *post*modernity. The presence of those features in modernity, however, is not seen as denying the paradigmatic nature of postmodernity. That nature derives not so much from the first occurrence of any particular feature (although the dedifferentiated and generalized nature of contemporary communication would be candidates on this criterion), as from the *coincidence* of the features, the *self-consciousness* with which they constrain action in the formation of cultural realities, and their historical *location* after a prolonged period of modernity, which may be seen as having failed importantly to deliver the instrumental benefits that impelled it.

The modernist epoch is referred to here as though it had passed. That it has indeed done so is, importantly, a contention underlying the work in this book. Nevertheless, it is acknowledged that strong currents of modernity still flow, just as do those of premodernist medievalism. It is also acknowledged that other commentators see the modernist epoch itself continuing, albeit in a variously, in some cases radically, modified form. Although the present work is not in harmony with the latter views, it is also not strongly in discord with them. It is, though, entirely discordant with those views in which, on modernist grounds, there is denial of the sort of cultural developments that are asserted in this work. To them, I commend a most particular reading of this and related works.[1]

The Modernist Epoch

The origins of modernity may be seen in the Renaissance humanism of the late fourteenth century.[2] In its decisive breaking away from the narrow confines of both religious dogma and secular tradition, the Renaissance opened the door to the modernist epoch of commitment to the power of the human will to work constructively and progressively in improving the human condition, in all of its dimensions.

That creative and instrumental awakening was increasingly and importantly secular, although it was, significantly, grounded in Christianity. Christianity, perhaps more than any other major religion, may be characterized as a religion of *transcendental humanism,* in which God is an idealization of the human, a projection of humanity's fears and aspirations into a timeless, all-powerful, all-knowing entity which is presented as having created humankind in its own image and given it custodianship of its other material creations. More perspicuously, in Christianity, Man[3] may be seen as creating God in his (Man's) own image; making Him (God) omnipotent and omniscient; giving Him dominion over all the universe; presenting Him as creator of that universe, with Man as His ultimate creation, the remainder of creation being available to serve Man's needs; and, finally, delegating the management of that whole dominion to Man for his use in the name and for the glorification of God. A perfectly self-serving circle.

Such a religion, as has been argued elsewhere (e.g., Black, 1970; Roszak, 1972), frames a worldview that is strongly instrumental and profoundly anthropocentric, in which the death of God leads only to His natural (and more authentic) replacement by humankind itself. That death, which has tended to occur progressively throughout modernity, and which was loudly announced by Friedrich Nietzsche in 1882 (Nietzsche, 1887/1974a), made little difference to the modernist project. The ongoing tension in modernity between the secular and the (institutionalized) sacred has been more a matter of which tradition exercised power in the formation of human identity and culture, than of competition between importantly different worldviews. As Toulmin (1990, p. 144) has observed, "the alleged incompatibility of science and theology was thus a conflict *within* modernity." The modernist show continued, regardless of who ruled. Nevertheless, the progress (and the decline) of modernity may be seen as greatly facilitated by the progressive secularization of the Western civilization which defined its cultural domain. That secularization was, crucially, not only of knowledge, but also of rationality itself. It therefore also secularized or anthropocentrized all material power, freeing the human will and mind to engage in a self-disciplined, self-liberating mission of discovery, conquest, and colonization: the project of modernity.

A new and even more powerfully instrumental current of modernity was ushered in at the end of the Renaissance: Cartesian rationalism. This is popularly dated from the 1630s, with the publication by René Descartes of his *Discourse on method* and *Meditations*.[4] Some commentators see Cartesian rationalism as the essence of modernity, with the start of modernity dating from this period.[5] However, it is more instructive to see it as one of two major currents of modernity, the other being secular humanism, with its origins in the Renaissance. These two strands—each essentially a mirror image of the other, each highlighting that which the other denied—remained in constant tension throughout modernity. Certainly, rationalism was dominant in various forms over most of the epoch: as the quest for certainty during the Age of Reason—the high point of modernity—in the eighteenth century Enlightenment; as evolutionary Darwinism from the middle of the nineteenth century; and as revisionist positivism from the 1920s until the 1960s and the demise of modernity. Humanism was, though, always important and was clearly dominant for over half a century in the Romantic period from late in the eighteenth century. The apogee of the rationalist current, and its magnificent last gasp, may be seen as state Marxism, in which deterministic, dialectical materialism was postulated and affirmed as the totalizing, universal organizing principle for the history, the contemporaneity, and the future of cultural reality.

Modernity, in its origins and its history, was a fundamentally Western tradition. Postwar Japan is perhaps the most notable exception to this generalization. However, that and similar cases remain ambiguous. The extent to which Japan's recent cultural history has been a matter of its occidentalization (and hence of its modernization) or of its redefining and submerging modernity within its own nonoccidental culture is a question left unaddressed here.

Modernity may also be characterized as a fundamentally elitist tradition, to the extent that it was directed and experienced most directly by those levels of society where there was the time, the learning, the resources, and the power (especially over one's own earthly destiny) to actively engage with it. Certainly there were periods of mass modernistic engagement, such as the French cultural revolution and, to a lesser extent, the popular Marxist revolutions of the twentieth century. On the whole, though, the experiences of modernity for the mass of Western humanity were through the trickling-down of its outcomes and consequences from above, be these industrial products, advances in medical science, political rights and duties, new work regimes, improved housing and welfare, changes in the nature of work, or whatever.

In its formulation, in those who created the modernist realities, modernity may also be seen as essentially a *male* worldview: a point which has been strongly articulated by many feminist scholars.[6] It thereby both gives expression to male cultural power and serves to strengthen that power. The corrosive effects on modernity of feminist criticism, and the emancipatory alternatives which their discourses have opened up have, indeed, done much to usher in the postmodern epoch.

Modernist Perception

Underlying modernity was a *representational* view of human perception. In that view, our perception of the world around us—through our various human senses and their technological extensions—was pictured as reflecting, mirroring, or representing the features of that world. This is what Michel Foucault (1970, p. xxiii) identifies as "the theory of representation," and Richard Rorty (1980, p. 12) as "the notion of the mind as mirror." Representationism depends upon a *realist* world view: one in which the true form of the world external to human consciousness is accepted as being open to objective perception by the subjective consciousness of the human subject. It is founded also on the dualism—most forcefully articulated by Immanuel Kant in 1781 (Kant, 1781/1934)—between the perceiving subject and the object of perception, between mind and matter. "Sense data" or their equivalents were regarded as being *given-off* by the objects of perception in various forms: as light, sound, aromatic compounds, and so on. Those sense data actually carried the perceptual information—the facts about the external world. Properly trained, our senses may accurately perceive those data, allowing our minds to see the facts, to compile a true picture of the world as it is.

Human subjective *interpretation* of the sense data was seen as being open to many errors arising from our emotions, our values, and our existing mistaken beliefs. Nevertheless, those errors may progressively be overcome through the application of procedures appropriate to the task: the methods of rational and empirical, especially scientific enquiry.

Reinforcing this representationalist or mimetic view of perception were two other dualisms: those that separated reason from the emotions, and matters of fact from matters of value. The first of these made it possible to see the emotions as unfathomable interferences to the power of pure reason: for the rationalists, as human weaknesses to be suppressed or overcome. Pure reason could then be brought to bear in properly interpreting our perceptions, and in clearing away the confounding effects of the emotions. Matters of fact were seen as being matters *of* the external world: matters to be perceived, understood as truths. In contrast, matters of value were either entirely or at least partly cultural creations—artifacts developed socially that become components of cultural tradition—and to that extent neither true nor false, but rather right or wrong (with respect to actions), or good or bad (with respect to entities or states of affairs), depending upon one's value framework. Thus separated from value and the emotions, pure reason could show us the way to a fully veracious perception of the world around us: the world of facts.

A more sophisticated conception of value—and one that became dominant in the course of the nineteenth and twentieth centuries—recognized two distinct types of value: intrinsic and extrinsic. Intrinsic value was seen as a stable, invariable, absolute quality of those entities that possessed it. In some sense, it was seen variously as being either a nonnatural property of entities or as reducible to natural properties of them. Even in those cases where intrinsic value was perceived as being analytically assigned to entities by conscious beings, there was taken to be an objectively *correct* assignment in each case. In any given case, the recognition of this intrinsic value was a matter of objective fact, requiring reference to no other entity of value and no context of meaning. On the other hand, an entity had *extrinsic* value—a quantitatively variable quality—to the extent that its elucidation was judged to demand or properly involve reference to other entities in terms of its contingent, instrumental contribution to the attainment or maintenance of those other entities. The latter may have had intrinsic value and/or instrumental value to the attainment of yet further entities. However, all such extrinsic or instrumental value was regarded as constituting value only in a derivative, and hence secondary and subordinate, sense. There may have been chains of such instrumental justification but, ultimately, they all ended in one or more entities of purely intrinsic value (Bagnall, 1990b; J.P. White, 1973, p. 8).

By some appropriate means, such as through intuition of the nonnatural property of value, or the interpretative perception of the natural properties in which the value was expressed, one could come to know of the existence (or otherwise) of intrinsic value in any entity or type of entity (Frankena, 1973, pp. 95-107; Nielsen, 1967). One could, though, be mistaken in one's intuitions, perceptions, or assignments of value in any given case. In contrast, the characterization and quantification of extrinsic value was seen as a culture-dependent matter of empirical, prudential, and rational analysis. It was variable over time and across social groups, because of its dependence on cultural norms, technical knowledge and skills, and so on.

In this more sophisticated modernist model or picture of value, an entity had intrinsic value if, and only if, it was an end in itself, not in any degree to the extent that it was instrumental to the attainment or maintenance of another entity, regardless of whether or not the latter had intrinsic value. Intrinsic value was thus both logically prior to and normatively superior to extrinsic value. The model was clearly one of normative atomism—each entity (or category of entities) had intrinsic value (if it had it at all) independently of the value possessed by any other entity, and that value could be ascertained entirely independently of any other entities and of any extrinsic value which the entity might contingently have.

On either of these models of value, the perceiving and intuiting human subject was in a position to observe facts *objectively*. With the perceiving mind separated from the objects of its awareness, and with our perception cleansed of cultural values and irrational emotions, we could objectively observe the world: calmly, dispassionately, disinterestedly, reasonably, and accurately. Fully objective perception was made possible, and was evidenced in, different individuals perceiving a phenomenon or entity in exactly the same way.

Modernist Belief, Knowledge, and Meaning

Modernist epistemology was grounded in its representational view of human perception. Through the senses, the external world was represented to the mind. The mind, as the knowing subject, possessed the intellectual skills to reconstruct the world in knowledge or theory. This "dualist model of mimesis," as Lash (1987, p. 361) has termed it, presupposed a transcendental model of knowledge, in which knowledge was an entity which existed entirely separately from its objects—the material world (Price, 1969). Knowledge pictured, mirrored, or reflected that world, but was not a part of it and did not affect it. The nature and being of the material world were entirely independent of the truth or falsity of the knowledge claims. Nevertheless, the central concern of modernity was with the elucidation of knowledge about the material world, and its articulation in theory. To that extent, the project of modernity may be seen as *epistemological*, in contrast to the more metaphysical concerns of premodernity.

Like the premodern metaphysics, modernist epistemology was strongly *foundationalist*. However, in contrast with premodernity, the foundations of its knowledge were not so importantly, and were diminishingly, seen as being some sort of divine will. They were, rather, naturally occurring features of the universe, through which claims to knowledge were legitimated: the universal, essential regularity of the material world (whether God-given or not); its objective transparency to human perception; and the power of the rational human intellect to interpret those perceptions in the formulation of knowledge about the world. Regardless of the views held about the ultimate origins and meaning of material reality, the modernist project was driven by a commitment to the secular demythologization of belief (Vattimo, 1992): the emancipation of reason through the eradication of myth, ignorance, false consciousness, and superstition. Its mission included the discovery and portrayal of the material world as it really was. Whether that reality was an expression of God's divine will or of some entirely physical set of forces, it was taken as having underlying regularities which were expressed in "natural" laws. The task was to discover those laws through the interpretation of the perceived facts.

In that interpretative task, modernity may be seen also as an epoch in which there was a preoccupation with *ordering* (Bauman, 1991a). There were developed autonomous, differentiated academic disciplines, each with its own modes and techniques of disciplined (rule-governed) inquiry, and each with its own criteria for evaluating knowledge claims. Within each of those disciplinary fields, the central task was seen as one of discovering the natural order of the world. That order was expressed in theoretical constructs and models: descriptive and predictive frameworks through which the variability of contingent reality could be *classified* or categorized on the basis of its essential constitutive and relational properties.

In its ordering, modernity was essentially *reductionist:* the properties of any entity in the material world being taken as adequately represented by the summative and coordinated properties of its individual component entities. Thus, for example, an adequate knowledge of each of the organ systems of the human body was seen as being combined without important addition to give an adequate understanding of the functioning of the human body itself. In spite of the limitations of such a view, it proved to be a powerful tool of empirical science, and hence of the modernist project as a whole.

Also central to the modernist project was a humanistic view of the *improvability* of the human condition via the application of instrumental reason. Through instrumental reason, disciplined inquiry was seen as leading humanity progressively to an overcoming of the ambiguity, incoherence, disorder, irrationality, superstition, and privation of experience. Modernist knowledge was, accordingly, strongly *instrumental* in nature. It was judged as *valuable* to the extent that it gave humankind *power* over the physical world—power that could be used to improve the lot of humankind.

Embedded in the notion of the improvability of the human condition was the *progressivism* of that instrumental knowledge which informed it. Successive pictures (models, theories) of material reality were seen as moving progressively closer to the truth—closer to the universal natural laws by which the material world was ordered, as evidenced in the facts of our perceptual experience. In so progressing, they became more powerful tools for the instrumental manipulation of the material world, to the end of human improvement. Their power was measured in the extent to which they could serve in the accurate explanation, prediction, and control of particular (located) events. The local, the particular, actual events were therefore seen as the (real-world) testing beds for the generalizations which constituted modernist knowledge. In assuming the material world to be driven by a limited number of universal, timeless, elegantly simple natural laws of immense explanatory, predictive, and manipulative power, the instrumental epistemology of modernity was given the task of progressively discovering and better representing those laws.

Progressively better pictures were thus seen as being those that were both more general (temporally and phenomenally) and more powerful (and hence more accurate) in their explanation, prediction, and control of material reality. Within those primary qualities, the natural laws to which they were seen as giving expression also indicated a favoring of theory that was *simple* in its expression. Progress in knowledge was achieved, on the one hand, through the progressive development and refinement of those perceptual and analytical tools with which knowledge was elaborated: technologies to extend the senses and more powerful procedures for analyzing and synthesizing data. On the other hand, it was achieved through the cumulation of particular knowledge, and the generation and testing of more refined theoretical models to explain the data.

Modernity thus allowed for human *fallibility* in its knowledge of the material world. Errors were seen as arising particularly from the limitations of available perceptual and analytical tools, but also from the interference of emotions and values. They were accepted as leading to knowledge that should always be presumed to be open to transcendence by more perfect knowledge. Modernist knowledge was thus open to an infinite progression of ever more perfect representations of the material world, each one more general and more powerful than that or those it replaced, but always carrying with it the presupposition of further fallibility.

Knowledge that was at the forefront of this progression was accepted as being true, on the grounds that one had the best available justification for believing it to be so. Such knowledge was seen as having been demonstrated, openly, to be superior to all rival claims through the established procedures of rigorous formal testing against the facts of the material world. Claims to knowledge that had been falsified, or that had not yet been subject to the proper formal procedures of rigorous testing against the observed facts, were regarded as (mere) belief. Modernity thus formalized an important distinction between "belief" and "knowledge." *Beliefs* were claims which were either demonstrably false or lacking in good and sufficient grounds as claims to be true. *Knowledge,* on the other hand, identified claims for which there were good and sufficient rational, objective grounds for accepting them as true, independent of social convention or tradition: what modernists came to present as "justified, true belief" (Scheffler, 1965).

Modernity also drew an important distinction between "knowledge" and "meaning." Knowledge was an objective, demonstrably true reflection of the natural order in the material world. *Meaning,* on the other hand, was what human interest saw *in* that knowledge and envisaged it as amounting *to.* The same knowledge could, and most probably would, have different meanings to persons from different cultural traditions and perspectives. Meaning was thus informed by contingent human culture, by values and emotions, and it was seen as being limited by that context of tradition, value, and emotion.

This distinction between knowledge and meaning contributed to an interesting development in the status of knowledge in modernity. Although the modernist *pursuit* of knowledge was *instrumentally* justified (and therefore valued) in terms of its potential to alleviate human deprivation and privation, there was a tendency for that pursuit to become of intrinsic value—an unqualified good in itself. This may be seen as a partial function of the alleged purity of modernist knowledge; cleansed of human interest it was an unalloyed, rarefied, and reified quantity of value in itself, regardless of the ends to which it was being or may have been put. Also contributing, though, to the intrinsic value of modernist knowledge was, on the one hand, its value in traditional Christian idealism, wherein the deity Himself was understood as pure reason (Gordon and White, 1979) and, on the other hand, the modernist acceptance that all knowledge had potential, even if yet unknown, instrumental value waiting to be realized.

The task of progressively interpreting the material world, of building better and better pictures of it through disciplined inquiry, was undertaken within the *academic disciplines*, especially the sciences. Each discipline had its own refined and tested techniques for discovering the truth, and criteria for judging claims to the truth—for legitimating knowledge claims. There existed a generally accepted hierarchy of disciplines, based on their perceived ability to generate theory that was not only true, but also precise, instrumentally powerful, and of great generality and elegant simplicity. The epitome of theoretical formulations so perceived, were purely symbolic and quantified mathematical formulations. Accordingly, mechanics and, later, physics tended to remain supreme throughout modernity, although the positions of the lower-order disciplines changed somewhat over time—powerful new discoveries, such as evolutionary theory and tectonic theory, giving a discipline a competitive advantage. Physics also had the advantage in that the object realm of its concern—the fundamental nature of the material universe—was seen as being foundational to all other disciplinary realms and the one to which the knowledge discovered in them may ultimately be reduced.

There was thus seen in modernity a general *unity* of knowledge. The academic disciplines were seen as providing different approaches to discovering the natural order of different object-realms of material reality. Since the natural laws governing order in the material universe were taken as being universal and integrated, knowledge of that order would, ultimately at least, be no less universal and integrated.

Modernist Identity

The modernist individual was seen as being an integrated, self-identical, autonomous, rational monad, separable from (although dependent upon) both culture and the external physical world (Lash and Friedman, 1992; Usher, 1989b; R. Williams, 1988). Culture was created *by* such individuals—acting either on their own or in collaboration with others; always *as* the creative center, albeit within an historical and contemporary context of knowledge, belief, meaning, aspiration, opportunity, and restraint. Culture thus informed and constrained modernist human action, but it was essentially a *context* of that action—a context which could be objectively perceived, understood, and manipulated.

Individuals were seen as being autonomous in the sense that, and to the extent that, they acted, or were capable of acting, as independent agents: independent of each other, of their nonrational emotions, and of their cultural contexts. Such autonomy had both intellectual and moral (practical) dimensions. The intellectual dimension was, as Gibbs (1979: 121) put it,

> to be equated with critical intelligence, independence of thought and judgement, discernment, involving not necessarily a high degree of intellectual originality and enterprise but at any rate a readiness to think things out for oneself free from bias and prejudice; and to do so not only in taking everyday practical decisions, and in pursuing particular artistic, technological and scientific projects, but also in reflecting on and determining answers to questions of universal interest and ultimate importance; [in] morality, politics, religion.

Moral autonomy, on the other hand, was "fundamentally a moral virtue or anyhow a disposition of character rather than intellect: self-mastery or self-discipline, having command of one's own feelings and inclinations" (Gibbs, 1979, p. 121). Thus perceived, individual autonomy was both something which everyone had *as* a human being, and something which all *could* have to a greater degree than they contingently did. In other words, it both defined each person's humanness and made that humanness an unattainable ideal in its full immanence. Thereby, the path to full autonomy could be (and was) defined as a desirable route for each person to travel throughout his or her life span. Late modernist humanism, through the work of gestalt psychologists such as Abraham Maslow (1970) and Carl Rogers (1969), developed this progressive aspect of individual autonomy to its highest point. It came, therein, to *define* personhood, maturity, and normality. Conversely, to the extent that it was not immanent, a person was perceived as being immature, abnormal, or deviant.

Individual autonomy presupposes a relatively unitary, integrated, coherent individual identity, or at least one in which there is an attainable hierarchy of influence—such as the conscious will over unconscious drives, and the rational over the emotional. Modernity, accordingly, saw different features of individual identity essentially as being integrated into the whole or, regardless of Sigmund Freud, as hierarchically manageable in any reasonably normal (autonomously acting) human being.

Within the rationalist strand of modernity there was a sense of a strong dualism between the mind and the body. Following René Descartes, the perceiving, reasoning, knowing mind, in all of its perfectibility, was seen as separate from—albeit undeniably located within and physically sustained by—the body. The latter was the contingent, imperfect, even burdensome corpus in which our wonderful minds with their powers of transcendent wisdom were regrettably grounded. The body, with its physical and emotional needs and limitations, was as much a restraint to the triumph of Reason as it was the physical sustainer of that Reason. This dualism not only had its basis in the exaltation of rational thought, but it also heightened that exaltation through the attribution of negative qualities to the body. The Christian idealist perception of God as pure reason, and that of salvation through the understanding of God's ways, further reinforced both the mind-body dualism and the exaltation of enlightened thought itself.

Free enterprise capitalism, the major current of modernist social theory, was transparently based on individual autonomy—the rational, sovereign individual subject—and on the exaltation of the creative intellect. Marxism—the apotheosis of grand modernist social theory—retained the essentially autonomous model of human identity. It sought not so much to deny the Cartesian dualism between mind and body, as to invert their status: exalting the physical over the intellectual.

Building on the dualism of the intelligent, autonomous subject, the modernist model of identity saw intelligence itself as a decontextualized, unitary, and generalized property of each individual. It was an essentially natural quality, initially seen as being God-given, later as biologically inherited, albeit complexly and unpredictably so.

It could be diminished or destroyed through misadventure, neglect, or abuse, but it could not be supplemented or added to. It could, though, be trained, both morally and cognitively, to the extent of a person's natural intelligence, in the arts of just and rational thinking. The greater the intellect, the more powerfully could it be trained in moral leadership, analysis, synthesis, and problem solving.

Marxism aside, the greater the power of a person's intellect, the greater his or her social value in modernist society, where reason was so highly valued. Intellectual skills, such as the use of language, logic, and mathematics, were of the mind and therefore highly valued. Manual skills on the other hand, were of the body, not the intellect. They were, accordingly, devalued—as the province of persons who did not have the intellect for the cultural vocations of the mind.

Since individual intelligence was a largely biological, generalized, decontextualized quality, it could (theoretically at least) be measured as such: independently of a person's culture and educational background, and largely independently of age (once the intellect had reached its biological maturity). Thus was developed the concept of the "intelligence quotient" (IQ). The IQ tests of the twentieth century were seen by their protagonists as measuring that core of natural, genetic intelligence.

Modernist Communication

With the modernist exaltation of transcendental *reason,* there was a corresponding exaltation of the symbolic over the concrete, the linguistic over the iconic, and the written over the oral. The senses not centrally concerned with language—touch, taste, smell, kinesthesia, and proxemia—were progressively devalued with the advance of modernity.

These value hierarchies were reflected in modernist communication, where the representational conception of perception served as the foundation for a highly *differentiated* model of communication. The material world—the world out there (outside the mind)—to be perceived by the senses and known to the mind was seen as being represented in images. Those images were most importantly linguistic and written: in key terms, phrases, sentences, and passages. They more or less adequately—more or less veraciously—represented the true nature of the imaged world. They did so in the *content*—the ideas, concepts, theories, etc.—that were encoded in them, signified, or denoted by them. That content was thereby seen as being a *function* of the signifier image, and as *representing* the referent. As Scott Lash

(1990) has elaborated at length, any act of communication allowed the transparent unpacking (differentiation) of the explicit (signified) content from the medium of representation (the signifier) and what it was about in the object world. The content was, importantly, seen to be encoded *into* (and fixed within) the signifier by its source: the object of the image in the case of images of the material world; the author of the signifier in the case of text or other symbolic medium.

There was, therefore, an objectively *correct* interpretation of every image, of every representation: both natural and artificial. The correct interpretation of a natural image was a true knowledge of its object. The correct interpretation of an artificial image (a symbolic representation or text) was the understanding and meaning that its author(s) intended to encode within it. The task of the sciences, and of scholarly, literary and artistic interpretation, was thus seen as being centered on the elucidation of the *true* content of the images with which they were concerned.

That task, increasingly, was undertaken through and regulated by the academic disciplines. The academic disciplines—both sciences and humanities—were centrally *defined* by the frame or zone of images with which each was concerned. Within its (fiercely defended) frame of images, its field of signification, each discipline was largely responsible for creating the public frameworks of knowledge or signification pertinent to that frame. In other words, it was largely responsible for the legitimation of knowledge in that frame. With the growth in the influence of the modernist academic disciplines, there was, accordingly, a parallel growth in the interest and the influence of the state in their control: through the universities, research institutes, and academies. That control was exercised through an increasingly closed and structured framework of disciplinary apprenticeship, membership, and contribution. Each discipline established progressively more lengthy and penetrating programs of enculturation for its aspiring masters and professors. Before one could pronounce publicly as an expert in a modernist discipline, one was subject to an increasingly prolonged immersion in its ways of perceiving, analyzing, and presenting reality: an immersion that came to build on foundational work in secondary school, and to extend throughout tertiary study as well as an apprenticeship or internship.

Elaborate systems of communications gatekeeping were also established, to insure that only work appropriate to the disciplinary tradition was legitimated and made public. Any claim to knowledge within a discipline was subject to ruthless scrutiny by disciplinary experts before it was accepted as valid. Printed publications—as the main medium of informed communication—were carefully controlled by editorial policy, expert refereeing, and codes of publication practice.

The precision, the rigor, the calculated and studied conventions of communication from each disciplinary stance, were thereby assured. With such a well-oiled, smoothly running, integrated, and conservatively constraining system for regulating the legitimation and communication of knowledge, the words of pamphleteers and other iconoclasts could quickly be drowned out, ridiculed, diminished, or dismissed, if not completely silenced. Claims to objective knowledge outside the framework of the academic disciplines were so marginalized from the mainstream of rational scholarship, that they posed no serious threat to the hegemony of the disciplines in the legitimation of knowledge.

With the advent of electronic communication, this differentiated and disciplined orderliness began to come under threat. Nevertheless, until recent decades (roughly, the 1960s onwards, depending somewhat on the country concerned), various factors—state controls, the conservatism of public tradition, computer software limitations, and the high costs of input and access to the electronic media—maintained a tight rein on what was publicly communicated. Those persons whose views were heard, read, and seen continued to be the experts in their fields: those who had earned their right to be so through established reputations of a traditional scholarly or professional nature.[7] Alternative visions and voices were largely unseen and unheard, and, when they were seen or heard, they tended to preserve their privilege of being so permitted by staying close to the norm.

The Modernist Frame of Mind

The modernist frame of mind was founded on the totalizing confidence of modernity in the power of reason and science to liberate humankind from deprivation, pestilence, and ignorance. To be modern was unquestionably an intrinsic good—absolute and invariable. To be otherwise was perverse. The modernist frame of mind was not only confident—supremely self-confident (Boyne and Rattansi, 1990)—it was *triumphant*.

In its triumph, it sought—quite naturally, properly, unreflectively, and uncritically—to command, to control. The object of control was, first and foremost, culture: its formation and its reproduction. Control was exercised by targeting and diminishing the value of competing realities, any set of beliefs or other cultural reality that was different from the modernist mainstream. Such beliefs were categorized, labeled, and marginalized as ignorance, false consciousness, myth, superstition, or irrational convention.

The modernist frame of mind may therefore be seen as more concerned with epistemological than with ontological matters (Bauman, 1991a). In other words, it was more concerned with questions about the nature of knowledge, and the criteria and procedures by which that knowledge was legitimated, than it was with questions of being or the nature of the material world. Given a sound epistemology, the transparent truth of material reality would be revealed. The modernist task in this respect was to expose the latter (the transparent truth of material reality) through refining the former (the epistemology).

Certainty breeds contempt for and intolerance of difference (Bagnall, 1991b; K. Harris, 1979; Nowell-Smith, 1954; Wain, 1987). In the case of modernity, the certainty was not of the truth—knowledge was too fallible for that—but rather of the modernist project itself: its foundations, its methods, its singular direction, its emancipatory mission. The modernist frame of mind thus tended strongly to self-righteous intolerance of difference in those respects (Bauman, 1991a). Cultural traditions that were not driven by a commitment to the Enlightenment project of human liberation through the progressive power of reason, and those persons who were not on the single true path of progressive human history to enlightenment and liberation, or who were not moving forward tolerably close to the contemporary modern, were seen as being less than fully human. They were thereby the proper objects of pity, scorn, and ridicule. The modernist frame of mind was certainly often compassionate and charitable, and even generous in its charity, but always demeaning and patronizing, and never giving (in the sense of letting go) of its modernity.

Those persons and groups who were different tended to be faced with the choice of assimilation into the dominant mainstream or marginalization as "primitive" or "deviant." Such marginalization brought great threat to its (human) subjects since, being less than fully human, they could properly (ethically) be the targets of inhumane treatment, with the denial of all human rights.

If one was less than enlightened by contemporary standards, one was fair game for those who were more so. That was the natural order of things. Through programs of charity, reform, sequestering, or even genocide, the progress of modernity could be assured and seen as inevitable. Social programs of these types were commonplace in one form or another, especially in areas of modernist colonization.

And the nonhuman world was even worse off. As an instrument of modernity, it had little if any intrinsic value, excepting some marginal, questionable, and dispensable aesthetic value. If it lacked evident extrinsic (instrumental) value it was open to reprocessing or annihilation: ecosystems, plants, animals, species of organism, landscapes, seascapes, and so on. Nothing was immune to modernity.

Modernist Culture

In the broad, then, what sort of cultural realities characterized modernity?

First, it was a "cult of reason" (Calinescu, 1977, p. 41), in which individual human minds—through formalized procedures of critical and analytical rationality—were seen as having the capability of coming to grips with the universe and the place of humanity within it. That coming to grips, while rational in analytic process, was empirical in its grounding within a realist world view. It entailed an instrumental view of knowledge, in which the power to predict and direct events was its driving force and ultimate justification. It esteemed the rational intellect, diminishing the influence of the emotional, the corporeal, and the nonrational in the formation and reproduction of cultural realities.

Second, it was a "struggle for order" (Bauman, 1991a, p. 6)—a project for the production of order in the known universe. It was directed to classifying the apparently chaotic diversity of the natural world, using universal principles underlying that diversity to reveal the true uniformities. It also sought to use those principles to *redesign* the world for the betterment of humanity, through the manipulation, management, and engineering of nature.

In that program, modernist culture itself became organized or differentiated into autonomous cultural spheres. Each sphere was seen and lived as a self-legislating (self-regulating or autonomous) field of cultural formation. It was also, nevertheless, foundational in its conception of its central mission: the discovery of the truth through the exercise of human reason, of beauty through human creativity, or whatever. This cultural differentiation occurred initially in the Renaissance, most notably with the differentiation of the secular from religious culture. It was greatly strengthened from the eighteenth century Enlightenment with the Kantian differentiation of three spheres: the theoretical, the ethical (moral or practical), and the aesthetic (Lash, 1990). There was developed also a firm differentiation of the private from the public. Matters of belief, and actions that did not cause injury to other persons or adversely affect their legitimate interests, were seen as being outside the public interest and therefore beyond legal sanction or state control.

Third, modernity was a project of human *liberation* from the bonds of ignorance, fear, myth, superstition, irrational convention, privation, and pestilence: of liberation through the "Enlightenment" (Adorno and Horkheimer, 1979, p. 3) of thought and action, both practical (moral) and technical; the "demythologization" of belief (Vattimo, 1992, p. 29); "the ideal of freedom defined within the framework of abstract humanism" (Calinescu, 1977, p. 41). Such an emancipatory project was necessarily, then, highly instrumental: not only in its view of knowledge, but also in its whole approach to the world. The nonhuman world was seen as a commodity for the instrumental perfection of the human condition. Even time itself was thus commodified: quantified, measured, valued, bought, and sold.

Fourth, and correspondingly, modernity was driven by "the doctrine of progress" (Calinescu, 1977, p. 41): a view of the progressive improvement of the human condition as both possible and desirable. It became a cult of the modern, of progress centrally perceived as "the obsolescence of yesterday's solutions" (Bauman, 1991a, p. 15). It was a quest for the *development* of all aspects of culture (Anderson, 1984): a quest in which both the action committed to it, and the (successful) outcomes of the action were highly valued. It was, therefore, "inherently future-oriented" (Giddens, 1990, p. 177).

Fifth, modernity was an epoch of *social connectedness*. That connectedness was multifaceted: centrally to one's (increasingly nuclear) family, more loosely to one's neighborhood, to associations or organizations to which one belonged, to one's workplace (or that of one's husband or father), and to the nation state (Foucault, 1970). All of these connections carried quite firm sets of expectations, duties, and rights, and were relatively stable over time. They located the individual in the social world, giving each person a sense of rootedness, historicity, belonging, citizenship, orderliness, purpose, certainty, and predictability.

Sixth, modernity was essentially a *unilinear* project (Vattimo, 1992, pp. 2-6). It developed and was based upon a vision of a single, linear time; a single, progressive, modernist history; the reasoned (ideally consensual) convergence of different views to the modern; and the universality of a single truth and morality. Difference was evolutionarily or developmentally deviant or prior. Progress onwards through modernity was the one true way.

Finally, and summatively, modernity may be seen as being expressed in its major institutions:

- *Scientifically,* it was the search for the objective, universal truth—for those general, veridical statements and theories that progressively more closely represented reality, whether natural or social (Feyerabend, 1978; Habermas, 1981/1983; Lyotard, 1979/1984a; Randall, 1962).

- *Ethically,* it was the search for those universal moral principles—natural or consensual—which may be taken as the normative guides for all civilized action (Bauman, 1993; Habermas, 1981/1983; Randall, 1962, pp. 365-386).
- *Aesthetically,* it was the search for general standards of beauty, taste, and harmony—dimensions of form common across particular instances and situations (Foster, 1983; Habermas, 1981/1983; Wellmer, 1991).
- *Technically,* it was the search for ever more totalizing ways of harnessing, constraining, molding, and directing nature for the emancipation of humankind (J.R. Jacob, 1994).
- *Economically,* it was the search for those universal principles of commodity constraint, restraint, incentive, regulation, and taxation through which the potential for cultural development could be optimized (Allen, Brahm, and Lewis, 1992; Bell, 1979, 1980; Lunn, 1982; Marx and Engels, 1867/1971, pp. 327–329).
- *Politically,* it was the search for those principles governing the optimal distribution of power within society for the realization of human potential in the interests of patronage nation states (Allen, Brahm, and Lewis, 1992; Bauman, 1991a, p. 278; Kumar, 1988).
- *Architecturally,* it was the search for the most effective and efficient ways of meeting perceived human needs for space (Ghirado, 1984/5; Jencks, 1987, 1991).
- *Industrially,* it was the search for the most efficient means of managing labor and capital investment for the greatest consumable production—culminating in the 'Taylorization' (Allen, 1992; Braverman, 1994; F. Taylor, 1972) and the 'Fordization' (Harvey, 1989; Montroux, 1961) of the twentieth century industrial sphere (S. Hall and M. Jacques, 1989; Rose, 1991; Rustin, 1989).
- *Organizationally,* it was the search for the most efficacious way of structuring power within, ownership of, and commitment to the goals of the organization; that structure being determined through both the dominant (the leading) organizational theory, and through consensus (Boje, 1994; Chia, 1995; Hassard, 1993; R.F. White and R. Jacques, 1995).
- *Individually,* it was a search for personal improvement, development, and enlightenment, with the correlative assumption of ever greater individual autonomy: entailing both responsibility and freedom (Bauman, 1991a; Lash and Friedman, 1992).
- *Socially,* it was the search for the most rational organization of

everyday social life, consistent with the foregoing imperatives—a search which generated a perpetual process of modernization through the rejection of the past and its reconstruction in a more perfect present as the path to an even more perfect future (Anderson, 1984; Habermas, 1981/1983; Kumar, 1988).

- *Educationally*, it was the search for the optimal means by which individuals could be molded into the social programs inspired by the foregoing enterprises (A. Green, 1990; Marx and Engels, 1867/1971, pp. 485–511; Whitty, 1992).

It is with this last institution of modernity, and more particularly with its *adult* education realities, that the next chapter is concerned.

Chapter 2

The Modernist Inheritance 2: Denying Adult Education

Modernist education was concerned with the molding of individuals into appropriate functional roles within the project of modernity.

That molding was undertaken within a strict framework of *constraints*: both procedural (deontological) and with respect to outcomes (teleological). The framework, or rather the frameworks, were defined by, encapsulated in, the competing grand theories or practical philosophies of social and educational development. These theories gave expression to different combinations of and emphases within the major currents of modernist thought:[1] humanistic education emphasized the realization of each individual's unique potential for creative goodness through the facilitation of individual human development; liberal education emphasized the liberation of human minds from the tyrannies of ignorance, myth, superstition, and culture, through initiation into the academic disciplines; progressive pragmatism emphasized the modernist commitment to life as an endless process of defining and solving problems, presenting education as initiation into the knowledge, skills, and dispositions indicated by that process; behaviorism emphasized the application of empirical science to education, in the manipulation or molding of individual behavior through the management of environmental contingencies; and radical education emphasized the transformative release from oppressive and exploitative cultural structures, by educationally empowering individuals and groups with the authentic knowledge of their contingent realities.

Modernist education was preoccupied with the molding of each person's inherited intelligence, through appropriate management of the learning environment. In the case of humanistic education, that management was seen centrally as the removal of unnecessary cultural constraints and restraints to the flowering of each individual's natural and naturally good talents. In the case of liberal education it was seen as immersion in the knowledge of the academic disciplines. In progressive education it was seen as being centered on engagement in the realities of life situations, in the form of real or simulated problems. In behaviorism it was the regulation of individual variables defined either as instruction or as rewards for correct behavior. In the case of radical education it was the presentation of challenging alternative realities and possibilities.

The intellect to be molded was seen as comprising not only the technical, cognitive intelligence of rational thought and action, but also the moral, practical intelligence of correct behavior, and the aesthetic intelligence of artistic creativity.

The role of education was seen in modernity as that of molding these zones of intelligence to the limits of each individual's inherited capacity. Those judged to have inherited a weak intellect were seen, accordingly, to be unsuited to prolonged or extensive education of the mind. They were suited, rather, for nonintellectual pursuits of the body: for manual or routinized occupations, which required not a liberating education of the intellect, but a training of the senses, the body.

Training—as instruction directed to the uncritical and unexamined learning and refinement of skill routines—was thus differentiated from *education* (see, e.g.: Lawson, 1979, pp. 105–108; Paterson, 1979, Chapter 2; R.S. Peters, 1965). Training was concentrated on the learning of technical, manual or psychomotor, and social skills. More particularly within the social realm, it was concerned with the learning of morally correct responses to the contingent temptations, threats, and opportunities of everyday experience. It also included—in late modernist behaviorism and neobehaviorism—the learning of intellectual skills prerequisite to education, such as the skills entailed in reading, writing, and arithmetical calculation (Gagné, 1977; Skinner, 1968).

Education, on the other hand, was concerned with the refinement of cognitive powers, with the development of theoretical and practical intelligence in the direction of prudential, ethical, theoretical, and critical understanding and, ultimately, wisdom (Paterson, 1979; R.S. Peters 1965). Education was concerned with the cultivation of individuals capable of independent thought and judgment; persons who could assume, within the social and cultural frameworks in which they were located, a high degree of moral, intellectual, and technical self-determination—of individual autonomy in all spheres of their lives (Boyle, Grisez, and Tollefsen, 1976; Candy, 1991; Chené, 1983; Gibbs, 1979). Training, in contrast, acknowledged the intellectual limits that nature had imposed on the possibility of many individuals gaining significant autonomy, or at least of doing so within particular spheres of their lives. It sought to ameliorate the effects of such deficiencies through providing for the development of functional routines by the afflicted individuals, sufficient for them to be happy and grateful in their work, social intercourse, leisure, and other spheres of civilized existence (K. Harris, 1979; Wain, 1987). Education was a serious business, demanding some objectivity, and therefore distance from the messiness of day-to-day living. It was, accordingly, seen as being properly undertaken in special institutions: schools, colleges, and universities. Training, in contrast, was less demanding and more appropriately embedded within the social engagements through which the training was to be practiced. It was therefore undertaken, not only in training organizations (such as polytechnics and technical colleges), but also on the job, on the parade ground, and elsewhere in "real life" situations.

Throughout modernity, education was increasingly focused on and structured by the knowledge of the academic disciplines and the honorable professions (such as medicine, architecture, and engineering). The disciplines were seen as both preserving the accumulating knowledge of the past and as leading to the discovery of new knowledge.

Within the education-training dichotomy, the gray areas—such as the formal learning of intellectual skills required in education within the academic disciplines, and the creative components of craftswork—provided no great threat to the dichotomy itself. That dichotomy was, indeed, of such profound importance in modernist education that it came to be expressed in all aspects of the education institution: in curriculum (e.g., between technical training and academic education); in teacher recruitment (e.g., between manual trades experience and academic achievement); in component institutions (e.g., between technical colleges and universities); and in vocational outcomes (e.g., between the trades and professions). In all of these distinctions, the persons involved with education, and the positions which they occupied, were of higher social status than were those of training, and they tended to attract higher material rewards. Students who were judged to be "better," "brighter," more "capable," and of higher "intelligence" were streamed without question into education. Those judged to be intellectually weak—the dullards, the troublemakers, the lazy, and the poor performers—were correspondingly channeled into manual training (M. Collins, 1991; Oakes, 1985).

Modernist education and training were seen very much as laying the foundation of a modernist *vocation*. The focus was on developing sufficient practical and theoretical understanding to slot each individual into their rung on a vocational ladder—the rung representing their level of intelligence (and hence their level of educational attainment, individual autonomy, and possible contribution to society). The strict status and reward hierarchy of vocations was, accordingly, paralleled closely by the level of educational attainment required for entry to them: most recently, professions such as medicine and law being of the highest status (and hence attracting the highest incomes), and those such as primary school teaching and nursing being among the lowest (e.g.: Congalton, 1969; Encel, 1984; Western, 1993).

Those vocations for which the required formal learning was judged to be of the nature of *training*, rather than education, were commonly seen (pejoratively) as mere "occupations." They were of lower social status, and they tended to command lower material rewards than did the professions. There was, within them, also a hierarchy of value, similarly correlated with the amount of formal training or basic education required: the various trades being the most highly valued. Work seen as requiring no formal training was, even more pejoratively, just a "job," requiring only "labor" for its execution.

In thus molding individuals to particular work roles and careers, the modernist education institution served to socialize its charges into the world of modernist dichotomies and hierarchies in which it was embedded and which it served. Those dichotomies and hierarchies were, accordingly, generally viewed as both real and natural.

The natural essence of being human was seen clearly as being, or as being expressed in, the power of the human species to understand the world, to codify and communicate that understanding in language, and to use it manipulatively to change the contingent nature of the material world for humanity's own benefit (Bauman, 1992; Davis, 1979). Those powers clearly were located in and identified with the rational intellect, the mind. The body served merely as the instrument by which the mind was nourished and informed, and through which the products of its creative activity were expressed. The superiority of education (which cultivated the intellect) over training (which cultivated the body) thus gave expression to the essence of what it was to *be* human. It was in that sense an entirely *natural* value hierarchy. It sought not only to enhance humanity in its humanness, but also to use the essential (intellectual) qualities of being human in the process. The derivative distinctions and hierarchies of the educational institution which served the process were therefore no less real and natural. The distinctions and hierarchies of the social order into which the educational institution was socializing students were viewed similarly.

The cultivation of the intellect—the task of education—was concerned with the acquisition of knowledge, both practical and theoretical, about the natural, social, and artifactual worlds. That knowledge was seen increasingly as being accumulated and refined within the academic disciplines, and as thereby being legitimated by them. Modernist education, correspondingly, came to be focused largely *on* the academic disciplines (Bowen and Hobson, 1987; Hirst, 1974). The curriculum was centered on them. They defined what counted as knowledge and what were acceptable means of acquiring it. They defined the epistemic criteria for assessing educational achievement and the standards of acceptable educational attainment.

Within the sciences, the concept of the progressive advance of knowledge held total sway over any thought of valuing the wisdom of historical "discoveries." Conversely—and on the other side of the great divide between what C.P. Snow (1956/1963) articulated as "the two cultures"—the humanities tended to be dominated by a view of their best scholarly output as potentially encapsulating and presenting timeless, general truths appropriate to their field, regardless of the historical period in which each was generated. Accordingly, the concept of the scholarly or, more precisely, the literary *canon* developed (Eliot, 1920; Hirsch, 1987; Scott, 1990a, 1990b). Included in the canon from throughout both modernity and premodernity were those works which were judged as perspicuously and insightfully identifying and presenting important social, moral, aesthetic, political, existential, or other truths which were seen as valuable in informing human action at *any* time, geographical location, or cultural circumstance. The "Great Books" program was one of the more notable and explicit projects to encourage the more general study of the (Western) literary canon. It was developed very strongly in the United States of America over the last 50 years of the modernist epoch (Adler, 1959; Van Doren, 1943). More pervasively, though, the canon was influential in defining the core curriculum of *any* sound modernist education. An intimate knowledge of its works, correspondingly, defined what it was, essentially, to be an educated person (A. Bloom, 1987; H. Bloom, 1994; Fish, 1993).

Since the extent and nature of an individual's intelligence were seen as being, from birth, a God-given or a naturally (biologically) inherited property, and since the task of education was primarily to mold that intelligence quantum, education came to be identified with the creation and management of an environment that was optimally supportive of such molding. This encouraged the development of agricultural metaphors to define and describe the educational task. Accordingly, education was commonly seen, at its best, as the "cultivation" or "nurturing" of the individual intellect. It sought to facilitate the "growth" of the individual learner in practical and theoretical understanding. It included such tasks as the "weeding out" (for training) of the intellectually weak, while the fortunate could "reap the benefits" of their education. Educational approaches were developed that incorporated the concept of "sowing the seed" (or the "germ") of key concepts in students' minds. "kindergartens" were developed as places for nurturing the early growth of small children. Sound education resulted in the "flowering" of individual intellectual potential, in response to a "thirst" for knowledge. Such metaphors were dominant and, through that dominance, they importantly determined the cultural construction and meaning of education (Candy, 1986).

Given this construction of the educational task as the cultivation of a predetermined intellectual quantum, modernity was, understandably, preoccupied with the concept of educational *opportunity* (Cohen, 1981; Paterson, 1979; Strike, 1982). Educational opportunity was seen in terms of what the individual's natural intelligence required to reach its full (natural, given) potential. That potential was perceived, in the early centuries of modernity, as essentially linked to social class, but it came increasingly to be recognized as biologically idiosyncratic. Increasing concern with equalitarian conceptions of justice therefore led to the generation of the guiding concept of "equality of educational opportunity." Through the expression of that concept, public educational institutions sought to provide identical educational experiences for all their charges, regardless of individual cultural background and circumstance, in the expectation that such experiences would allow the development and expression of whatever natural intelligence each individual possessed as part of their universal human nature (Bagnall, 1995a).

Correlative to that task of providing equality of educational opportunity in order that each individual could achieve to the limits of his or her natural intelligence, the educational institution had the responsibility of weeding out students on the basis of their intellectual (in)capabilities. This meant a focus on student assessment and grading (Levin and Clowes, 1991). Based on their respective gradings, students were sorted into hierarchical levels of capability for further education (of different levels of intellectual difficulty), or for training preparatory to entry to the workforce (DiLisi, 1980; Kulik, 1993).

In time, particularly with the development of IQ (Intelligence Quotient) tests, the process of weeding out students was made much more efficient (Hernstein and Murray, 1994; Mensh and Mensh, 1991; Oakes, 1985). Measures of general intelligence, as provided by IQ tests, allowed early determination of a child's educational potential, obviating the wastage of expensive educational opportunities on persons of weak intellect. Such children could be channeled early into manual training and domestic crafts—avoiding not only the futility of attempting to give them an education, but also certain frustration and dissatisfaction on their part at their own inability to respond to educational opportunities.

Modernist education was thus the education of youth for adulthood (Hunter, 1994; Newman, 1979). It was the schooling of immature persons for entry to the more or less stable, although progressively evolving, social framework of adult society. Adult education, on the whole, was a marginal sector of relatively little importance (Clark, 1958; M. Collins, 1991). To the extent that modernist schooling—primary, secondary, and tertiary—played its part in educating, assessing, and categorizing its charges, there was nothing left for a nonschool, an adult education, sector to achieve. Nineteenth and twentieth century programs of university adult education may be seen as having been as much public relations exercises in response to increasing levels of state support as they were genuine programs of university outreach (Whitelock, 1974). To the extent that they were genuinely educational, they were perceived as being properly watered down, simplified, made digestible to those members of the nonacademic general public who would seek to engage with them.

Extending the concept of modernist adult education as an educationally marginal enterprise, two perspectives of it may be adumbrated. The first perspective—that of adult education as the poor cousin of the educational institution[2]—is seen as the primary and dominant characterization. The second perspective—that of adult education as the social conscience of the educational institution—is dependent on the first and, in that sense, is derivative of and secondary to it.

The image of adult education as the educational poor cousin foregrounds its marginality. Even in those times when adult education was seen as being of some considerable social importance—such as the British and colonial army education programs during the two world wars (Dymock, 1995; T.H. Hawkins, 1947), the Scandinavian folk high schools over the last century (Blid, 1990; Lund, 1949; Paulston, 1980), and the agricultural extension movement in the United States after the spectacular agricultural disasters early this century (Boone, 1970; Matthews, 1960)—it remained steadfastly marginal to schooling (primary and secondary) and to formal higher and, more recently, to further education (M. Collins, 1991, pp. 1–2; McMaster and Randell, 1992; Maureen Smith, 1991). Its marginality was evidenced in all measures of social significance, such as: the level of public expenditure devoted to it; its political importance; the attention that it received in government policy; the social status accruing to its practitioners from their engagement in it; the level of remuneration associated with that engagement; the level of formal education required to practice as an adult educator; the level of recognition accorded it as a field of professional practice; and the derivative nature of its informing social theory and scholarship.

Public expenditure on modernist adult education was always small, relative to that on formal education. It consistently trailed the rapid development of public expenditure on formal education in the nineteenth and twentieth centuries (Tsang, 1996; Woodhall, 1989a). Only in times of large scale "public education" (propaganda) campaigns, such as those instituted in times of war, did the public fiscal commitment to adult education look at all serious. Even then, it is doubtful that it measured up to the formal educational sector. It is only by including private expenditure on in-house training, within business and industry, that the financial commitment to adult learning rivals that of formal education, and then only in late modernity (Catley and Rann, 1992; Lusterman, 1978; Mincer, 1962; Woodhall, 1977, 1989b).

Similarly, politically, modernist adult education rated as very weak, although it was of considerable importance in empowering a small number of individuals. The importance of the Workers' Educational Association (WEA) in New Zealand in the education of Labour Party politicians, cabinet ministers, and a former prime minister is a notable example here (Shuker, 1984; A.B. Thompson, 1945).

Adult education did not feature strongly overall in government policy. There were, though, notable exceptions, occurring when particular programs were being formulated, such as the Cooperative Extension Service of the United States, established effectively with the Smith-Lever Act of 1914 (Boone, 1970), and the Australian Trade Union Training Authority, established in the Trade Union Training Authority Act of 1975 (R. Morris, 1991).

The social status accruing to the practitioners of modernist adult education from their engagement in it was, similarly, generally not great relative to that from other forms of educational engagement, most notably those in the secondary and higher education sectors. The marginality of adult education as a field of social practice allowed it to be used as a testing ground and as a site for educational innovation and experimentation for the educational institution as a whole. Correspondingly, it tended to attract (often quite radical) social reformers—individuals who perceived the marginality of the field as affording them greater freedom to develop and realize their reformist agendas or missions. Their activities and personalities, in turn, reinforced the marginality and lower status of the field. That status was reflected in the correspondingly lower levels of remuneration accorded teachers and other leaders in adult education. Indeed, much work in the field was traditionally seen as voluntary. There developed a pattern of large numbers of voluntary workers, smaller but still large numbers of part-time or casual employees, and a very small elite of full-time professionals. This pattern was conceptualized by Houle (1970) as a pyramid of leadership in adult education. Not surprisingly, the majority of those towards the (professional) apex of the pyramid were men, while the proportion of women was higher (generally predominant) toward the (voluntary) base (J. Thompson, 1983).

The levels of formal education required for practice as an adult educator in modernity also tended to be below those of other educational sectors. Since much modernist adult education was developmental, social, vocational, issue-based, problem-based, or craft-based in nature (nondisciplinary, and therefore marginal to education proper), it was judged to be reasonably taught by persons who were experienced in the area of its particular concern, with less attention commonly being paid to the levels of formal qualifications held. In contrast to the school sector (but not that of higher education, where academic qualifications performed the basic gatekeeping function), adult education was largely seen also as not requiring regulated formal teaching qualifications of its practitioners.

The research and scholarship that informed modernist adult education practice was almost entirely derivative—primarily through the behavioral sciences and social philosophy, and secondarily other fields of education. Throughout history, the dominant theories, concerns, and interests in the field were those of its formal counterparts. This is well illustrated by the rise of the adult education movement in the USA, where the development of adult education theory was focused almost entirely on the application of social philosophy and the social, behavioral, and political sciences *to* the field: teasing out the implications of those disciplines for practice in the field and using their research paradigms and techniques to illuminate and inform that practice.[3]

Adult education emerged as being of any cultural importance only in periods of rapid social change, such as: when Christian churches sought to consolidate their authority, in the face of the threat from secular science, through Bible study and related adult literacy programs (Kelly, 1970; Knowles, 1977); when minimal levels of workplace literacy became economically desirable with the industrial revolution (Graff, 1987; Harrison, 1961); and when re-education in both occupational and civic knowledge was increasingly demanded in the course of the twentieth century by the accelerating rate of intragenerational obsolescence in instrumental knowledge and technological change.[4] This last factor saw the rapid growth of programmatic activity in late modernist adult education. It was accompanied by the development of adult education as a field of professional practice, distinct from the knowledge with which it was educationally concerned (Darkenwald and Merriam, 1982; Knowles, 1994). Embedded in that professionalization was the development of adult education as a field of scholarly inquiry—examining the practice, informing it, and giving it academic authority (Jarvis and Chadwick, 1991; Jensen, Liveright, and Hallenbeck, 1964).

The second perspective of modernist adult education here articulated is that of the field as the social conscience of the educational institution. As such, it must necessarily be both derivative of and secondary to that institution. In this sense, modernist adult education was characterized by its responsiveness to the failings, limitations, and injustices of the more formal primary, secondary, and tertiary sectors of the educational institution. That responsiveness took a diversity of more or less radical forms.

Toward the less radical end of the spectrum, the field was primarily, but variously, concerned with such projects as: the offering of second-chance education (such as adult basic, including literacy, education) to adults who had failed fully to capitalize on or to benefit from the formal system (Inbar, 1990; Kozol, 1980); the offering of a (necessarily watered down) version of mainstream education to those adults who were outside the mainstream, through, for example, the liberal education programs offered by university extramural departments (Whitelock, 1974; B.M. Williams, 1978); responding to the social contingencies demanding education which the formal system was ill-equipped to provide, through, for example, citizenship education programs for immigrant adults in the United States (Hazard, 1948); and responding to the demands for retraining and resocializing arising from shifts in the political economy (Foley and Morris, 1995).

The more radical end of the spectrum was characterized by a concern for social or political change of one sort or another. More formal modernist education, by its very nature, was socially and politically conservative, more focused on individual development and the transmission of cultural heritage (Briton, 1996; Usher and Edwards, 1994). The child- and youth-centeredness of its clientele gave it a very long lead time—essentially an intergenerational one—as an agent of social change. Such a lead time was, on occasions throughout modernity, and increasingly toward its end, quite inadequate in coping with the demands for social and political change. In such circumstances, adult education developed forms of engagement more radical than those which could be accommodated within the formal educational system. Such forms, while various in their programmatic expression, were all structured around the concept of individual or collective empowerment of politically, economically, socially, or culturally marginalized, disempowered, and oppressed individuals and groups. The focus was on experimental and creative ways in which adult education could be used, instrumentally, in the service of individual and collective empowerment, liberation from oppression, and release from deprivation. The traditional distinctions between education and sociopolitical change were thus blurred or lost entirely in programs of this sort, with adult education becoming a *part of* the sociopolitical ends to which it was directed (Boughton, 1994; Paterson, 1973; Thomas, 1982). The learning being sought was, correspondingly, typically directed to achieving solidarity and capability in social action, and to developing a more politically aware construction, on the part of those involved, of their social realities (Foley, 1991; J. Thompson, 1980).

In their responsiveness to contingently perceived injustices, programs of radical adult education relied heavily on the continuation of both the particular injustices on which the programs were founded and the will to address them. In so far as the programs were successful, or the will to engage in them defeated, the programs diminished and died, or became less radical (Foley, 1991). This strongly contextualized nature of radical adult education resulted in its programs exhibiting greater ephemerality than did other programmatic areas in the field.

Programs of radical adult education date at least from nineteenth century social movements such as the Chartist movement of social reform in mid-nineteenth-century England (Briggs, 1959; Johnson, 1988; Youngman, 1986). Earlier this century, notable programs were the Antigonish Movement on the eastern seaboard of Canada and the Highlander Folk School in the United States (Lovett, 1980), the latter continuing in modified form in later modernity. In the twentieth century, such programs have been framed strongly by Marxist and neo-Marxist ideology, through such critical activists as Freire (1972, 1978), Boal (1979), and Lovett (1982).

Conclusion

In sum, then, the field of modernist adult education may be characterized as a diverse heterogeneity of ideologically driven interests, competing for resources, attention, and commitment—both public and private. While much of it was responsive to particular perceived needs and interests, it tended to be so within well-articulated and researched theoretical and philosophical frameworks. As a whole, it was driven by a commitment to progress: to a progressive growth in knowledge (technical, moral, aesthetic, and theoretical) as underpinning the progressive liberation of humanity from deprivation, ignorance, prejudice, pestilence, and dependency. Such progress was made possible through a humanistic, essentially secular, commitment to the power and universal superiority of reason over the emotions and all other natural forces of disorder and degeneration. Given the continuing triumph of reason, the contemporary was seen as part of the essentially timeless march of progress. In it, accurate accounts of human history were seen as contributing importantly to humanity's appreciation of the need for continuing commitment to the project, through an understanding of the value and fragility of its achievements. The value of modernist adult education derived from that mission: encompassing both the instrumental value and the intrinsic value of understanding and proficiency as liberating ends in themselves. Given the importance of education as both a social and a socializing institution, the manner in which it was conducted was seen as being of no less importance than the ends to which it was directed. There was a tendency, therefore, for it to be seen as essentially interactive, and ideally group-based. It emerged as having been importantly both a public and a private good, although the ways in which and the extent to which it was so depended upon the prevailing social theory. The focus and mix of state and private funding were correspondingly various.

Significantly, modernist adult education was an activity marginal to the rest of the educational institution. Mainstream education was concerned with cultural transmission and cultural induction. It was therefore concerned with the education of children and youths. Adult education was relevant only when the pace of sociopolitical change demanded an educative response more rapid than could be achieved through the generational cycle of schooling, and in those cases where schooling had so signally failed to deliver the educational outcomes expected of it that remedial (adult) education was called for. It was also present, though, as a current of liberal progressivism, that sought to give adults educational opportunities for self-improvement through organized learning outside the formal system.

Modernist adult education may be seen, from a postmodern perspective, as suffering from two signal limitations. First—and in spite of the efforts of educational reformers such as Birkbeck (Kelly,

1957), Lindeman (1926/1961), Buckingham (Turner, 1934), and Knowles (1980)—it failed to bring adult learning in from the educational and cultural margins. Adult education was, overall, a minor component of the modernist cultural machine. The educational focus of modernity was on schooling—primary, secondary, and tertiary—as a means of cultural transmission. Second, modernist adult education was constrained within a very narrow set of competing progressive ideologies: the Enlightenment frameworks of liberal, humanistic, and technicist normative belief which defined the limits of the permissible cultural universe. The value of perspectives beyond that field was vigorously denied, and the perspectives suppressed.

In these respects, modernist adult education may be seen as the embodiment of its own denial. It denied the centrality and importance of adult learning to the nature of individual and social being, and it denied the potential of realities beyond the narrow range of its own Enlightenment vision. Nevertheless, important parts of modernist adult education rendered it much more like its postmodern successor than did those of more formal modernist education, most notably those programs where it was, genuinely, situationally responsive, contextually embedded, heterodox, open, diverse, ephemeral, and participative.

Part Two

Postmodernity

The three chapters in this section examine the nature of postmodernity. Chapter 3 begins with an articulation of postmodern perception, belief, and identity. Chapter 4 continues in the same vein with a focus on postmodern communication and on the postmodern frame of mind. It then draws together some summative features of postmodern culture. Chapter 5 reconfigures the material from the previous two chapters in a framework of six tensions, two in each of the domains of belief, identity, and sociality.

Chapter 3

Postmodernity 1: Seeing, Believing, and Being in a Fractured World

Postmodernity is seen here as a transformative cultural change—transformative in the sense that, contrasted to modernity, it marks a profound shift in the way in which we perceive, understand, and communicate about ourselves, realities external to us, and our location within those realities. It incorporates modernity, in the sense that its inherited cultural realities (its beliefs, traditions, mores, meanings, symbols, myths, values, and artifacts) are essentially modernist, while including also some premodern elements. Importantly, though, it problematizes that cultural inheritance, in the sense that it questions, challenges, casts profound uncertainty over, and deconstructs the modernist frameworks of belief and meaning upon which the project of modernity was founded and in which it was constituted. Postmodernity is, importantly, the result of the modernist project turning critically in on itself; the transformative maturation of modernity. It is culture reconstructed and (more importantly) in the process of *being* reconstructed, from the self-conscious deconstruction of modernity. That deconstruction may be seen as a *fracturing*, a *rending*, of the certainties and verities of modernity. It is the central, the pivotal, postmodern impulse, from which all other important features of postmodernity flow in their culturally contingent difference.

Postmodernity is a cultural condition, self-consciously underpinned by and incorporating a worldview, a frame of mind and mood. That postmodern worldview is generated and informed by three general elements: (1) an *epistemology* of the nature of belief and its relationships to noncognitive realities, perception, and action; (2) an *ontology* of being or human identity; and (3) a *technology* of communication. These elements may be drawn together and recombined in the summary definition given in the introduction—

> Postmodernity is culture that is self-consciously and sympathetically informed by an understanding of: the interpretative nature of human perception; the indeterminate, contextualized, and fragmented nature of knowing and being; and the de-differentiated and generalized nature of contemporary communication.

As a cultural condition underpinned by a worldview, postmodernity may best be seen as fundamentally a *paradigmatic*, rather than an epochal, concept. In other words, it may best be seen as a cultural phenomenon which stands in opposition to continuing and emerging elements of the modern (and of the premodern). Those currents and elements may, conceivably, recombine and reform to overwhelm postmodernity as the dominant influence in cultural formation. Alternatively, postmodernity itself may give way to cultural influences not yet envisaged. In other words, while postmodernity may be seen *as* contemporary, it is not *the* contemporary, and it may well lose its contemporaneity. Nevertheless, *as* a contemporary cultural reality, it may be seen as a *periodizing* change, in the sense that it follows the modernist epoch (see Chapter 1) in time. It is also periodizing in that its incorporation of modernity means that it must necessarily *follow* that modernity which it incorporates. This applies also, and perhaps even more pointedly, to the communication technologies which it importantly incorporates and which inform it.

The extent to which postmodernity is an *epochal* change (one of both profound and general cultural—and hence historical—import) is a function not only of its transformative and periodizing nature, but also its *contingent cultural importance*. The increasingly contingent importance of postmodern realities is a matter of common observation and heated exchange. Whether we can reasonably label—in expectation or in hindsight—that continued contingent reality as "epochal" is a matter secondary to the nature of postmodernity itself, although a number of commentators have chosen to so label it.[1]

This chapter and the next are directed to unpacking the foregoing definition of postmodernity. They do so by paralleling the elucidation of modernity presented in Chapter 1. Through that structure, it is intended to highlight the way in which postmodernity incorporates but problematizes modernist realities and, in so doing, moves importantly beyond them. The present chapter focuses initially on the understanding of human perception that informs postmodernity. It then examines the nature of postmodern belief and individual identity. The following chapter continues the dissection, with an articulation of communication in postmodernity, and of the postmodern frame of mind. It closes with an attempt to examine more broadly the cultural institutions and currents in postmodernity.

Postmodern Perception

Postmodernity problematizes the modernist representational or mimetic view of human perception and the realist world view on which that representationalism depends. Realism, you may remember, is the belief that the world external to human consciousness is open to objective perception by the subjective consciousness of the human mind. Representationalism, then, is the belief that the perceptions of our senses represent or mirror the objective realities of their objects—the objects of perception in the external world. Such a view, you may further recall, is dependent also on a fundamental dualism between the perceiving subject or mind and the objects of perception or matter.

Postmodernity, though, fractures the certainty of that dualism, and with it both realism and representationalism. Human perception is seen as embedded inseparably in our existing beliefs and subconscious figurations about the world. Those beliefs and cognitive frameworks determine which realities we expect and which we regard as possible in our perceptual world.[2] The external world, therefore, is not represented or mirrored in our perceptions of it, as modernity presupposed. Rather, the external world is *interpreted* in and through our "perceptions" of it. In perceiving, we take to the external world a complex array of mental templates, through which we make sense of that world, by crafting images of it. We can no more perceive the external world (in the sense of forming comprehensible images of it) without those templates, than we can imagine the unimaginable.

This is not to deny the existence of the external world. Philosophical idealism—in the sense that nothing exists outside the mind of a knowing subject — is nonsense if taken at face value. To that extent, realism is correct. However, it is incorrect in its commitment to the possibility of the objective—the subjectively independent—perception of that external reality by human minds. We cannot perceive but through an active process of interpretation. That is what is meant by the "interpretative nature of human perception" in our summary definition of postmodernity.

If perception is never purely objective, unmediated by prior understandings and expectations, how, you may ask, do we develop those understandings in the first place? The answer is, in part, progressively throughout life, and certainly to some degree from birth (Gadamer, 1977; Lacan, 1977). There is a continual reflexivity between what we perceive on the one hand and what we believe on the other. That is to say, what we perceive continually and variously confirms or modifies what we believe, and what we believe continually and variously conditions what we perceive.

A "fact," then, is not something that exists in the external world. There are no facts to be perceived without frameworks of belief and cognition to define them. Similarly, "truth" exists only *within* particular frameworks of belief and cognition. To that extent, truth is relative to those frameworks. However, this is not to say that anything is true because we choose to believe it. Truth is defined by the (intersubjective) interpretative frameworks that we bring *to* our perception and understanding of the world. Within those frameworks, what counts or doesn't count as evidence, what is seen as fact or fiction, and what is true or false is, to varying degrees, clear-cut, non-arbitrary, and not subject to individual or collective whim.

Indeed, our frameworks of belief are ineradicably embedded in language. It is through our use of language that we categorize and symbolize our realities, and it is through language that we generate beliefs about the relationships between those realities and their various component qualities (Halliday, 1978; O'Sullivan et al., 1988). Human perception is thus conditioned not only by our beliefs but also by the linguistic conventions through which we structure our beliefs.

Furthermore, those beliefs and conventions are ineradicably normative (Barthes, 1973; Gadamer, 1977; Phillips, 1981; Wain, 1987). By this is meant that their very nature is determined by considerations of what is worthwhile, what is of interest, what is of value, and what it is right to do and good to be. A belief may well be construed as describing (or constructing) a matter of fact in the world, but it is also irreducibly determined by matters of value. The tidy modernist dualism between matters of fact and matters of value is thus denied in postmodernity. With that denial, and with the psychocultural embeddedness of all perception—its interpretative mediation by our cognitive frameworks and beliefs—that perception itself is seen as fundamentally normative in nature, as essentially value-based (Eagleton, 1983; Vattimo, 1988). Therein is denied in postmodernity the modernist commitment to the *objective* perception of facts in the world, cleansed of cultural value.

But what of emotion? You will recall that modernist perceptual theory was founded also on a dualism between reason and emotion, the latter being seen as a human weakness, interfering in the process and diminishing the power of pure reason. Rationality, then, sought to conquer the emotions. Postmodernity problematizes this nicety too—arguing that our reason, our rationality, and the beliefs (including knowledge) generated through its application, are irreducibly influenced by our emotions. To believe that we can separate out the emotive components from the rational and objective components of our thinking and believing is seen as simplistic nonsense. The process and nature of rationality are thereby seen as irreducibly influenced by our emotions and, more particularly, by desire.[3] So too, then, is our perception. If perception is based in our frameworks of belief, expectation, and subconscious figuration, and those frameworks are importantly emotive in nature, so too must our perception importantly be a function of our emotions.

In sum, then, while modernity embraced a representationalist model of perception, postmodernity embraces an interpretivist one.

Postmodern Belief

If all perception is interpretative, then all belief must be underdetermined by the material reality to which it relates (if it relates at all). That belief must also be a function of—be contingent upon—the perceptual frameworks through which it is mediated. Postmodernity thus problematizes the tidy modernist distinction between knowledge (as justified true belief) and mere belief (as that which may be false and is uncertain). The truth of any belief is seen as being dependent upon its informing framework of understanding—the view of the world in which it is embedded. And all belief (including "knowledge") is *indeterminate*—underdetermined by any other realities, and therefore tentative, uncertain, and subject to contestation—a feature which is distilled out in the summary definition given earlier.

Belief is thus subjectively and intersubjectively determined. It is a function of value and of emotion, both of which we take to any project of understanding. Ultimately, there are no value-neutral grounds on which we may distinguish fact from value. Problematized, then, in postmodern epistemology is the modernist distinction between these categories—between what is and what should be, between the empirical and the normative.

With the erosion of perceptual representationalism, postmodernity also erodes the foundationalist epistemology of modernity. The assumed objective transparency of the external world in modernist epistemology is shifted to opacity in postmodernity. No longer can our perceptions of the external world be taken as the empirical foundations of the natural order of that world, cleansed of subjectivity, value, interest, and emotion. No longer can the rationality of the human mind be seen as providing a universal set of procedures for interpreting those perceptions in an objectively pure manner. The foundations of our knowledge have become fragmented into epistemic pockets of provisional, interpretative belief, infused with cultural interest, emotion, and value.

The grand modernist project of secular demythologization, the emancipation of pure reason, has collapsed into a plethora of (frequently contesting) programs and traditions. With the project of secular demythologization has gone the universally progressive search for transcendental, timeless truth. Epistemic heterodoxy is implied, expected, and celebrated. The traditional grand narratives, theories, or philosophies of modernist legitimation—whether they be of an empiricist, rationalist, Marxist, or whatever nature—are diminished in status to that of competing programmatic perspectives. By extension, postmodernity involves the diminution of grand, universalizing social or developmental theories. It is anticanon, in the sense of its questioning the notion that any intellectual tradition has epistemologically privileged authority. It is antiholistic, in the sense that it questions the coherence and universalism that underpin holism.

Belief is also importantly articulated through *language*. The concepts that we take to an understanding of the world, and the relationships between those concepts, are constrained and restrained by the possibilities, limitations, and power of the language(s) that we use in the process. All perception is interpretative, and it is largely interpretative through language. What we perceive and what we believe are not unmediated images of an external reality. They are linguistically mediated and generated pictures of and stories about imagined external realities.

Those stories may exist as *artifacts* in text, graphics, formulae, or similar codifications. However, they attain meaning *as* belief only in particular cultural (including sociolinguistic) contexts. Only within a cultural system—including its conventions of language use, conceptual meanings, interests, priorities, expectations, power relationships, value commitments, and beliefs about the world—do stories or other interpretations acquire any particular meaning. Problematized, then, is the clear modernist distinction between knowledge (as a function of facts in the world) and meaning (as human interests in the world). Knowledge—or more correctly, belief in general—is inseparable from meaning. Interpretations have meaning in particular contexts of belief. They have no meaning outside particular contexts; that is to say, they have no context-free status as beliefs. In other words, postmodern belief is seen as being *contextualized* in the phraseology of the introductory summary definition.

Belief, knowledge, then is necessarily embedded in cultural contexts. It therefore loses the transcendental properties assumed for it in modernity. The dualist model of mimesis that informed the modernist conception of knowledge thus loses its meaning; if knowledge is embedded in cultural contexts and those contexts mediate and constrain our understanding of the material world, the basis for any rigid separation of knowledge from its object dissolves.

Cultural contexts of belief are, potentially, infinitely diverse, although transcultural influences have historically limited the realization of that potential. The globalization of value through the influence of contemporary communications media may well be enhancing that process of convergence, although there are also countertendencies immanent in such media (of which more in the next chapter). The important point to note here, though, is not the extent of potential diversity, but rather the *reality* of diversity—the reality of different cultural contexts of belief and (most importantly) the lack of any necessary commonalities between them. By this last point is meant that there are not evidently any necessary beliefs, values, or conventions between contexts. While *some*—perhaps many and profoundly important—commonalities contingently *do* prevail, it is not necessary that they do so. It is also contingently evident that there is, indeed, a great diversity of belief between cultural contexts. That diversity is potentially incompatible or incoherent across contexts. What is true in one context may be denied in another, and what is meaningful in one context may not be so in another. In other words, belief is *fragmented* or fractured, to varying degrees and in differing ways, across cultural contexts of meaning—another point that is captured in our summary definition of postmodernity. The assumed *unity* of all knowledge in the modernist epistemological project thus collapses into fragments.

With the fragmentation of that unity, the modernist concept of the *advance* or progress of knowledge is also fragmented. Indeed, the very notion of the progressive advance of modernist knowledge—tied as it was to such values as greater epistemic generality, power, and simplicity—is seen as contingent to particular types of cultural contexts (instrumental, scientistic, and so on). In postmodernity, then, knowledge may certainly be seen as progressive, but only in particular cultural contexts, particular sociolinguistic traditions which, notably, themselves are unstable and changeable over time.

The modernistically tidy hierarchy of academic disciplines is thereby also problematized in postmodernity, since it is denied its universal foundations. If there is no one correct model of the progress of knowledge, no one set of epistemic values in which to ground such a model, there can be no one correct hierarchy of disciplines based on such a model or such a set of values. Uncertainty and difference prevail, with contestation where there are competing claims to epistemic value.

You will recall that, with the modernist commitment to the Enlightenment project—to the use of knowledge gained through the power of instrumental reason for the improvement and emancipation of humankind—a strongly instrumental conception of knowledge developed. That conception is clearly incorporated into postmodernity, but it loses its grandeur. Postmodernist belief is more situational than instrumental—more concerned with illuminating and exploring local regions of meaning and with sensitizing its travelers to the epistemic intricacies, than it is with discovering a powerful theory through which nature may be harnessed for the grand project of human emancipation.

With the loss of certainty as to the one true path to enlightenment, so too is lost the certainty of modernity as an epistemological project, as a project committed to the elucidation of knowledge about the natural world. The certainty of that project contributed (with Christian idealism) to a commitment to knowledge as being of *intrinsic* (as well as of instrumental) value. The fragmentation of the one true path into a potential infinity of different—variously contradictory and mutually incoherent—paths, diminishes and opens to question the wisdom of a commitment to traveling determinedly and imperiously on only one of them. Postmodernity tends to be more concerned with the nature of *being* and identity. Its concern is, in that sense, more ontological than epistemological. Gone with the certainty of the modernist epistemological project is its component preoccupation with the ordering or classification of contingent reality. The focus, rather, is shifted to the infinitely rich diversity of contingent reality, and to its many meanings and interpretations.

In all of this it should be noted of postmodernity that—contrary to the enunciations of some of its critics and its overenthusiastic apologists—it is not a project committed to denying rationality. It is recognized in postmodernity that reason serves as the framework through which experiences are related and extended, through which ideas are translated into action, and through which (together with trust) we can communicate with other persons—however inadequately—our perceptions, visions, concerns, and aspirations, both within and across traditions.

Postmodernity does, though, recognize important *limits* to rationality, most importantly the lack of any extrinsic foundation constraining our commitment to rationality itself. In other words, it is accepted that this commitment is a matter of (rational) instrumental choice—a choice that cannot be justified beyond our (solipsistic) appeal to the utility and reasonableness of so choosing. Postmodernity may thereby leave an individual or group to choose freely the option of rejecting rationality. The choice, however, if genuine, would result in a profoundly isolated and meaningless existence. It is one which few, if any, persons would either be likely or able to take.

Postmodernity also recognizes the *insufficiency* of reason to the leading of anything like a full life. Creativity, research, social interaction, indeed, all of our everyday experiences draw heavily upon the nonrational. To perceive of rationality as (modernistically) displacing or ridding us of such other aspects of human experience, is to impoverish that experience, to drain it of much that is rich and valuable, except, perhaps, in those cases of the most trivial, reduced, and technicist human action.

The third and crucial limit to postmodern rationality derives from the pluralism of the postmodern social context. To the extent that different frameworks of belief and action are incompatible or incommensurable, to that extent there cannot be rational coherence between or among them. Coherence—the central criterion of rationality—cannot hold in such instances. We must therefore (rationally) accept the (rational) irreconcilability of those differences: their opacity or impermeability to rational understanding or reconciliation. In such a situation, insistence on rationality, insistence on reasoned coherence, can only be dismissive and repressive of difference. Pluralism and tolerance thus demand (reasonably) that these situations—constituting perhaps a large part of our individual and social existence—are beyond the limits of rationality.

In sum then, in the shift from modernist to postmodern belief, we see the following sorts of component shifts in focus: from necessity to contingency, from the general to the local, from the universal to the particular, from instrumental knowledge to situational knowledge, from the timeless to the timely, from foundationalism to relativism, from objective to subjective knowledge, from transparency to opacity, from progressive to alternative, and from demythologization to the demythologization of demythologization (Vattimo, 1992, p. 40)—what Bauman (1992, p. x) sees as the "*re-enchantment* of the world that modernity had tried hard to *dis-enchant*."

Postmodern Identity

Postmodernity similarly problematizes the modernist conception of the individual person as an autonomous, coherent, rational monad, clearly separable from culture and from the physical world. The emphasis, rather, is on the cultural and the subconscious determination of individual action, the incoherence of individual being, the fragmentation of individual identity, and its embeddedness in the historical contexts of its formation.

Any claims to essential properties of humanness are regarded with the utmost suspicion. Human identity, rather, is seen as being importantly grounded in the discourses or cultural contexts within which each individual acts over the course of the lifetime.[4] Culture, thereby, is not just the *context* of human action—as modernity postulated—but is its very genesis, as well as its impulse. Identity is thus *contextualized* in the terminology of our summary definition. It is contextualized, though, in and through the subconscious, in a complexity of different, disparate, separate, and partial selves. It is thus contextualized in two important ways. On the one hand, it is *informed* by the discursive contexts through which each individual journeys. On the other hand, the emergence of any particular identify will be *triggered* by particular discursive or cultural contexts (whether willed or otherwise).

The many and diverse contexts of those contextualizations, are therefore seen, not as molding a single coherent identity, but rather a diversity of identities within any one individual. The mutual incompatibility and incoherence of cultural contexts of identity formation thus contribute to the generation of an array of potentially incompatible and mutually incoherent identities within any one individual. Also contributing to that diversity is the particularity of the processes through which identities and identity fragments are reworked and recombined in each individual. Individual identity is therefore highly *fragmentary* in nature (to refer back again to the summary definition). It is fragmented among an open set of shifting and partial identities constructed from and through different discourses, associated with different life situations and different life roles, and mediated by profoundly indeterminate subconscious influences. An individual may thus be seen as a portfolio of such personages.

What numerous recent events of the most horrifyingly inhumane proportions have told us—the Holocaust, the ethnic violence in postcolonial Rwanda and postcommunist Yugoslavia, and so on—is that each individual has the potential to embrace the most disparate selves. Diabolical evil can coexist with overwhelming good, great compassion with profound brutality, unflinching selfishness with selfless generosity of spirit. Such experiences are seen as expressions, and as evidence, of the fragmentation of identity, of the power of the various discourses in which our identity is embedded over the idealization of the autonomous individual. Rejected, therefore, as unrealizable, is the liberal humanist call for the rational reconciliation of our individual identities into coherent unities.[5]

Individual identity is therefore also *indeterminate,* in the sense that its nature can never be fully and finally known, since there is always potential for the development of new identities and the evolution of existing ones: a quality which is also brought out in our summary definition.

Individual identity is always, therefore, *provisional*—in the process of change and open to new and different possibilities, including possibilities that are consciously and actively *selected* by the individual. Such selection should be seen as constrained by the frameworks of belief and subconscious figuration within which an individual is operating but, within those constraints, the freedom to select may be seen to exist. The opportunity to experience that freedom is clearly dependent on the choices that are available—on the range and diversity of alternative models of identity that are sufficiently clearly and appealingly presented to constitute alternatives from among which one can choose.

Here the mass media of late modernity, and of postmodernity itself, have contributed and are contributing most significantly, in presenting a wide range of heroes, antiheroes, common persons, outrageously different persons, and alternative persons in ways which are believable, and replicable as identity models. From magazines, newspapers, television, film, video, and the Internet, we are presented with a vast array of identity alternatives, from which we can select, and from which we do select within our epistemic and ontological constraints. From that selection we contribute to the fragmentary complexity of individual identities—to that extent contributing to our own creation, but always so within the limits imposed by existing identities and the frameworks of belief that importantly inform those identities.[6]

The contingency, indeterminacy, and openness to self-selection of postmodern identity encourage the retrospective integration of self-identity with self-constructed senses or stories of one's personal history of experiences, meanings, and relationships. In this sense, postmodern identity may be seen as showing a tendency to historicism, albeit a fragmented historicism—a feature of postmodern identity that has been developed pedagogically by Middleton (1992) through the use of life-histories.

The provisionality of individual identity extends importantly (for the purposes of this book) to the concept of intelligence. The modernist conception of intelligence as a decontextualized, natural (biologically inherited), generalized property of each individual is turned on its head in postmodernity, where intelligence is seen as a quality that is specific to—defined by and only meaningful within—specific cultural contexts. While clearly we inherit (biologically) variable potentialities with respect to intelligence, the possibilities for the formation of those potentialities are infinitely diverse. Intelligence is not, therefore, inherited in any important sense. And it is certainly not a generalized property across different cultural contexts—a point that is heightened with epistemic contradiction and incoherence across those contexts. The notion of generalized, culture-free, objective intelligence tests is therefore a nonsense. Intelligence, rather, takes various forms, depending on its context. It is not necessarily intellectual anymore than it is manual. An important basis on which modernity exalted the creative intellect over manual skill is therefore lost.

The fragmentation of individual identity and its cultural contextualization seriously undermine the notion of the individual as an autonomous monad. If identity is indeterminately embedded in and fragmented among a shifting set of discourses, the idea of the individual as autonomous, free of those discourses, does not make a great deal of sense. Similarly, and more fundamentally, the coherence of the individual monad is quite contrary to the postmodern notion of identity as fragmented and contextualized.

Humanistic notions of individual development as the realization and efflorescence of innate potential are thus problematized by postmodernity, since they depend on the individual possession of essential human properties, and on the natural determinacy of human potential—both of which are questioned in postmodernity. Similarly problematized is the humanistic conception of personhood and individual maturity. If autonomy is denied, what is left of such a conception? Modernist humanism may have displaced God with humanity as the center of the intelligent and moral universe, but postmodernity displaces both God and humanity, in denying the veracity of any center. The meaning of our existence is as open to the contingency of circumstance, life history, and self-construction as is the identity that gives that meaning its existential and empirical expression.

Also problematized in postmodernity are the clear modernistic hierarchies of influence within the individual: the conscious over the unconscious and the rational over the emotional. Identity (and thereby thought itself) are, rather, seen as importantly influenced by the human subconscious and the human emotions. To that extent, at least, human thought and action are nonrational, nontraditional, and not subject to individual will or cultural molding.

The clear distinction—in Cartesian rationalism at least—between the individual mind and the body in which it is located (and which nurtures it and is the instrument of its rational will) is similarly questioned in postmodernity. There is seen to be a veritable avalanche of evidence for the mutuality of mind and body, for their interdependence at different levels of their functioning and in diverse ways.

Also problematized by the postmodern conception of individual identity is the individualistic foundation to free enterprise capitalism. Capitalism is based on the (individualistic) assumption that individual persons, on the whole, act rationally in their own enlightened self-interest. So long as that self-interest is sufficiently informed as to the possible consequences of particular actions, then individual action will be socially responsible through its taking into account the possibility of retributive response, punishment for wrong-doing, future loss of benefit, payback, and such like. All of that, though, presupposes the possibility of individuals acting in a thoroughly informed, coherent, rational, responsible, and self-interested way, independent of those expectations, fears, passions, mores, loyalties, commitments, fetishes, and norms which characterize the discourses framing their individual identities.

In sum, then, in the transition from modernist to postmodern identity, we see a shift from the integrated to the fragmented, from the autonomous to the contextualized, and from the essentially determinate to the contingently provisional and partial.

In the next chapter, we examine the remaining categories of contrasting features by which modernity is seen as being problematized in and by postmodernity: most particularly communication, but also the general frame of mind, and the broader cultural features.

Chapter 4

Postmodernity 2: Conversation and Hope in a Cultural Implosion

In this chapter, we continue the elucidation of postmodernity begun in the preceding chapter. The same approach is used: drawing upon the articulation of modernity presented in Chapter 1, the important ways in which postmodernity has problematized modernist realities are teased out. The nature of communication is first examined as a key constitutive feature of postmodernity. The distinctive postmodern frame of mind is then sketched, the chapter being drawn to a conclusion with an attempt to characterize the cultural institutions and currents of postmodernity.

Postmodern Communication

Postmodern communication is seen as being importantly characterized by what Lash (1990) has termed the *de-differentiation* of signification. You will recall that modernity presented communication as a highly differentiated process, in which the explicit (signified) content could be clearly distinguished from the medium of representation (the signifier) and the object of representation (the referent). The *de*differentiation of communication in postmodernity is seen as arising most importantly from the interpretative nature of human perception. In such a view of perception, the distinction between the objects or referents of the communicative representations and both the representations (signifiers) and the meaning or content of the representations (signifieds) is eroded. The referents cannot be known or communicated about, independently of the interpretative representations, and the meaning of the communication becomes more a function of the communicative context than of the representation. The clear modernist differentiation of these communicative elements is therefore eroded.[1]

The idea of the content being encoded into and fixed within the signifier by its source—either its author or the material object that it represents—is rendered highly uncertain. The content, the meaning, of the message is seen, rather, as multiple and a function of the interpretative context rather than the communicative source. The modernist notion of an objectively correct interpretation of every representation is correspondingly problematic. Representations are, rather, seen as being open to multiple interpretation and to deconstructive interpretation as a function of the frameworks of belief that are brought *to* them.

Thus, a seemingly contradictory feature of the dedifferentiation of signification is the postmodern phenomenon of meaningful signifier autonomy: the breaking of the dependence of the signifier (image, representation) on the object or referent that it (modernistically) represented. Such autonomy may, and demonstrably does, arise both in strictly narrative signification (i.e., in which the signifier is linguistic) and in iconic or figural signification (in which the signifier is a picture, film, model, video, or simulation of some sort). With the contemporarily great importance of the mass media and electronic communication, there is thus a tendency for the experienced world to become increasingly dominated by representations or signifiers lacking any original, any represented entity: what Baudrillard (1983) has termed "simulacra."

The dedifferentiation of signification also arises importantly through the influence of contemporary communication technology. In this regard, we see—through the mass media, the Internet, video, etc.—the proliferation of images of images, so that the referent is effectively a signifier (representation). Similarly, we see the representations becoming increasingly symbolic—lacking referents but carrying meaning within interpretative contexts. That symbolic meaning is not something that was encoded into the image or representation by its author or by the object of the representation. It is, rather, something that has come to be associated with the representation through its use within a communicative context.

Another effect of contemporary communications technology has been to reinforce the epistemic erosion of the modernist superiority of symbolic, linguistic, and written signification over concrete, iconic, and oral communication. Contemporary communication technologies such as film, video, and compact disc make extensive use of nonlinguistic imaging, frequently with the symbolization of nonlinguistic images. More generally, postmodern epistemology is seen as diminishing the superiority of textuality. While the communicative importance of textuality is certainly not denied (and is actually enhanced with the use of the Internet), the status of nonlinguistic images is strongly enhanced relative to the written and the oral. Thus, communication through touch, taste, smell, kinaesthesia, and proxemia tends to be valued more in postmodernity than it was in modernity. The privileging of the word is diminished; unimodal communication becomes multimodal.

The second important, defining, feature of postmodern communication is seen as being its *generalized* nature. By this is meant, on the one hand, the pervasion of all aspects of culture by communication and, on the other, its democratization or egalitarianization.

The pervasive invasion of contemporary culture by communication is seen in the importance of the mass media, film, video, and so on, in such domains as identity formation, sport and recreation, the exchange or purchase of goods and services, in entertainment, education and training, politics, and so on. Few, if any, domains of our social or more broadly cultural engagement are not mediated by contemporary communications technology. And, as Marshall McLuhan and others have argued (e.g.: McLuhan, 1974, 1990; Kerckhove, 1995; Press, 1995; Rosen, 1990), the communication medium or technology does not just passively carry messages that previously would have been carried through speaking face-to-face or in other traditional ways of communicating. Rather, the nature of the medium importantly influences the messages conveyed. This feature of contemporary culture has been captured by Vattimo in his notion of postmodernity as constituting "the society of generalized communication" (Vattimo, 1992, p. 54), and by Baudrillard (1983, p. 127) in his characterization of contemporary culture as "the universe of communication."

The democratization of contemporary communication technology is not meant to suggest anything like the ownership of the mass media by the masses. Indeed, the reverse trend is clearly the case. The point, rather, is the enhanced accessibility of communications technologies to input from the population at large, and the erosion of the power of expertise through the influence of media personalities. Fueled by the loss of epistemological clarity and certainty, the modernist control of communicative legitimation through the academic disciplines and honorable professions is challenged and eroded in postmodernity through the babble of opinions from individuals and groups previously marginalized into public silence in modernity. The importance and uniqueness of each academic discipline's field of signification or frame of images is also challenged in postmodernity by the importance and power of cross-disciplinary and often nondisciplinary enquiry. With this erosion of the modernist monopoly of the academic disciplines and honorable professions over the legitimation and communication of public knowledge, there is also eroded the dominance of the universities and research institutes in knowledge legitimation, preservation, and transmission. The academic and professional institutions therein lose their monopoly over the gatekeeping of knowledge: its generation in research and scholarship and its use in professional practice. With the loss of that monopoly is eroded public acceptance of the arcane wisdom of professional institutions and professionals themselves. Accordingly, consensual and public codes of conduct come to replace the mystery of in-house professional expertise as determinants of professional conduct. Correspondingly, that practice becomes more open to public scrutiny, review, and accountability—a point that has been developed by, among others, Bennett (1991) in his apologia for university accountability.

The legitimation of knowledge thus becomes diffused much more throughout society, through the communication media. With that diffusion is diminished the perceived need for (indeed the impact of) government control over the legitimation of knowledge, its preservation, and its communication. Rather than governments (modernistically) *controlling* the generation and communication of knowledge through universities and research institutes, and discouraging nongovernment involvement, they tend in postmodernity to *regulate* the excesses of those activities, and to *encourage* private investment and control within the regulatory framework—a framework that tends to be minimal in its constraining and restraining of human action.

The need for public investment in long periods of initiation into the academic disciplines and honorable professions is also thereby opened to question and challenge. The contextualization of meaning combines with the pressures for democratization to encourage a more *situated* approach to education and training through engagements that are structured by the workplace (learning-on-the-job, internships, and the like), rather than through institutions of learning (universities and such like) structured by the nature of the academic disciplines.

Contemporarily, the democratization of knowledge generation and dissemination is being further and greatly facilitated through the spread of the Internet, through which the thinking and voices of all who have access to it may be aired. While this is certainly occurring under increasing regulation, it is far removed from the hegemony of the dominant discourses that characterized modernity.

In sum, then, we see in the shift from modernity to postmodernity an important dedifferentiation of communication: an erosion of the traditional chains of signification. There is a parallel cultural pervasion and democratization of communication. Those shifts are generated not only by the postmodern epistemology of contextualized knowledge and the postmodern interpretative conception of perception, but also by the *technology* of contemporary communication. Through that technology, we live in a world populated by images—a hyperreality of imaginings grounded only indeterminately in any physical reality beyond their immediate being.

The Postmodern Frame of Mind

The modernist frame of mind, you may recall, was characterized as one of supreme, totalizing, triumphant, uncritical confidence in the power of reason, in the rightness of action taken in its instrumental application and in the goodness of the cultural progress to which that application gave rise. Such a view may be seen as emanating from other features of the modernist paradigm, most particularly its epistemology and conception of individual identity.

The postmodern frame of mind, similarly, may be seen as emanating particularly from its epistemology and its model of individual identity. In this case, though, the mood is one of ambivalence, uncertainty, and tentativeness. The indeterminate, contextualized, and fragmented nature of belief have eroded the foundations of clarity and certainty as to the direction and meaning of progress. The indeterminate, contextualized, and fragmented nature of identity, and its social consequences, have eroded faith in the value of the modernist project and its capacity to emancipate humanity from privation, pestilence, and fear. Progress tends to be seen, not (modernistically) as the unilinear path of enlightenment and emancipation, but as the addressing of one set of problems by their substitution with another. The postmodern mood is more one of existential insecurity and anomie, than one of triumphant confidence in the modernist agenda and one's place within it.

The modernist certainty of the rightness and goodness of its project led to the assimilation or the marginalization as primitive or deviant of any beliefs that were not essentially modernist, orthodox, or mainstream. The intolerance of difference was an unavoidable central feature of the modernist hubris. Postmodernity, in contrast, seeks strongly to tolerate and embrace difference, and to present it as such, not as something to be pitied, ridiculed, or scorned. Diversity, heterodoxy, is encouraged as an essential part of the postmodern condition. This raises, of course—and much more acutely and problematically than was the case in modernity—problems of the limits of tolerance, of decisions as to when celebrated difference becomes antisocial and destructive. Such problems were relatively readily addressed in modernity—as matters of general philosophical principle, derivable from the features of the modernist project and its conceptions of individual identity, knowledge, and progress. In postmodernity, each such question must be addressed as a contingently and uniquely grounded situation. General principles, while informative, are generally in conflict with each other and are never adequate or decisive.

The modernist perception of the nonhuman world (and also sectors of the human) as the rightful instruments of human emancipatory progress is problematized in postmodernity and may be seen as replaced by a more general concern and respect for human impact on the environment and for the reflexive effects of that environment on individual and collective identities. While postmodernity can offer no firm foundation for a love of nature or, indeed, of fellow human beings, it does at least erode the foundation of that arrogant, self-righteous certainty in the modernist project which allowed the oppression, colonization, marginalization, and annihilation of cultural difference and the possession, reprocessing, and extermination of any desired nonhuman reality.

The supreme confidence in the modernist project of emancipatory enlightenment, through the power of reason, meant a preoccupation with matters epistemological. Postmodernity, in contrast—as was noted in the previous chapter in the section on belief—tends to be more concerned with matters of an ontological nature, especially with respect to the nature of individual identity. In postmodernity, belief is to be explained through identity, in the discourses that constitute it. In a sense, then, postmodern ontology *is* its epistemology.

The postmodern erosion of the grand modernist narratives of emancipatory enlightenment through reason-driven progress encourages a view of the postmodern frame of mind as one directed to the cultivation or the pursuit of *desire* (e.g.: Rojek, 1993; Siebers, 1994; Usher, Bryant, and Johnston, 1997). The desire here is a desire to experience or to experiment with that which is different (heterodox)—a desire to consume realities for the sake of experiencing them (i.e., as autotelic, as ends in themselves). In this way, postmodernity represents an *aestheticization* of experience—the pervasion of experience by engagements, commitments, and goals that are valued in and of themselves, rather than as means to other (emancipatory or material) ends; that are valued for the pleasure that experiencing them is envisaged as bringing.

Most importantly (and here we return to our summary definition) postmodern culture is *self-consciously* informed by an awareness of the postmodern condition. The postmodern frame of mind is therefore one in which there is an awareness of the sort of postmodern features that are articulated in this chapter and the previous one. Postmodern culture is not the mechanical by-product of cause-and-effect relationships. It is, rather, a *cultural condition* made possible and real by the self-conscious awareness of those who frame it and respond to it. Had we all remained steadfastly committed to modernity, postmodernity as we understand it could not have developed. The ontological and technological elements of postmodernity would not have been sufficient on their own to generate what we understand as the postmodern condition. It is in this sense that postmodernity may be seen as being notably *epistemological* in nature, but it is an inversion of the modernist epistemology: from a public framework of epistemic rules, to a private reflexive awareness of the complicity of one's own epistemic commitments in the determination of cultural realities.

Also, though (and here we return again to our summary definition), postmodernity depends to some degree on a conscious commitment to it—a *sympathetic* awareness of its dimensions. To what extent such an identification is necessary, I cannot be sure, but, to take an extreme view for the sake of argument, if we (meaning the cultural constructs of our identities) all were steadfastly determined *not* to allow our actions to be influenced by our understanding of perception, belief, being, communication, frame of mind, and culture in a postmodern world, then it is hard to see how that world could be postmodern in its characteristics. To some extent and in some ways it would be so—under the influence of contemporary communications technology. But even that influence, and certainly that of our individual identities, could be largely suppressed and marginalized, as it certainly was in the case of identity in modernity itself.

The awareness of the postmodern condition, and particularly its epistemological elements, itself tends to encourage a mood of playful irony (Bove, 1980; Hutcheon, 1994; Jameson, 1991; Lyotard, 1979/1984a); willful contradiction (Dooley, 1995; Habermas, 1990; Hutcheon, 1988); skepticism (Bagnall, 1994d; Kroker, 1992; Norris, 1994; Raes, 1992; Rosenau, 1992; Seguin, 1994); or, more negatively, of cynicism (Antonio, 1989; Burbules, 1986; M.E.G. Smith, 1994). The loss of epistemic foundations, the fragmentation of belief, and the acceptance that our beliefs will, unavoidably, lead to contradictions, are seen as encouraging certainly the use of irony, to the extent that some commentators see irony as *characterizing* postmodernity (Rorty, 1989) or, at least postmodern*ism* (Hassan, 1971). Relatedly, Terry Eagleton (1985) has argued for the importance of parody in postmodern culture, at least in parodying the modernist avant garde—an activity which may be seen as a major preoccupation of postmodern critique (Huyssen, 1981). Others, most notably Hutcheon (1988), see the acceptance, creation, and celebration of contradictions as characterizing postmodernity. Cynicism, at least for those who view postmodernity negatively, is also a common response to the postmodern condition, and thereby a feature of it. I have also argued elsewhere (Bagnall, 1994d) for the existence of postmodernist skepticism as a powerful leveler of belief: a skepticism that denies *a priori* superiority not only to any particular path to knowledge, but also to knowledge claims themselves. Any claim to the *a priori* privileging of knowledge is argued to be open to abuse on the part of its protagonists and as grounds for intolerance toward, and the suppression of, belief other than that which is privileged. Just such abuses are seen as underpinning the cultural genocide that, from a postmodern perspective, characterizes the history of modernity.

In sum, then, we see in the shift from modernity to postmodernity a significant loss of self-confidence—of confidence in one's ability to know what is right or wrong, good or evil, true or false, beautiful or ugly, and authentic or contrived. There is also a loss of confidence in the modernist project of emancipatory enlightenment through reason, and especially through science. With that loss there is an erosion of intolerance of difference, although any enhanced tolerance is tempered by the removal of any firm foundation upon which to ground a concern for other persons. As Bauman (1991b) has argued, there is the danger in postmodernity of a callous indifference to the suffering of others—a difference based on an unrestrained tolerance of difference. Also gained, and necessarily so, is a degree of sympathetic self-awareness—of the postmodern condition and, with that awareness, a tendency to irony, contradiction, skepticism, and cynicism. Present too, to some degree at least, is a sympathetic identification with the postmodern condition.

Postmodern Culture

In broad, then, what sort of cultural realities characterize postmodernity? I shall tackle that question by using the comparative ideas introduced in the equivalent section in Chapter 1.

First, modernity was noted as being a "cult of reason." Postmodernity, while incorporating the reason of modernity, is much more broadly based in admitting the validity and in raising the standing of other forms of knowing. Existential knowledge, the emotions, the subconscious, the nonrational, the serendipitous, the inexplicable, the metaphorical, the analogical, the spiritual, and the aesthetic are all admitted and accepted to the point that the place of reason is unclear. The role of knowledge itself is also much less a function of the modernist preoccupation with instrumental knowledge, and much more a matter of happenstance, interest, delectation, recreation, exploration, passion, pleasure, and engagement: of desire.

Second, modernity was noted as being a "struggle for order," through highly differentiated spheres of cultural formation. Postmodernity, in contrast, embraces the value of difference, accepts the chaos, esteems the disorder. In so doing, it seeks to break down the modernist cultural differentiations and the autonomous fields of cultural formation that those differentiations protected. Cultural deconstruction and reconstruction is seen as being a fluid, shifting, undifferentiated ebb and flow of unpredictable and unbounded activity, characterized by particular discourses, themselves subject to constant re-formation.

Third, modernity was noted as being a "project of human liberation" through enlightenment, demythologization, and the instrumental commodification of all serviceable reality. Postmodernity is much less sanguine about the possibilities of human liberation,[2] all humanity being seen as caught in its particular frameworks of understanding and identity formation. Its project (if it has one) may even be characterized as the demythologization of demythologization (Vattimo, 1992, p. 42): a negative program from the perspective of modernity. And, while it is characterized by the commodification of *cultural* realities (Fox, 1990; Haug, 1987; Wexler, 1989), it is much more uncertain and ambivalent about the commodification of material realities.

Fourth, modernity was noted as being driven by a "doctrine of progress, " as constituting a cult of the modern, a quest for development that was inherently future-oriented. Postmodernity, in contrast, sees progress as more localized and ephemeral—as situated within, and dependent upon, particular informing frameworks of belief. More broadly, a postmodern view of progress is cynically that of replacing one set of problems with another—the "solution" of any one given problem laying the foundation for, or exacerbating, another "problem."

Fifth, modernity was noted as an epoch of social connectedness, with its attendant sense of rootedness, historicity, belonging, orderliness, purpose, certainty, and predictability. Postmodernity, in contrast, may be seen as a culture of fragmentation, of social dislocation, of ephemeral social relationships. The fluidity of contingent opportunities for and commitments to work, family, social relationships, location, and interests encourages perceptions of deracination, isolation, disorder, purposelessness, uncertainty, and unpredictability.

Sixth, modernity was noted as being a unilinear project: temporally, historically, perceptually, and epistemically. Postmodernity, in contrast, is irremediably pluralistic or pluriform: a heterogeneity of potentially incommensurable patterns of belief or action. There is no sense of a postmodern project, and no unified sense of the past, the present, or the future. Unilinearity is replaced with a situated conception of time, multiple histories, diverse visions, and contrasting views of reality.

Seventh, the commitments informing and constituting the major institutions of modernity are all seen in postmodernity as problematic—

- *Scientifically*, postmodernity recognizes the explanatory, predictive, and manipulative power of the sciences, while recognizing also their limitations through their imprisonment by those qualities (Lyotard, 1979/1984a; Perez-Martinez, 1995; Roberts, Schumacher, Vogel, and Rouse, 1991; Ward, 1996). Science, as a paradigm, is seen on the one hand as just one approach among many to human understanding. On the other hand, it is seen as encompassing a great range and diversity of different approaches to knowing. None of these approaches is more centrally "scientific" than the others; none is free of subjectivity or value; all draw variously upon nonrational approaches to the generation, legitimation, and affirmation of belief; and all are seen as open to recombination in potentially infinite diversity with elements of the others.
- *Ethically*, postmodern belief is grounded in particular discourses—which situation is recognized as leading inevitably to differences across discourses, differences calling for recognition and variously for acceptance, contestation, or negotiation (Bauman, 1993, 1995; R. Green, 1994; Hunter, 1988; Kitwood, 1990; Shusterman, 1988; Wellmer, 1991). Following Toulmin (1990), postmodern ethics may thus be characterized as Aristotelian (situational), rather than Platonic (an ethics of general principles)—the latter being seen as underpinning modernist ethics. The modernist commitment to individual moral responsibility within a framework of universal moral principles or rules is challenged in postmodernity by a recognition of the power and legitimacy of situated moral influence and commitment. That situatedness challenges the validity of the principled impartiality of modernist justice—replacing it with a recognition of justice as a quality that is uniquely negotiated between competing interests (Bagnall, 1995a; Young, 1990). In the absence of any firm or consensual ethical foundation, postmodern morality tends also to be aestheticized, in being framed by aesthetic qualities, such as "balance," "difference," and "opposition" (Bagnall, in press; Lash, 1994).
- *Aesthetically*, postmodernity is similarly a discourse-dependent

set of sensitivities, values, and commitments (Arac, 1987; Burgin, 1986; Featherstone, 1992; Foucault, 1990; Haug, 1987; Hutcheon, 1988; McHale, 1987; Pearse, 1992). It tends strongly to parody, irony, and cynicism—turning the grand narratives of the modernist arts in upon themselves; using their own values and commitments to underline the uncertainty, fragility, and artificiality of their missions; diminishing their standing through a corrosive self-criticism of their own foundations; using technology both as aesthetic in itself and to aestheticize our experiences of the world as virtual realities (Kroker, 1992). Indeed, postmodernity may be seen as "the aestheticization of everyday life," to take a phrase from Mike Featherstone (1992, p. 265).

- *Technically,* postmodernity is the fragmented search for solutions to particular problems (Jones, 1990; Kroker, 1992; M. Peters, 1989). It is focused on the immediate, the local, incident, event, or situation. It is essentially project-based and project-constituted. It is, though, not just outcomes-driven, but is also importantly committed—however briefly—to the qualities of the engagement itself. In its project commitment, it draws eclectically together perceptions, scenarios, theory, values, and techniques, with scant regard for their origins and with even less respect for traditional disciplinary boundaries and proprieties.
- *Economically,* postmodernity tends to be market-driven and market-seeking, rather than authoritative (Bauman, 1992; Jameson, 1991). In its contemporaneity, it is also strongly global and transnational. The protective barriers around modernist nation states are eroded. Economic planning loses its ideological commitment, to be driven by populist desires for change and opportunity on the one hand, and by the expectations of multinational companies for their investments on the other. Economic control is through regulation of the extremes, rather than through promulgation of the central path. There is no central path; the direction of economic growth and policy are contingently defined by the play of market forces: nationally, regionally, and internationally. Knowledge itself is strongly commodified and highly capitalized; knowledge industries are of central economic and political importance (Duderstadt, 1992).
- *Politically,* postmodernity denies the state any *a priori* substantive grounds for privileging one set of beliefs over another (given the denial, in postmodern epistemology, of the *a priori* superiority of any one path to knowledge and of any particular knowledge claims). The principles upon which postmodern governance are based, therefore, become matters to be taken

empirically from the pluralistic and shifting cultural context. They cannot be drawn self-evidently from prevailing ideology or common sense, since both ideology and common sense are culture-specific. The political institution becomes, then, not so much a field of contesting socio-economic ideologies as an arena of shifting and confusing uncertainties in the socioeconomic realm (Doherty, Graham, and Malek, 1992; Gibbins, 1989; Heller, 1988; S. White, 1991). It is an arena of mass-media massaging of popular public opinion, and reflexive sensitivity to the changing allegiances of that opinion. Political management replaces political leadership. Immediate solutions replace projected visions. Solid and lasting political allegiances—by either politicians or the populace—are quaintly old-hat. The role of the state becomes primarily that of procedural regulation of the market, in such a way as to optimize its operations: minimizing harm to individuals and traditions from the activities of individuals in other traditions, without stifling the essential freedom of the market, while moderating and resolving conflicts of interest between groups and cultural entities. This involves a not inconsiderable commitment to dismantling the ideologically driven projects of modernity (such as state enterprises and programs of social welfare). Nevertheless, the state must maintain some degree of responsibility for welfare and educational support to compensate those persons who may be unjustly or unduly disadvantaged, marginalized, or oppressed by the market (such as persons who have been unemployed for some time, are severely handicapped, or are vocationally under-skilled).

- *Architecturally*, postmodernity is a search for the expression of the particular in buildings and constructed landscapes (Ghirardo, 1984/5; Jencks, 1987, 1989, 1991). The particular here embraces both that which is situationally sensitive and expressive and that which may be mined from other styles, other times, other places, and other cultures. The latter impulse encourages the eclectic use of pastiche in architecture, in the creation of that which is unique, and variously: for its own sake, for its emotional impact, for its market value, or to parody those aspects of correctness and tradition in modern architecture which pose as superior values in and of themselves. Architectural design thus denies the modernist privileging of the functional. It foregrounds the playful and the disjointed, fragmentary influences of diverse cultural traditions on any given place and construction, seeking, as Jencks (1991, p. 13) has argued, a "radical eclecticism."
- *Industrially*, postmodernity sees a privatization of labor. Worker

mobility, flexibility, and responsiveness replace the qualities of loyalty, expertise, and commitment. Production is fragmented, outsourced, and moved around across national and regional borders to maximize its efficiency. Markets are shifted similarly to capitalize on the purchasing power of novelty. Market differences are cultivated and supplied with an endless progression of cultural ephemera. In business, contingent opportunity replaces traditional mission; the immediate project replaces long-term commitment; regulatory constraints and restraints are determined and negotiated in an *ad hoc* fashion, rather than on the basis of a planned projection of the past into the future; planning is short-term, opportunistic, and responsive, rather than long-term, ideological, and directive. Companies amalgamate, diversify, and internationalize in endeavoring to survive within an unpredictably shifting set of cultural realities in an essentially capitalist context (Dunphy and Stace, 1990; Halal, 1986; Rose, 1991). The worlds of work and production are both "Post-Fordist" and "Post-Taylorist" and, more broadly, "Post-Industrialist" (Edwards, 1993b; Jones, 1990; Rustin, 1989; Westwood, 1991a).

- *Organizationally*, postmodernity is caught between the press of the open market and that for the recognition of multiple organizational voices. The modernist organizational structures of hierarchical power reinforced by the hegemony of consensus are deconstructed as intolerant and oppressive of difference, as coercing organizational members into inactive conformity under the veiled threat of sanction for deviance from the consensually and theoretically validated norm (Best and Kellner, 1991; Dreyfus and Rabinow, 1992; Foucault, 1979). In place of those structures, the postmodern organization tends to seek, on the one hand, to be optimally responsive to the changing cultural context in which it must function—a context demanding of immediate performativity, accountability, and competitive efficiency. On the other hand, the postmodern organization seeks to give expression to the multiple voices within it—both in recognition of the productive capability that is thereby generated through the commitment flowing from ownership of the organizational culture, and as a response to demands for recognition of and from those voices. In seeking to bring together the shifting and multiple demands of the organizational context and its own cultural pluriformity, postmodern organizations tend to lurch from one organizational fad to another, each purveyed by its apologists as the answer to every important contemporary problem (Rhodes, 1996; Winsor, 1992). Employee loyalty to the organization tends to be fragile, shifting, ephemeral, and often multiple—under the impact of the constant, responsive, organizational restructuring, the downsizing and casualization of its workforce, and the outsourcing and subcontracting of its component operations (Freeland, 1995; Handy, 1990; Kanter, 1989; Kincheloe, 1995; Poole, 1991).

- *Individually*, postmodernist action is infused with ambivalence, uncertainty, irony, and contradiction—willful contradiction, as Hutcheon (1988) has argued. It thus tends to be heterodox rather than orthodox, eclectic rather than consistent or programmatic, and experimental rather than constrained by principle (L. Appignanesi, 1989; Benhabib, 1992; Castoriadis, 1989; Hunter, 1994; Szkudlarek, 1993). There is a sense of immediacy and spontaneity within a framework of historicist reflection. There is a tendency toward collective action, although group allegiances are shifting and open to renegotiation or termination. In its response to contingency, postmodern action is also strongly consumerist—a consumerism that may be perceived as focused particularly on the consumption of "life-style alternatives" (Hunt and Hunt, 1987; Usher, Bryant, and Johnston, 1997, pp. 107-110), driven by the foregrounding of desire in postmodern commitments and the commodification of culture directed to feeding that desire. In a (postmodern) free market, choice and responsibility tend to be privatized, that is, to rest with the individual. However, given the role of cultural tradition in constraining individual choice, and in molding individual identity, there is a strong tendency to shift that responsibility to those cultural traditions which are seen as constraining choice in any particular situation. Choice and responsibility are thus strongly indeterminate: complexly embedded in the postmodern pluriformity of discourses.
- *Socially*, postmodernity is strongly market-based, in the sense of its being open to the confrontation, resolution, and exchange of realities and meanings between and among its constituent pluriformity of discourses (Bauman, 1992; M. Peters and J. Marshall, 1996; Seidman, 1994). In the absence of the constraining and restraining normative frameworks of modernist social philosophy and theory, not only value, truth, and beauty but also the standards by which they are determined and assessed are relativized. That is to say, they are contingent upon the particular situations, discourses, or cultural traditions of their generation and application. The social mechanisms for the setting of standards (of value, truth, beauty, authenticity, and form) must, then, be a function of individual and collective choice, within and between discourses, exercised through cultural exchange. In a

cultural pluriformity, this task requires a context in which there may occur the free exchange of all entities of potential value, claims to truth, conceptions of beauty, and images of harmony: in other words, a free market. In such a postmodern free market, value, truth, beauty, authenticity, and form are therefore determined, variously, by consumer choice, negotiation, manipulation, or domination and oppression—depending upon the values and the distribution of power involved. The social thus becomes a zone of difference and contestation (N. Smith, 1992), including that between long-oppressed "indigenous" cultural interests and those of more recent colonizers (Jacobs, 1996), that between different identity discourses, such as homosexual and heterosexual (Gitlin, 1994), and that between social interest groups (such as conservation organizations) and the interests of free-enterprise capitalism (Newman, 1994).

- *Educationally*, postmodernity is concerned with situating learning in particular contexts—those in which knowledge is generated and applied—most notably work or vocational (in the sense of occupational) contexts (Garrick, 1994; Kincheloe, 1995; Usher, Bryant, and Johnstone, 1997; Usher and Edwards, 1994). There is an emphasis on the learning of discourse-specific capabilities, but at a level of generality that optimizes mobility across contexts (through national frameworks of awards, competence-based approaches, and the like). There is also, though, an emphasis on learning through grounded, situated reflection on the nature and effects of one's actions and their informing beliefs and capabilities. Learning is recognized as being fragmented and of limited transferability or generalizability across contexts or discourses. Educational engagements are crafted, correspondingly, into self-contained, particularized packages or modules, which may be taken in isolation and simply aggregated to obtain recognition in awards for specified quantities of learning in broad and shifting domains. There is also a recognition in awards of the valued learning obtained through experiences other than those of formal education.

Overall, postmodernity sees an erosion of the distinctiveness of the modernist realms of discourse (such as the theoretical, the moral, and the aesthetic), just as it does of the modernist institutions (such as education, health, and politics) and the modernist organizations serving those institutions. There is a breaking-down of categorical boundaries, an invasion of territories across the old modernist borders: education permeating the vocational, the political becoming culturally diffused, and so on. The modernist elites, whose status depended on those old borders, correspondingly see their standing diminished. The academic disciplines and the professions see their power, status, and position eroded. Previously disempowered and oppressed sectors of society—women, ethnic, and cultural minorities—experience a renaissance of their values and power (Iragaray, 1985; Owens, 1983; Spivak, 1988).

The rightness and clarity of the modernist distinction between the public and the private realms of discourse are also eroded, with the private invading the public and vice-versa. On the one hand, individuals and groups openly present and project their private lives into their public roles in politics, work, entertainment, and so on. On the other hand, the private lives of individuals and groups are freely invaded through monitoring and surveillance mechanisms, seen as being in the public interest. Public entertainment is brought into private homes and lives via contemporary communications technology which, in turn, takes and disseminates information on the private lives of those who use those technologies. The use of electronically mediated cultural exchange procedures (in purchasing, banking, traffic control, communication, and so forth) places massive quantities of modernistically private information into the public realm, or into the hands of individual agencies or corporations from which it may be disseminated through sale or theft.

In these ways (and referring to the subtitle of this chapter), postmodernity may be seen as a cultural *implosion*: a dissolving of the modernist distinctions and certainties, in which the solutes are intermelded, through and among each other.

Chapter 5

Formal Tensions, Contingent Realities: Reconfiguring the Problematic

The task of this chapter is to present a reconfiguration of the ideas in the foregoing two chapters: to transform those ideas into a simpler framework that may be used then to guide the analyses of adult education which constitute the remainder of the book.

A major challenge of any such project is to avoid the (modernist) trap of defining a core, a center, an essence of the object of our concern. Importantly, postmodernity is characterized by its diversity, its pluriformity, and, in that sense, its lack of a center. Responding to this challenge, we may approach the task of reconfiguring and simplifying our conception of postmodern diversity by recognizing that the diversity itself may be seen as importantly informed by a number of major *tensions*.

The concept of tension here derives from the sense in which postmodernity is *post*-modernity, that is, the sense in which it problematizes modernity itself. By *tension* is meant two opposing or contrary inclinations, such that for each there are good reasons for inclining toward it, but that to do so—and to the extent that one does so—is to limit, compromise, or threaten the possibility of satisfying the contrary inclination (Bagnall, 1994b). Both poles of the tension may be seen as acting simultaneously, but differentially, in different events or situations. In other words, the relative attractive power, or the relative impelling force (depending upon how one chooses to construct a given tension), will vary across situations and across discourses within situations. The range of that variability is theoretically from almost complete dominance of one pole over the other, to the converse situation. Nevertheless, assuming that there *is* some degree of (postmodern) awareness of the postmodern nature of a situation, the tension must be there. Were a situation or a component discourse not to evidence a tension, one would be inclined, on that ground alone, to question the postmodern nature of that situation or discourse.

The notion of tension here is one of inherent conflict or dissonance between the realities identified by the tensional poles. To be a part of the postmodern condition is to be aware of the tensions and to live them. The dissonance, the tension, is not resolvable, except through a premodern or modern ignorance of the postmodern condition, or a (narrow-minded) fanatical denial or rejection of it. The more we understand the nature and reality of the tensions, the better informed may be our actions with respect to them, but the tensions, the conflict, the dissonance, will remain.

In opposition to the modernistically functional niceties of such constructs as Kurt Lewin's Force Field Analysis (Lewin, 1951/1975), the contingent realities with respect to a (postmodern) tension should not be seen as indicating a balancing of the forces entailed in the tension—an equilibrium of those countervailing forces—even if there is a degree of apparent stability over time. The rational, natural-law-abiding, consistent, fully determined, and in principle explicable nature of reality that is assumed in all such conceptions of balance or equilibrium is inconsistent with postmodern epistemology. The contingent realities with respect to a tension may be no less illogical than they are rational, arbitrary than natural-law-abiding, inconsistent than consistent, indeterminate than determinate, and inexplicable than they are explicable.

Correspondingly, temporal change with respect to a tension does not necessarily entail any shift in a posited equilibrium or balancing of forces—such as through the empowering of one set of considerations over another. It may contingently do that, but no less than it may alternatively not do so. Empowering no more leads necessarily to a tensional shift than does a tensional shift necessarily indicate a shift in the balance of power. Indeed, if anything, it may be argued that empowering through understanding of and capability in manipulating through a tension is more likely to lead to greater degrees of arbitrariness in the situational expression of the tension, than it is to lead to greater degrees of determinate directionality in that expression. However, such is not the point here.

Insofar as postmodern realities with respect to the tensions *are* under conscious control, a tension may be seen as presenting situational players with a choice between the realities implied by the poles of the tension. In education, it is just those realities with which we are particularly concerned—hence the focus on individual choice in the author's earlier work on "semantic" tensions (Bagnall, 1994b). Nevertheless, it must also be accepted that there are indeterminate, yet assuredly major and important components of the tensional realities that are outside conscious control, at least in any given contingent situation. The tensions are certainly "semantic" in the sense that they define dimensions of meaning in the world. However, the meanings are also ontologically grounded, most particularly in the case of those tensions which pertain to individual identity and to sociality.

The tensions are presented here by characterizing both the general tensional quality and the two poles of the tension. Those poles are arranged iconically as ranging from left to right. The left-hand pole in each case may be seen as identifying those tensional realities that are more modernist in nature—as defining the relevant modernist realities which postmodernity incorporates and problematizes. Contrastively, the right-hand pole in each case may be seen as identifying those tensional realities that are more strictly postmodern in nature—as defining the relevant realities toward which the postmodern problematization of modernist realities tends to draw the latter. Extreme caution, however, must be exercised in taking this point on board, since postmodern realities are characterized here as defined by the *tensions* between the poles: the tensions between the incorporated modernist realities and those to which the postmodern problematization directs them. Postmodernity in this sense has no meaning as just the right-hand pole of each tension. The characterization here of the two poles in each case seeks both to describe the sort of realities defined by the pole and to sketch the impulse to seek or construct realities through that pole.

The tensions presented here have been crafted from a potential infinity of alternatives. Those presented are seen by me as capturing the more notable qualities of the postmodern condition. They are seen as doing so particularly in virtue of the following features:

1. they are at a high level of explanatory generality, in the sense that each entails or indicates a broad spread of related qualities of postmodernity;
2. they embrace the main domains of postmodern variability—those of belief, individual identity, and sociality; and
3. they are selected as focusing attention on those qualities which I see as being of particular importance, both in the nature of postmodernity itself and in its implications for adult education.

Nevertheless, the subjectivity of their identification should be recognized in deliberations on the substance of this and the subsequent chapters.

The six tensions (Table 5.1) are distributed across three broad domains of postmodern reality—belief, individual identity, and sociality—two tensions being located in each domain. The concept of *sociality* follows its use by Bauman (1992, pp. 190-191) as a postmodern alternative to the modernist "society," replacing the notion of the modernist "social system" and its reliance on rational, ordered, efficient, effective, evolutionarily progressive, and goal-directed processes, which draw upon identifiable inputs in the production of planned outputs. That notion is replaced by one of culturally contingent realities, the nature of which is multifaceted, constantly shifting, uncertain, and importantly arbitrary, and which exist only as the ongoing process of dialectical interplay between and among the myriad of contesting interests and tendencies. The two tensions in the domain of *belief* are those of *situatedness* (defined by the tension between *transcendence* and *particularization*) and *ambiguity* (defined by the tension between *singularity* and *plurality*). The two tensions in the domain of *individual identity* are those of *determination* (defined by the tension between *holism* and *fragmentation*) and *control* (defined by the tension between *autonomy* and *embeddedness*). In the domain of *sociality*, the two identified tensions are those of *homogeneity* (the tension being between *differentiation* and *dedifferentiation*) and *temporality* (the tension being between *developmentalism* and *presentism*). The tensions are here articulated (and in future chapters are used) in that order. However, no epistemic significance should be read into the ordering.

Table 5.1: The Six Tensions of Postmodernity

		Tensional Quality	Modernist Pole	Postmodern Pole
Domain	Belief	Situatedness	Transcendent	Particularized
		Ambiguity	Singular	Plural
	Individual Identity	Determination	Holistic	Fragmented
		Control	Autonomous	Embedded
	Sociality	Homogeneity	Differentiated	Dedifferentiated
		Temporality	Developmentalist	Presentist

Situatedness

The first tension here articulated pertains to the domain of postmodern belief. It identifies the situational particularity of belief—the extent to which belief relates only to singular, ultimately unique, events, rather than to more general situations based on particular properties of events. It is generated from the postmodern problematization of the modernist commitment to the objective universality of truth, goodness, beauty, and authenticity. That problematization sees belief grounded in the discourses of its generation—ultimately in the particularities of each unique cultural event. A tension is therefore created in postmodernity between the impulse to generate, recognize, and use beliefs that transcend particular events and the impulse to recognize the uniqueness of events and the beliefs that define and inform each one.

The "transcendent" pole of the tension (the left or modernist pole) values belief (or "knowledge") that is situationally specific across a potential infinity of particular events: temporally without limit and spatially over all like instances. Belief is thereby *de*contextualized, in the sense that it transcends particular contexts or events. Individual events are then illuminated through their being identified as instances of the general (the transcendent) category to which the belief pertains. Action in those events is, correspondingly, informed by their categorization. Also valued in this pole is the quality of *simplicity* in belief (since increasing complexity of belief parallels the increasing acknowledgment of contextual difference—ultimately, each different case being accounted for). Similarly valued in this pole is instrumentally more *powerful* belief, since the more general the domain of realities to which belief applies, the wider the range of more particular uses to which it may be put.

In the sciences, the arts, and the humanities, what is valued is not the rich description of detail but the elegant simplicity of profound generalization, of underlying (or overarching) concepts that *subsume* the detail. Theory in human affairs is seen as being properly applied *to* particular instances of practice. Once we have our (general) theoretical constructs, we can apply them to a potential infinity of particular instances. What is gained in this process of generalizing and categorizing the qualities in specific events is a powerful epistemic simplicity. What is lost is all of that variability which is not expressed in the categorical properties or the generalizations. That specific variability is thereby marginalized and diminished in value (or denied *any* value). The knowledge generated by modernist science is paradigmatically of this sort.

The impulse to transcendence is to acquire and create more general, more elegant, and more powerful belief. It is to understand our experience (and that of others) as instances of more general situations. It is therefore realized in a desire to categorize, to classify realities, and to define and quantify general relationships between and among those categories. Such knowledge we may then take with us (individually or collectively) from event to event, applying it to interpret or inform those events where it is applicable. Such knowledge can also be seen readily as contributing to the stock of *public* knowledge, available to humanity as a whole.

The "particularized" pole of the tension (the right or postmodern pole) recognizes belief as situated in particular contexts or events. Those contexts include the discourses and individuals involved in the generation of the knowledge, as much as they include the nonlinguistic and objective realities of events. Belief is valued, correspondingly, more for the richness of its detail than for the simple generality of its application. Theory in human affairs is seen as being embedded (contextualized) in practice, as arising from that practice, and as being particularly applicable *to* that practice. It may, though, *sensitize* us to possibilities in other events.

The particularized impulse is to create and use knowledge that is true to the individuality, the uniqueness, of each cultural event. Such knowledge therefore does not distort events through molding them into general categories. Neither does it distort them through the artificial extraction of individuals and discourses from the realities of those events. The impulse is to value the richness of detailed description or prescription; to acquire and create knowledge *within* events, *from* the experience of those events, and to apply it *to* those events. It is an impulse to respect the uniqueness of each event, but to value also knowledge of other events in enhancing our awareness of other possibilities.

Ambiguity

The second tension also pertains to the domain of postmodern belief. It identifies the extent to which there are good grounds for accepting a number of different epistemic pictures of what is good, true, beautiful, and authentic. In other words (and conversely) it identifies the extent to which there are no good grounds for accepting that there is one correct interpretation of any reality, in relation to which all other interpretations may be ranked according to the extent to which they approach the ultimately correct interpretation. The tension is generated from the postmodern problematization of the modernist commitment to a mimetic or representational view of perception and belief. That problematization questions the epistemological foundations on which representationism depends—opening up the possibility of multiple correct interpretations of any given reality. A tension is therefore created in postmodernity between the impulse to advance knowledge through the pursuit of the (ultimate) truth, goodness, and so on, and the impulse to recognize the validity of alternative (and potentially contradictory) interpretations.

The "singular" pole of the tension (the left or modernist pole) recognizes the in-principle existence of a single, ultimately correct, interpretation of every reality. Those realities may, of course, be various—ranging from material objects and sociocultural events, to plans of action, codes of conduct, or the ideas represented in works of art. Acceptance of the in-principle existence of an ultimately correct interpretation of any reality allows us to identify particular interpretations as approximating that ideal to a greater or lesser extent. It allows us, then, to rank order competing beliefs according to the extent to which each does so approximate the truth, goodness, and so on, of the ideal. We can settle disputes between competing claims by deciding which is the more correct. We can recognize which belief has been replaced (for all time) as inferior by more correct belief. We can recognize and track the progressive, historical advance of knowledge, through the aggregation of all such advances, and we can plan intelligently to advance knowledge in those culturally important areas where our present beliefs fall well short of the ultimately correct, ideal situation.

This pole, then, may be seen as representing the impulse to create, value, learn, or otherwise acquire belief (knowledge) that is hierarchically closer than are competing claims to the objective reality that it represents. The impulse is the search for truth (in theoretical knowledge), for goodness and rightness (in moral knowledge), for formulaic conformity, problem resolution or situational change (in technical knowledge), for authenticity and meaning (in existential knowledge), and for form (in aesthetic knowledge). There is also represented within this pole the impulse to locate contemporary belief—and one's contribution to it and understanding of it—at the apex of a progressive historiography of knowledge. There is, too, the impulse to be clear and certain about what is true or false, right or wrong, good or evil, beautiful or ugly, and authentic or contrived. Such certainty gives a feeling of empowerment. It allows us to arbitrate between rival claims to knowledge and to diminish all others as being less correct than our own beliefs.

The "plural" pole of the tension (the right or postmodern pole) recognizes beliefs, claims to knowledge, as essentially located in cultural space. The meanings which they are accorded therefore derive from that cultural space. Within it, they have particular value relative to other competing claims and, from the perspective of that cultural space, they may be ranked with those competing claims on the basis of the criteria immanent to the culture. What is more or less good, true, beautiful, and so on, is, then, seen not as a matter that can be determined solely in relation to any objective reality. It is, rather, dependent also on the cultural space in which one is operating—the frameworks of belief or the discourses that one is bringing to the epistemic task. Between and among discourses there is recognized to be a degree of incommensurability—of incompatibility, denying the comparability of beliefs precisely *because* they have been developed within different discourses. Any given reality therefore has a plurality (a potential infinity) of valid and correct interpretations—limited only by the interpretive frameworks that are brought to the task.

The impulse of the plural pole of this tension is to acknowledge and respect the alternative beliefs of other persons working through other frameworks of belief. It is even to acknowledge that, as individuals, we may harbor within ourselves incompatible sets of belief thus generated. That acknowledgment and respect, however, tend towards an egalitarian acceptance of the more or less equal *un*importance of all beliefs—of their fragility, their ephemerality, their lack of any firm foundation—and of their ultimate ridiculousness, rather than of their importance. There is, therefore, the impulse to see all belief as open to deconstruction, (re)interpretation and to ironical, parodical, and skeptical criticism. The impulse, on the one hand, is a freedom from obedience to inherited wisdom, from respect for the beliefs of the past. On the other hand, it is the freedom from the constraint of commitment only to belief that is at the forefront of the advance of knowledge. If epistemic progress is discourse-dependent, then alternative discourses are open to adoption, generation, and advocacy. If the beliefs that we inherit are open to deconstruction and reinterpretation in the light of (future) realities, what sense is there in our accepting an obligation now to adopt and construct only belief that advances our present understanding? To do so would surely be irrational.

Determination

The third tension pertains to individual identity. It identifies the extent to which the determination of individual identity is, or is potentially, through an aggregation of independent, incompatible, contradictory, and isolated partial identities, none of which necessarily is, or is able to be, in reconciliatory communication with the others. In other words, and contrastively, it is the extent to which individual identity is determined as a unitary, integrated entity, more than the sum of its parts, since there is a reconciliation of any differences between and among those parts. The tension is generated from the postmodern problematization of the modernist commitment to the individual as an integrated, unitary, monad, capable of action as an autonomous individual and as properly held responsible for the consequences of all such actions. That problematization questions the veracity of each of those modernist concepts, arguing that individual identity is more elemental than integrated, fragmentary than unitary, and embedded in the discourses of its formation and expression than it is independently autonomous.

The "holistic" pole of the tension (the left or modernist pole) sees individual identity as integrated into a coherent unity. That unity derives from the individual's determinate inherited potential to be an individual of a particular sort or, rather, to become one within a determinate range of contingent possibilities. Individual identity is "realized" through individual development, even though that realization may involve some molding by contingent circumstance. An individual's different beliefs, values, commitments, and so on, are therefore seen as interactive, as interdependent. New learnings are related to those existing, and are integrated with them—extending or modifying them. Individual response to any given situation is therefore (in theory at least) predictable on the basis of a knowledge of individual identity, and is more or less uniform across instances of importantly similar situations. Differences across the span of beliefs, values, and commitments defining an individual's identity may well exist but, where they do, they are seen as creating tensions that are accessible to efforts at resolution or reconciliation on the part of the individual (with or without the assistance of counsellors, educators, or other helpers).

The impulse to holism is to accord persons a status as unitary individuals, to see them (and ourselves) as integrated wholes, capable of self-knowledge and of having the capability to perceive and address internal contradictions, differences, and inadequacies in any aspect of their individual identities. It is the (humanistic) impulse to see individuals as mature to the extent that they demonstrate self-knowledge and the extension of that self-knowledge to responsibility for the consequences of their own actions. It is the impulse to accord individuals the social status and the social responsibility befitting that demonstrated (or presumed) maturity. Social, political, economic, and other interpersonal relations may then be premised on the presumption of individual responsibility—errors therein being located in irresponsible or deliberately antisocial behavior. In other words, individuals can be held accountable for their actions. Particular individuals can be identified as the proper targets for blame and consequential punishment. Conversely, individuals can be recognized and rewarded for their achievements and for the good that they do.

The "fragmented" pole of the tension (the right or postmodern pole) recognizes individual identity as essentially fragmented among a plurality of different, partial, frameworks of belief, value, and commitment. Individual identity, in other words, is "decentered." It is determined only provisionally and partially—leaving the development of identity both open *in toto* and open to multiple framings. Individual identities are contingently acquired, rather than realized, and they may be deliberately so. Between and among their component partial identities, there may be vast differences in what is believed and valued, but such differences are not necessarily in tension, except contingently in the event of their coming into play simultaneously. They may coexist unproblematically in being brought into play in different situations. New learning therefore does not necessarily require integration into or reconciliation with that which exists. It may, rather, come to frame a new identity (however partial) in itself. Individual response to any given situation is, correspondingly, open to the play of different identity elements. It is not necessarily uniform or predictable.

The impulse to fragmentation is the freedom that it gives to act as the mood takes one—unfettered by constraints of consistency and rationality. Acknowledging the importance of nonrational elements—the emotions, the subconscious—in our actions, and accepting the fragmentation of individual identity and its concomitant lack of consistency across fragments, is liberating from the constraints imposed by individual autonomy. Whatever one does, it can be justified in terms of a feature of accumulated identity fragments. The erosion of social consensus as to what is acceptable and unacceptable individual behavior, expands the cultural space available for alternatives, loosening the restraints to expressiveness, encouraging diversity and experimentation. The impulse to fragmentation is thus also the freedom that it gives us to enhance our repertoire of identity fragments, through the crafting or the drafting of additional partial identities from models presented to us ever more strongly through the contemporary mass media.

Control

The fourth tension also pertains to the domain of individual identity. It identifies the extent to which an individual's actions may be seen as deriving from the discourses in which those actions are embedded. The focus is not on the traditional modernist debate between free will and determinism (causation), but rather on the tension between the possibility of action that is defined by the integrity of the individual against that which is constrained and restrained by the discourses defining individual identity. Free will, in that sense, is presupposed by the tension. What defines the tension is the way in which that free will is realized. The tension arises from the postmodern problematization of the modernist commitment to individual autonomy. That problematization sees the determination of identity as embedded in—emanating from—the discourses defining individual identity, rather than from the individuals themselves.

The "autonomous" pole of the tension (the left or modernist pole) sees individuals as independent monads, as autonomous agents, empowered by (and to the extent of) their command over their realities: through self-awareness, technical and moral understanding, and so on. The control by individuals over their own destiny may therefore be enhanced through education that contributes to their self-awareness, technical and moral understanding, and so on. The holistic unity of individual identity serves as the source, the wellspring of those individuals' control of their own destiny. Individual development and maturity may be defined by the extent to which individuals are "together" and derivatively in control of their being. Other realities—natural and cultural—are to that same extent available to be used instrumentally by the individual (or collectivity of individuals) for the furtherance of their interests.

The impulse to autonomy is strongly that of individual empowerment—to be in control of one's own destiny, to be free to set one's own agenda in all matters—moral, spiritual, practical, and so on. It is not necessarily the will to power over others. That, insofar as it exists, may obtain and be realized no less in the oppositional pole of the tension. *Self*-control is, rather, the impulse, although inherent in that must be the freedom to draw upon other realities as resources—to use them instrumentally in achieving one's own (individual and collective) interests.

The "embedded" pole of the tension (the right or postmodern pole) sees individual action as embedded in the discourses of each individual's (fragmented) identity. Individual action is, correspondingly, constrained and restrained *by* those discourses. Individual autonomy is more of an illusion than an objective reality. What is being realized in individual action is not the self-control of the individual so much as the realization, through the individual, of the potential of their component discourses. Individual empowerment is, correspondingly, substantially an illusion. We (learn to) act through and in accordance with the discourses constituting our individual identities. Education may deepen our grasp of particular identity-forming discourses, and it may broaden the range of those that contribute to our identities. In so doing, it may be construed as enhancing our capabilities of acting within those discourses and, in that sense, as informing and possibly adding to our options. In that sense, then, education in the embedded pole may be seen as empowering. To use an analogy, it is not a freeing of individuals into the open expanses where they may exercise their individual autonomy. It is, rather, the giving to individuals of pigeon-holes from among which they may choose, while also enhancing their capabilities of operating within the pigeon-holes.

Embeddedness shifts from the individual the weight of responsibility for individual failure to live fully up to the expectations of society and to utilize fully the opportunities for development, advancement, and goodness presented by society to that individual. It sees individuals more as victims of their life circumstances than as masters of their own destinies. The guilt of responsibility for failures and shortcomings, and the blame for wrongdoings, are lifted from the individual. So too, though, is responsibility for successes and achievements, for the doing of great good. Heroes are victims no less than are antiheroes and the world's multitude of others in their largely silent desperation.

The impulse to embeddedness is a letting go of the burdens of individual responsibility. It is to acknowledge that, as individuals, we are complex heterogeneities of different frameworks of belief and subconscious figuration, and that those frameworks limit the possibility of and the opportunities for the exercise of individual autonomy. Through embeddedness, we see ourselves more as actors playing out a diversity of life roles than as individual champions. The impulse to embeddedness is also the desire to see ourselves as victims of circumstance—of the discourses defining our identities—and as therefore not fully responsible for the mistakes that we make, for our moral, legal, and other transgressions, for our failure to optimize all of the opportunities that have been given to us, for our failure to become heroes in the model of our sociality.

Homogeneity

The fifth tension pertains to the postmodern sociality. It identifies the extent to which that sociality is, or is not, strongly structured into discrete or lasting realms, whether they be domains of discourse, social classes, institutions, organizations, occupational categories, or individual life roles. It thus identifies the extent to which realms of social reality are, or are not, clearly and unambiguously recognizable as culturally distinct or lasting, in terms of their concerns, interests, traditions, inputs, outputs, and so on. It may also be taken as identifying the extent to which a realm is heteronomous, in the sense of its being nonselfregulating. The tension arises from the postmodern problematization of the modernist commitment to sectoral cultural autonomy. That problematization creates a tension between the impulse to construct sociality in autonomous, stable, solid, reliable, predictable, determinate, and self-referential realms, and the impulse to construct sociality as open, indeterminate, unpredictable, malleable, and therefore as subject to individual will.

The "differentiated" pole of the tension (the left or modernist pole) sees sociality (or "society") as differentiated into distinct spheres or realms of social practice. That differentiation is at all levels of social organization: most broadly, at the level of domains of discourse (the aesthetic and so on) and, beneath them, the social institutions (education, welfare, politics, commerce, and so on) and social classes. More specifically, it is recognizable at the level of particular organizations (dedicated businesses, welfare agencies, and so on), occupations (teaching, training, nursing, management, and so) and individual life roles (parent, worker, sportsperson, and so on). In all of these the social distinctiveness of the differentiated categories is seen in their goals, their norms of behavior, their procedures and criteria for legitimating both knowledge and players, in their general values and beliefs, and, consequently, in the expectations that may be held of them.

The impulse to differentiation may be seen, on the one hand, as the creation of individual and collective identity focusing on the differentiated realm. It is therein to create unities through which meaning and purpose may be accorded the lives of those persons who identify—through vocation, upbringing, life stage, and so on—with them. In this regard, the impulse to differentiation may also be seen as an expression of the will to power (Nietzsche, 1901/1974b)—to be in control of one's own individual or collective destiny through control of the social relations within which one operates. That power may be as crude as the right to set fees for services to the community (as in the case of most modernist professions), or as sophisticated as the evolutionary development of an exclusive and self-referential mystique defining membership of a social class.

On the other hand, and more broadly, the impulse to differentiation is the creation of a lived world—a sociocultural universe—of predictability, of certainty. The differentiation of distinctive values of cultural discourse gives clarity to those realms: the borders or boundaries are recognizable, the ways in which one should properly relate to each realm are knowable, the roles of insiders are comprehensible, and the ways in which outsiders are expected to relate to them are also knowable. Social existence thus becomes something into which one can be enculturated, tutored, and in which (once one is there) one has the confidence of knowing the social rules, of acting appropriately, of knowing the probable impact of one's actions on others, and of being able to predict the likely actions of others.

The "dedifferentiated" pole of the tension (the right or post-modern pole) defines sociality as an unstable, shifting, and relatively unpredictable miasma of social relationships. The differentiation into distinct social realms that does exist is both weak and open to challenge and reformulation or elimination. In contrast to the distinct borders of modernist realms, there is here a permeability of boundaries and, with that permeability, there is a lack of certainty and clarity to be derived from belonging to a realm, an uncertainty as to how to interact with aspects of the sociality, and of knowing how its players will act and respond to one's actions with respect to them. The power and autonomy of the more prestigious modernist realms (the honorable professions and the upper social classes, for example) is thus also comparatively less. Their domains are not the exclusive territory of a self-regulating gatekeeping, and they must seek support and sanction from others to survive. Occupational categories are more contingently and situationally defined and open to (possibly radical) redefinition. Life roles are a function of the shifting pattern of social relationships and concerns, defined by contingent discourses rather than social tradition.

The impulse to dedifferentiation is the situational freedom that is provided by a borderless, fenceless social world. If there are no barriers, nothing is sacred, nothing is beyond one's grasp, except through contingent circumstance, and contingent circumstance is subject to one's active will. One is not constrained to be a particular person, or to act in a particular way. Neither is one restrained from being something else or from acting otherwise. The world of social formation is opened to one's desires and interests. Individual and creative enterprise are free to acquire, to mold, to create realities of one's desire. The free market pervades, allowing the individual to benefit from the fruits of individual and collective enterprise and commitment.

Temporality

The sixth and final tension also pertains to the postmodern sociality. It identifies the extent to which individual and collective action in cultural formation and interpretation are focused on the immediate situation. In other words, it identifies the extent to which the perspectives of the discourses within which human action is framed are oriented toward the here-and-now. That focus or orientation is essentially with respect to time, both in historical reflection and in future cultural formation. The tension arises from the postmodern problematization of the modernist commitment to a progressive view of social development and, more broadly, of cultural formation. That problematization creates a tension between the impulse to construct cultural formation as a progressive process of evolutionary development and improvement, and the impulse to see it as a purely contingent response to immediate concerns, interests, and issues.

The "developmentalist" pole of the tension (the left or modernist pole) defines a temporal perspective that locates the present, the here-and-now, the immediate problems or issues, in an historically meaningful sequence. It is thus timeless in the sense that the meaning of what is perceived, interpreted, and constructed in cultural formation is a potentially lasting perception, interpretation, or construction. Timelessness here is not with respect to any lack of cultural location or situation, but rather applies to the meaningfulness of the location or situation in the history and forward march of sociality. What is seen or constructed now is done with a sense of its transcendent timelessness as a valid perception or construction—to the extent, of course, that it *is* valid for that location or situation. Concrete cultural constructions—such as buildings, landscapes, works of art, and implements—are accepted, equally obviously, as having a finite concrete existence, as being subject to decay, destruction, and loss of utility. What is timeless in them is not their material existence so much as the spirit of their construction, the perception of the social world as a meaningful and developing entity. In that meaningfulness and through that developmental process, what is seen and created now continues (potentially infinitely) to have meaning as a perception or a creation into the future. Accordingly, what was seen and created in the social past has meaning and developmental, historical situation, which may be captured in our historiographic interpretations of that historical social reality.

The impulse to adopt a developmentalist perspective is to see our social worlds as metaphysically meaningful (even if the nature of that meaning alludes us). It is to locate our own actions, and those of our predecessors, in an orderly developmental progression. The reality of that evolutionary advance is not denied by periods or pockets of apparent regression (such as the Dark Ages or the Holocaust). Rather, the timeless temporal perspective allows us to interpret, to understand those spells of regressive social formation. What we do now thus acquires sociocultural meaning in terms both of the history that precedes us and the future of humanity that is before us. Through that meaning (again, even if we do not understand it, or cannot grasp it) we acquire *significance* in the sociocultural scheme of things. What we choose to do, and not to do, may be seen as having lasting import—however minor—in the evolutionary development of humanity.

The "presentist" pole of the tension (the right or postmodern pole) defines a temporal perspective that focuses on the here-and-now, the demands of the present, of the immediate problems, concerns, or issues as if they were *ahistorical* events. In other words, the events of the present—while certainly perceived as situated in a broader context of influences, interests, and consequences—are nevertheless not viewed as part of an historical developmental or evolutionary sociocultural progression. The particular present event or situation, therefore, is not seen as carrying any timeless meaning and import into the future. Neither, then, does individual or collective action with respect to that event or situation carry any particular lasting significance into the future. That future is entirely unknown. How it will interpret and evaluate our present actions are open, unknown, and historically indeterminate realities. The actions that we take now will not necessarily have any particular significance or meaning in the future. Correspondingly, the sociocultural artifacts—traditions, social structures, hierarchies, works of art, buildings, made landscapes, and so on—of the past, of history, are seen as being open to our contingently present interpretation. Within the constraints of the discourses defining our actions, we are free to do with the past what we will: to reinterpret it, deconstruct it, reconstruct it, diminish it, esteem it, marginalize it, centralize it, fragment it, recombine it in pastiche, create our own (multiple) historicities from it, or whatever.

The impulse to adopt a presentist perspective is to deal with our present realities free of the constraints and restraints imposed upon us by history and our consideration of the future. We feel free to use the sociocultural artifacts of the past as we will in pursuing our interests and in addressing our concerns, problems, and issues. We may use history with cavalier disregard for the meanings that its authors ascribed to it. What remains is now ours to interpret, signify, fragment, deconstruct, and reconstruct as we elect. We may do so playfully, lightheartedly, for the weighty modernist obligations of respect for history and our impact on the future have been lifted. That future, we are confident, will have no stronger impulse than do we for respecting the cultural inheritance of the past. Why, then, should we be concerned about our impact on the future, when there is no good reason to believe that it will accord us and the artifacts of our cultural formation any particular respect? Our carefree attitude to the past is projected into our concern (or, rather, our lack of it) for the impact of our action on the future. If the meaning and value of our actions are open to the future to define as contingently and contrarily as it will, then why should we be concerned about how the future will interpret and value our actions? How *can* we effectively and logically *be* thus concerned? We cannot. We are, accordingly, freed of the past and freed of the future to *be* in the present.

So What?

What, then, can we do with these six tensions? More particularly, how may they be used to advance the concern of the present work? That concern, you will recall, is to elucidate and articulate a picture of the implications of postmodernity for practice, research, and the formation and professional development of practitioners in the field of adult education.

The tensions are seen, here, as providing a framework through which to structure that elucidation and its articulation. The tensions, in other words, will be used in the following chapters to organize an examination of postmodernity in the field of adult education practice: first, in looking at aspects of the tensions through a number of dialogues between the author and adult educators in professional development activities, as students of adult education, and, second, in focusing on a number of case studies of adult education practice, each of which exemplifies a particular tension. The final chapters will then move back away from (while presuming) that tensional framework, in teasing out general tendencies in the nature of adult education events (Chapter 8); in examining nodal forms of educational engagement that are seen as emerging in the field (Chapter 9); research in the field (Chapter 10); and the formation and professional development of adult education practitioners (Chapter 11).

Part Three

Adult Education in Postmodernity

The six chapters in this section examine the nature of postmodern adult education in different ways and from different perspectives. Chapter 6 presents a set of dialogues with students of adult education practice, on the nature of that practice in postmodernity, within the framework of tensions developed in the immediately preceding chapter. Chapter 7 uses the same framework to present a series of case studies of postmodern adult education. Chapter 8 re-examines postmodern adult education as a number of qualitative tendencies. Chapter 9 looks at two nodal forms of programmatic response to the postmodern cultural context. Chapter 10 explores the nature of adult education research in postmodernity. And Chapter 11, the final substantive chapter in the volume, looks similarly at the formation and professional development of adult education practitioners.

Chapter 6

Eternal Ambivalence: Learning in Postmodern Adult Education

The focus now shifts from what may be seen as the postmodern *context* of adult education to the implications of that context for adult education itself. Such a focus is not in any sense intended to deny the possible persistence or the creation in a postmodern cultural context of adult education that is essentially modern or even premodern. Pockets, islands, even archipelagos of such activity may be expected in postmodernity—the resolve of their architects and supporters steeled by the very threat to their existence which arises from the cultural context that would seek to absorb and redefine them. Our concern, here, is rather with those adult education engagements that are more directly and sympathetically responsive to the postmodern cultural context.

The *a priori* inclusiveness of the conception of "adult education" informing this analysis (and those of the subsequent chapters) follows that articulated in the introduction to this volume. There, "adult education" was taken broadly and procedurally as embracing activities that are intended to enhance worthwhile adult learning in ethically appropriate ways—the definition of which learning *is* worthwhile and which ways of enhancing it *are* ethically appropriate being determined by the more particular (postmodern) cultural contexts in which it is embedded.

In this chapter, there is attempted an examination of postmodern adult education through engagements with adult learners. The learners, though, are particular in being students *of* adult education practice. In other words, they are engaging in learning either as part of their preparation for work as adult educators, or as part of their professional development as adult educators. The engagements have been drawn from my experiences over the last fifteen years in working within both graduate and undergraduate programs for the formation and development of adult educators.

The engagements are crafted here as composite pictures, each drawing upon an open set of selective experiences. They are crafted as dialogues between me (as adult educator) and particular (but again composite and essentially mythological) individuals as students of adult education.[1] Each dialogue has been crafted to focus attention on one of the six tensions. They are exchanges *across* the tension in each case: I ('RB') being situated in the postmodern pole of the tension, the learner in the modernist pole. The dialogue in each case focuses on a substantive aspect of the tension itself, as it relates to adult education practice.

The dialogues are presented here under the heads of the tensions which they address. The tensions are ordered in the same sequence as that used in the previous chapter. In each case, the formal nature of the tension is firstly summarized as a reminder. The context of the dialogue is then briefly introduced, before the dialogue itself is presented.

The Situatedness of Belief

The situatedness tension, you will recall, identifies the extent to which belief is particular to the frameworks of preordinate perception and belief in which it is generated. The *transcendent* or modernist pole sees truth, goodness, beauty, authenticity, and so on as qualities of situations, regardless of the frameworks of belief in which they are generated. The *particularized* or postmodern pole recognizes belief as being situated in particular contexts or events. Truth, goodness, beauty, authenticity, and so on are therefore qualities of events, including (and importantly) the frameworks of belief that inform them and the identities of the individuals realizing and articulating the frameworks.

The dialogue presented here focuses on the nature and value of classification systems (and therefore, ultimately, of all systematic knowledge) in the planning of adult education activities. The author's interlocutor (Alex) is struggling to organize the mass of information about the relative value of different teaching/learning arrangements in such a way that the knowledge may be used in designing, managing, and evaluating specific educational tasks.

Alex: I have been reading about the use of classification systems in adult education. It seems that what I need is a good classification system of adult education events. I could then relate the research findings on the value of different teaching approaches to the categories—'taxa' I think they're called—in the system, using the knowledge applying to each category when I'm selecting or evaluating a teaching approach.

R.B.: Sounds good, but what sort of a system are you looking at, what sort of categories?

Alex: Well, I came across this nifty system developed by Coolie Verner.[2] He divides what he calls educational 'processes' into 'methods' and 'techniques.' The techniques seem to be what I'm really interested in. They identify the different sorts of ways in which we teach adults. The categories are pretty easy to understand, because they're mostly based on common-sense notions like 'lecture,' 'forum,' and 'group discussion.'

R.B.: So, what's so good about them?

Alex: Well, what Verner does is, first, to clarify the categories—defining each one clearly, articulating its central idea and its outer limits or boundaries—so that we know precisely when we are dealing with one category or another. We know exactly what category research findings relate to; we know precisely the nature of a good example of a category, when we are wanting to create one; and we can be clear about what category of processes an event falls into when we are evaluating it.

R.B.: Wonderful! What else?

Alex: Second, what Verner does is to develop a partially hierarchical classification system. For example, the category of 'film forum' constitutes two subcategories: 'forum' and 'discussion.' That way, we can develop not only practical knowledge that is specific to processes in the 'forum' and 'discussion' categories, but also more general practical knowledge that applies to both of them combined in the 'film forum' category. It is a really efficient way to organize, remember, and recall practical knowledge and to apply it in my work.

R.B.: Indeed, what more could we ask for? Before closing the deal, though, I would want to be satisfied with the answers to two general questions. First, *is* the world of adult education events really like that, and, second, if it is, *should* it be so? Let's look at these briefly. Take the lecture and group discussion categories. What defines the boundary between them?

Alex: In a lecture, someone talks *to* a big group, and in a group discussion there is a smaller number of learners, each of whom talks to the others, at various points, as part of an on-going conversation.

R.B.: So, we have at least three qualities involved here: the number of persons in the learning group; the extent to which one person does the talking; and the extent to which the talking is preplanned.

Alex: You could look at it that way.

R.B.: You could, and if you did, wouldn't you find that, on each of the qualities, there was potentially a continuous array of variability, for example, in the number of persons constituting the learning group?

Alex: True.

R.B.: What, then, happens to the clarity of your categories and the precision of the boundaries between them?

Alex: I guess that it's lost.

R.B.: It is, and what also of your willingness to generalize research knowledge across all of the diversity *within* a category, while not accepting that it applies to varying degrees across category borders, to events in other categories?

Alex: I guess it all looks a bit of a nonsense. But you must be wrong, because the fact of the matter is that we *can* recognize things like lectures and group discussions, and we don't have too much difficulty classifying particular events as one or the other (or, indeed, as some other).

R.B.: Maybe, but two things need to be said here. First, that *because* we believe in the reality of the categories, we tend to create policies and events that conform to them, even though anything else could be created instead. Second, and also because we believe in the categories, we tend to see the world as conforming to them, even if it does not.

Alex: O.K., but is that necessarily a bad thing? At least the use of categories allows us to do all of the really valuable things that I outlined earlier.

R.B.: It's not *necessarily* a bad thing, but I would argue that it is, *contingently*, a bad thing. On the one hand, we diminish the value of all that does *not* conform to the categories, denying learners the opportunities that such alternative arrangements present. On the other hand, we take knowledge gained from research and experience in particular events and we apply that knowledge to other, often quite different events, just because we put those events in the same category. In so doing, we may seriously diminish the quality of the learning that we are seeking to facilitate.

Alex: Thanks a lot!

The Ambiguity of Belief

The ambiguity tension, you will recall, identifies the extent to which there are good grounds for accepting alternative views of what is good, true, beautiful, authentic, and so on. The *singular* or modernist pole accepts the in-principle existence of a single ultimately correct interpretation of every reality. The *plural* or postmodern pole recognizes the potential incommensurability of interpretations across different frameworks of belief, and accepts the existence of a plurality of alternative interpretations of any given reality.

The dialogue here focuses on the relative value of alternative types of knowledge in informing adult education practice. The author's interlocutor (Rowan) is concerned to make the very best use of the limited time available to study, and seeks accordingly to identify the sort of knowledge that will be most useful.

Rowan: The situation is quite clear to me—as a teacher of adults my concern is to facilitate adult learning; learning is a change which is internal to each individual; if we are to facilitate it in the best possible way, we must have and act according to the most up-to-date understanding of how that learning occurs; only then can we truly claim to be acting in a professionally responsible (and fully accountable) manner.

R.B.: Certainly, clarity has been seen by many a great scholar and humanitarian to be a desirable state of affairs, even a virtue. Where, though, does this lead you?

Rowan: It leads me to the view that what is of greatest value in informing my work as an adult educator is that knowledge which deals most particularly with the learning process.

R.B.: And that is?

Rowan: Cognitive psychology, obviously.

R.B.: Obviously, but how will it help you?

Rowan: Stupid! I shall use the understanding that cognitive psychology has of the way adults learn, in structuring my teaching so as to help my students to learn efficiently and effectively.

R.B.: So efficiency and effectiveness define for you what is best in this regard?

Rowan: Of course! Don't they for everyone? What else is there?

R.B.: No, they don't do so for everyone. There is a great deal besides, many alternatives, like respect for traditions, and for persons, and an acknowledgment of different reasons for engaging in learning.

Rowan: Humph. You're just playing with words.

R.B.: I am not. This is of the most profound importance. Take your commitment to using only what you term 'the most up-to-date understanding.' How do you recognize it?

Rowan: Easy. You just follow through the argument logically. The most up-to-date knowledge is that which is at the cutting edge of the most pivotal discipline. As I said before, that discipline is obviously cognitive psychology, because cognitive psychology is concerned with the processes of learning.

R.B.: Perhaps, but surely that only applies if a large number of unarticulated assumptions are true.

Rowan: Such as?

R.B.: Such as that we have some sort of objectively valid way of gaining access to the way learning occurs inside people; that the knowledge gained about the way one set of adults learns can be applied to the way other adults learn; and that you, as a facilitator of adult learning, can morally treat your learners on the basis of those assumptions.

Rowan: But if we don't make those sorts of assumptions, what is left? How would we know what to do?

R.B.: Exactly. You don't know such things, and you certainly don't know them on the basis of the assumed *a priori* superiority of one type of knowledge over another.

Rowan: Hey, but that is just confused thinking—the advocacy of woolly thinking against clarity.

R.B.: Well, since you have raised it again, let me question the overarching importance that you accord 'clarity' as a value.

Rowan: You're mad!

R.B.: I don't think so, at least not in this regard. Let me for now offer just two general points of argument with respect to the value of clarity.

Rowan: Go for it.

R.B.: First, since conceptual clarity is not otherwise a notable feature of our cultural universe, its pursuit must be at the expense of a great deal of diversity that does not accord with it. What is unclear, 'woolly,' or whatever, is rejected or distorted to suit the conception of clarity. The pursuit of clarity is, in this way, strongly hegemonic. It diminishes or colonizes its opposition.

Rowan: What else?

R.B.: The second point derives from the first. It is that the attainment of clarity gives one a false sense of certainty and of empowerment through that certainty—a hubris not warranted in an uncertain and an unclear universe. That certainty is itself, then, a potentially antisocial and destructive state of mind.

Rowan: So we are left groping around in the mists of vagueness and uncertainty, trying to work out what to do without being able to see much past our noses?

R.B.: Not a bad analogy.

Rowan: So much for professionalism.

R.B.: Not so fast on the dismissal. I am not denying that there is an important place for disciplinary knowledge. What I do insist upon, though, is that we should not use it to *structure* our actions, but rather to sensitize us to alternative possibilities within the realities in which we engage and in the crafting of our actions within those realities.

The Determination of Individual Identity

The determination tension, you may recall, identifies the extent to which individual identity is determined as a plurality of partial identities. The *holistic* or modernist pole sees individual identity as integrated into a coherent unity, deriving from the individual's inherited potential to be a person of a particular sort. The *fragmented* or postmodern pole sees individual identity as fragmented among a plurality of partial identities, identity being only provisionally determined and underdetermined, and therefore open to the contingent addition of further partial identities.

The dialogue presented here focuses on the value of humanism. The author's interlocutor (Lindsay) has just completed an extensive study of the philosophical foundations of Western adult education—liberalism, radicalism, humanism, and so on[3]—and has come to the view that a broadly humanistic approach to work in the field is the best. Something the author said has made Lindsay doubt the author's commitment to humanism, arousing considerable consternation.

Lindsay: I have always seen you as a humanist, but now I hear you questioning humanism. How can you possibly question something that is through and through so good: in its recognition of individual value, its respect for humanity, and its acknowledgment of individual difference?

R.B.: The points that you make about humanism are fair ones. Humanism in adult education, and in social discourse generally, has many good features.

Lindsay: Well, what's wrong with you that makes you question its appropriateness?

R.B.: A practical educational philosophy like humanism is only as good as its assumptions. Traditional humanism, unfortunately, is founded on some assumptions that are difficult to sustain in the light of experience.

Lindsay: What assumptions?

R.B.: Perhaps most important is the assumption that the individual human being has some inherited potential and inclination to *be* a socially constructive person (a good person) and that, given an appropriately supportive social environment during upbringing, every individual will realize that potential and become what they should be. Another important and allied assumption is that an individual has an integrated individual identity, and the capacity—and the will if supportively nurtured—to reflect critically upon any negative aspects of their identity or personality, and to address those aspects, thereby becoming a better person. The development of individual identity is, therefore, seen as an ongoing and unidirectional progression.

Lindsay: Of course! What's wrong with that?

R.B.: It's beautiful, but it doesn't make a lot of sense. There's little evidence from experience to support the idea that an individual has more inclination to be good than otherwise. Morally, individuals appear to be capable of anything at all, so long as it is sanctioned by the frameworks of belief within which they are operating.

Lindsay: O.K., but how does that impact on adult education?

R.B.: Profoundly. For example, it questions the wisdom of a whole range of nondirective, interactive (group-based) educational activities that have come to characterize humanistic adult education in recent decades.

Lindsay: That's worrying, but perhaps we can put them aside as mistaken. Other approaches to humanistic adult education are surely constructed to optimize features—such as self-direction and self-reflection—that derive from the nature of persons *as* holistic, integrated, progressively developing entities. You mentioned those features earlier, but have not countered them.

R.B.: You are correct about the educational importance of what I would call 'progressive monadism.' Its unproblematic nature, though, cannot go unchallenged.

Lindsay: Go on then.

R.B.: It could be observed, for example, that the horrors of recent history reveal to us the ease with which unimaginable evil and sublime good can be co-resident within, and be acted out by, one individual, under the appropriate facilitating circumstances, regardless of any overall sense of individual identity development. Humanism holds such identities to be abnormal, schizoid, and exceptional. Our experience of the Holocaust and of numerous other pogroms of all sorts, before and since, is overwhelmingly that such identities are the *norm*, not the exception. Perhaps each and every one of us is similarly constituted.

Lindsay: What a depressing thought.

R.B.: Perhaps, but by facing up to it, we may be better placed as adult educators to help others in coming to a more realistic and mature understanding of themselves, and thereby to develop stronger mechanisms for self-realization and restraint when they are under the influence of inhumane frameworks of belief.

Lindsay: But isn't that possibility denied by the picture of individual identity that you have just been painting—of identity as fragmented into noncommunicative and irreconcilable chunks?

R.B.: Yes, to some extent at least.

Lindsay: Isn't it also likely that such a 'more realistic and mature understanding,' as you put it, is likely to lead to an *indifference* to evil—an informed tolerance of wrongdoing, the consequence of which may well be to *encourage* evil, both in oneself and in others?

R.B.: Yes, that may well be so.

Lindsay: So, you really *are* a humanist, even if you are lacking any justification of that belief. I was right and you are wrong.

R.B.: Not so hasty. What these last points indicate is rather, I might suggest, that we need to be open both *to* criticism of our own actions and *in* our criticism of the actions of others (as well as of ourselves), and to be situationally sensitive in our selection and application of moral principles—not just *devoid* of principles as you imply.

The Control of Individual Identity

The control tension, in summary, identifies the extent to which individual action may be seen as deriving from the discourses in which those actions are embedded. The *autonomous* or modernist pole sees individuals as autonomous monads, empowered by their command over their realities. The *embedded* or postmodern pole sees individual action constrained and restrained by the discourses in which individual (fragmented) identity is embedded.

The dialogue here focuses on positive or reverse discrimination (affirmative action) in adult education. The author's interlocutor (Chris) is offended at not being offered personal assistance that has been made available to a minority student (Edward) covered by equal opportunity legislation allowing positive discrimination in such cases.

Chris: My problem with this situation (aside from the personal disadvantage to me) is that what has happened does not appear to be just.

R.B.: How so?

Chris: Edward has been given learning assistance not available to me or to others, purely because he is a member of an historically disadvantaged group.

R.B.: True. Please explain the injustice.

Chris: Traditionally, justice in such cases is based on equality of opportunity (which is, ironically, the label given to the legislation under which the injustice here is perpetrated). In other words, every individual is recognized as properly being given the same opportunity to succeed, using their own wit, will, and effort. That way, we are all on an equal footing; the educational differences between us then will only arise from differences in our native intelligence, our desire to achieve, or the effort that we respectively put into the work. In the present case, that conception of discriminative justice has been violated, by Edward being given preferential treatment. Compared with others, he is now able to succeed with less native intelligence, a lower desire to achieve, or less effort on his part.

R.B.: Well, yes and no. The argument that you have presented is certainly true to what has traditionally been the case in matters of discriminative justice. It is clear-cut, straightforward, and ideal in those qualities.

Chris: So, what's wrong with it?

R.B.: The main problem with it is its assumption that individual qualities like the will to achieve and the individual effort that we commit to a task are functions *only* of our natural individual personalities or identities.

Chris: Ah, so this is the 'nature versus nurture' argument, and you are taking the side of nurture.

R.B.: Yes, but much more profoundly than is implied by the concept of nurturing.

Chris: How so?

R.B.: I would argue that the 'environment' of an individual—most importantly the frameworks of belief, meaning, and value in which one functions as a being—actually define, through subconscious reconfiguration, what the individual *is*. In other words, they contribute significantly to the determination of the individual's identity—an identity which is likely to be as fragmented as the frameworks of meaning in which the individual has participated. Without those frameworks, the individual does not exist *as* a person.

Chris: But what of native intelligence? Surely you acknowledge that!

R.B.: Only to the extent that we all clearly inherit limitations and potentials. I would argue, though, that they permit in all but the most retarded of individuals a truly vast encompass of possibilities. Intelligence as such only exists *within* particular frameworks of meaning—including those that we craft into the discourse of adult education.

Chris: And I suppose you would argue the same of the will to achieve, the inclination to work hard, and such like.

R.B.: I would.

Chris: So, how does this impact on my claim of discriminative injustice? I am certainly prepared to accept differential assistance to correct for the effects of individual disadvantage. That is not the case here. Indeed, Edward is probably much more capable and motivated than are many of us.

R.B.: Part of Edward's identity is that of the ethnic group with which he identifies and through which he is here being discriminatively advantaged. That group as a whole is seriously disadvantaged in contemporary society—a disadvantage that diminishes the group and the identities of those who identify with it. Society is judged in this case to have an obligation to correct that disadvantage, properly through the sort of individual assistance to which you are taking exception.

Chris: What a chaotic situation! So any identity-forming group, like bank robbers and pedophiles could claim similar disadvantage and seek similar assistance.

R.B.: Certainly, they could *claim* those things, but that is not the point. What is important here is what society legitimates as unjust disadvantage. That conception is certainly an openly broad one, but it is one which is contested and resolved for each particular category of claim and I cannot see it resulting in the recognition of bank robbers or pedophiles as constituting identity categories of unjust disadvantage.

Chris: I'll think about it, but I maintain that the sort of situation for which you are arguing is likely to be infinitely more uncertain, confused, and conflict-ridden than is the one from which I have been arguing.

R.B.: With that I agree.

The Homogeneity of Sociality

The homogeneity tension—to reiterate briefly the articulation in the previous chapter—identifies the extent to which sociality is not strongly structured into discrete or lasting autonomous realms. The *differentiated* or modernist pole sees sociality as divided into distinct and lasting spheres or realms of social practice: domains of discourse, social institutions, social classes, organizations, occupations, and individual life roles. The *dedifferentiated* or postmodern pole sees sociality as an unstable, shifting, and unpredictable miasma of social relationships, with social differentiation constantly open to, and the subject of, challenge and reformulation or elimination.

The dialogue here focuses on a qualified and experienced builder (Kim) who is seeking a midlife change to teaching. Kim plans to pass on to trainees in the building industry, the years of accumulated experience in this trade. Traditionally in Australia, such training has been provided through a variable mixture of workplace apprenticeships and classroom teaching in the technical and further education (TAFE) sector of the educational institution.

Kim: I'm getting pretty pissed off with all this fancy stuff in the course, about philosophies, theory, postmodernity, and such like. It's all a bloody waste of time. I'm here to learn how to teach carpentry. Teaching skills; that's all I need.

R.B.: Teaching skills to do what?

Kim: Like I said; to teach my trade.

R.B.: What sort of skills?

Kim: Well, look at what's happening—my job is going to be in TAFE at the classroom end of things, so what I need are classroom management skills. And CBT's[4] all the rage now, so I need to know how to manage that.

R.B.: Fair enough, but what happens if there isn't a job for you teaching carpentry in TAFE?

Kim: There will be. TAFE does that sort of thing.

R.B.: Maybe now, but there is increasingly a tendency to open up tertiary education to other providers.

Kim: So, I'll get a job with one of them.

R.B.: Perhaps, but it could be hard to sell your capabilities if all you have is a bundle of classroom and CBT management skills. Even if you *do* get a job, what will happen to you when CBT is no longer 'all the rage'?

Kim: I'll be right in the classroom.

R.B.: But what makes you think that classrooms are sacred, or that someone with a much broader range of skills, and deeper practical knowledge of how to use them, will not come along and take away your job?

Kim: The union would stop it happening.

R.B.: Sorry, trade unions, like all other social structures, are losing their singular power. Increasingly, it's an open marketplace in which we must work.

Kim: OK, I'll come back for retraining.

R.B.: Certainly, that's a possibility, but would it not be helpful, too, to look forward a little—admittedly into a very uncertain future—and to *prepare* yourself for what is likely to happen?

Kim: OK, so what if I did?

R.B.: Well, you wouldn't be seeking specific skills training for a particular job that is likely to be unrecognizably different shortly after you graduate; you wouldn't be seeking security in educational employing bodies that are rapidly losing their privileged positions as educational providers, or in trade unions that are losing their power to protect the privileges of their members. You would, rather, be seeking to make yourself as broadly employable as you can, so that you can effectively market your capabilities within a broad range of educational roles, facilitating learning from within a whole range of knowledge types.

Kim: But I'm a chippy [carpenter].

R.B.: Yes, and that is important, but redefine and repackage the knowledge that you have acquired as a builder. All of it, I'm sure, is applicable to other tasks and in other contexts. If you see those links, you can build on them and present yourself as encapsulating them.

Kim: So you're now going to tell me that all the shit you have in this course is to help me do that.

R.B.: Exactly. That is the intention.

Kim: Who wants that sort of a world? Not me! It's pretty rough and lonely.

R.B.: Maybe it is. We all contribute to its creation, in acting out our desires for individual freedom and autonomy.

Kim: Not me! I just want to get on with my life.

The Temporality of Sociality

Temporality—the final tension—you will recall identifies the extent to which individual and collective action in cultural formation and interpretation are focused on the immediate situation, the here-and-now. The *developmentalist* or modernist pole defines a temporal perspective that locates the presentness, the here-and-now, in an historically meaningful, developmental, or evolutionary sequence. The *presentist* or postmodern pole defines a temporal perspective that focuses strictly on the here-and-now: the contingent demands, interests, problems, concerns, or issues of the present, as if they were ahistorical events.

The dialogue presented here focuses on the proper nature of the curriculum for the formation and professional development of adult educators. The author's interlocutor (Lee) is arguing for a problem-based approach.

Lee: So, we seem to agree at least that the role of the adult educator is that of responding to contingent circumstances and facilitating desirable change in those circumstances through facilitating learning.

R.B.: Agreed.

Lee: I suggest, then, that the best way to equip a person for such a role is through a problem-based approach to curriculum design and management.

R.B.: Why so?

Lee: Because, what the adult educator's role clearly amounts to is addressing problems: contingent problems that have arisen in one aspect or another of life, and which may be addressed, at least partly, through learning.

R.B.: Perhaps. What do you mean by a 'problem-based approach'?

Lee: What I mean is basing curriculum design and management on real-life situations that adult educators face in their work—both the day-to-day happenings and those that arise only occasionally.

R.B.: OK, but what if the nature of those real-life situations changes? How would the graduate who is looking for a job be placed then?

Lee: Get real! Things don't change that quickly.

R.B.: Why not?

Lee: Well, for all sorts of reasons; like the traditional ways of doing things that we inherit and build upon; like our respect for what those before us have done; like the expression of human nature in the desire to build progressively on those historical achievements and to create things that future generations will respect and, in their turn, build upon.

R.B.: That sounds all very well and all very familiar, but I would argue that it describes a cultural world that is rapidly leaving us. We are facing not a respect for tradition so much as a disregard for it and a willingness to reconstitute it to suit our immediate desires. We are facing not a trust in the will of future generations to respect what we have done so much as a loss of confidence in the future to give more than a passing thought to our commitments, intentions, strivings, and creations.

Lee: Well?

R.B.: Well, if you accept those realities, then the arguments that you put forward for the progressive and gradual continuity of cultural change just don't hold water.

Lee: I suppose they don't.

R.B.: Then, I would argue, we are faced now with the prospect of cultural change being nonprogressive, deracinated, without heed as to its future impact, and therefore potentially highly radical and rapid.

Lee: OK, so let's get back to the curriculum.

R.B.: Right. I argue that a problem-based curriculum as you have outlined it just won't do, because it must be built on the basis of present and past work roles and patterns, and the exigencies that we face. That is not an adequate preparation for a radically unknown future.

Lee: Maybe, but what would be better preparation for such a future?

R.B.: A big question, but let me suggest at least that what we should be looking at is a curriculum based on an understanding of the sorts of things that we *can* reasonably predict about the future.

Lee: Like what?

R.B.: Like its highly pluriform nature; its highly changeable nature; the highly ambiguous nature of all realities and the ambivalence and uncertainty that is thereby generated; like humanity's awareness of its profound insignificance and meaningless; like ...

Lee: Enough! Where does that get us with the curriculum?

R.B.: Another big question, which I shall answer for now only by suggesting a curriculum structured by the concept of *enhancing situational sensitivity* in learners: a sensitivity across the range of knowledge types (technical, ethical, theoretical, existential, and aesthetic); a sensitivity that facilitates one's passage into radically unknown events, not with an armory of problem-identifying and problem-solving skills, but rather with an expectation of and a respect for the unknown, the unfamiliar, the radically different, the contrary; it is to so move with the will to learn, to respect, and to respond accordingly.

Lee: Once adult educators were seen as educational pioneers, heroes, change agents; now we seem to be heading into the role of wimps.

R.B.: If what I have described fits your description of a 'wimp,' so be it. I would suggest, though, that the macho Australian notion of a wimp is an historical anachronism, the death of which is long overdue.

Lee: What situational sensitivity!

In Conclusion

The foregoing dialogues leave far more unsaid than said. They do no more than touch upon the array of realities opened up in an exploration of the implications of postmodernity for adult education. As a selection of vignettes from my experience in the formation and professional development of adult educators, they are particularly limited, and selective, and should be seen by you as such. They no more define the world of postmodern adult education than does a modernist painting of a landscape scene define that landscape. Both are, though, one hopes and expects, important interpretative characterizations of their objects.

Another set of pictures of the landscape of postmodern adult education is presented in the next chapter. There, though, the perspective shifts a little from that of adult educators as students *of* practice, to that of adult educators *in* practice.

Chapter 7

Horsehair in the Undies: The Adult Educator as a Boundary Rider

Here we continue the examination of what postmodernity means for adult education practice. The focus, though, is shifted, both substantively and methodologically. Substantively, we move from issues arising in the formation and professional development of adult educators, to the actual *practice* of adult educators. Methodologically, we move from the examination of particular dialogues between me and students of the field, to the examination of *case studies* of adult education practice.

As was the case with the dialogues, the case studies, as they are presented here, are composite pictures (principally to protect, from undeserved ridicule, those whom I inadvertently misrepresent). Each of the six case studies focuses on one of the identified primary tensions of postmodernity. It is presented in such a way as to draw attention to the tension and some of its implications for adult education practice.

Those implications have been selected to complement and extend, rather than to reinforce or elaborate on, the implications drawn out in the previous chapter. They have been selected also to cover a range of practical roles and situations. Roles range from program planning, policy formulation, needs assessment, and marketing, through the management of learning situations and the recognition of prior learning, to instructional design and the assessment of learning. Practice situations range across various categories of adult education providers: from university and community providers, through workplace education and technical and further education provision, to self-directed learning and a private (commercial) provider of adult education. Other variations enter across the case studies, with the inclusion of distance- and resource-based programs, and one which has a particular focus on continuing professional education. There has also been generated some sort of a gender balance and a range of personalities.

In presenting each case study, the First Person is used. The adult educator in each case has been given the expectation of explaining the considerations that are informing his or her thinking with respect to the substantive (and hence the tensional) focus of the case study. The case studies have been drawn from my (vicarious) experience in and understanding of selective engagements of those practitioners who have studied and worked with me over the last twenty-five years.

In seeking to remove any hint of opportunity for personal identification, and to reconstruct the depicted experiences within the tensional framework here being utilized, there has no doubt been generated a certain sameness across the case studies. It is to be hoped that the substantive and situational appeal of each is sufficient to offset the tedium induced by that degree of uniformity, whatever it is seen to be. I apologize, also, to the individuals whose identities have been reconstructed in these vignettes, and I thank them for the quality of their professional practice which has so impacted on me as to induce the articulations here provided.

Each case study is briefly introduced, before the authorial voice is passed over to the player herself or himself. In case you are struggling still to remember the nature of the tensions, the summary description of each one from the previous chapter is reproduced here as an endnote to the opening of the pertinent case study.

The Situatedness of Belief[1]

The case study included here is that of Roger, in his role as an adult education programmer, working within a university extension department (recently renamed 'Unicom' and reconstituted as a commercial arm of the University). The concept of an adult education programmer is that of a planner, manager, coordinator, and evaluator of an area of adult education provision: variously recognized as a geographical region (e.g., metropolitan NW); a category of provision (e.g., study tours); a particular range of substantive focus (e.g., child development); or a client category (e.g., physicians). The programmer role *per se* excludes the planning, managing, and assessing of teaching/learning engagements themselves within the program (Bagnall, 1982; Boshier, 1978).

Roger is here reflecting on his first two years in that programming position, to which he moved after having worked as an industrial training officer, before taking a year out to study for a course-work master's degree in adult education. His new position covers all programming in the University's nonmetropolitan region—encompassing a strongly indigenous Australian population. In this reflection, Roger starts in the realities defined by the transcendent pole of the tension, but moves across to those defined by the particularized pole.

> The thing was, when I started here it was a new game to me. I'd worked in industry training, but nothing like this. But I'd spent the previous year boning up on adult education in my master's work. That included a lot on program development—partly because it's a particular interest of mine—different

theories of program planning, management, and evaluation, and what research there is that has been undertaken in that area.

Anyway, I had the job of setting up a program across this huge area. Nothing had been done before. The University apparently decided it wanted to look good in the community quality advancement stakes or something. So all eyes were on me; at least that's how it felt. So I went for my program development theory. The model that I reckoned would work best in that situation was the one by Pennington and Green.[2] It's a problem-based model, and I thought that the people in my area would be more interested in learning how to solve their problems than they would in normal university courses.

Well, I went out into the field with this programming model; identified all the right people; asked all the right questions; analyzed all the data; identified what courses needed to be offered; and put on this great program. Everything went like clockwork. I was feeling really good. Then, bingo! What happens? Right! Nobody turns up—well, almost nobody—a few old friends of the University, some retired schoolteachers, hobby farmers, and such like, but not really the people I thought I was programming for.

So, I then had to rethink the whole thing; what the hell I was doing. I started by taking a few days out to visit some of the key towns and camps. Nothing formal. Just mooching around, chatting with people about who I was and what I was trying to do.

Everyone seemed to know of me, but they had some weird ideas about what I was doing. They seemed to like my courses, but nobody thought that it was for them. They were mostly very nice about it, though. They seemed to respect the University, even though they didn't see its relevance for them. They left my program planning looking a bit sick. All that work for nothing.

Back to square one; I chucked the bloody programming model. What the heck do Pennington and Green know about anyone in this part of the world anyway? I started by talking and sharing with people who seemed to be important in some of the communities. I gradually built up lists of ideas about what I should be doing. But they were all over the place. Some were connected to this, others to that; some thought that things could only be done one way, others quite differently.

Gradually, though, I built up a few tentative programs in this way. We started them off; not quite sure what they were or where they were going. No fancy brochures, no persuasive arguments on value. A fair bit of arm-twisting, cajoling, pretty crude appeals to self-interest, trading on fears of being left out of something good, and what my colleagues in the Uni. would probably see as flagrant misrepresentation.

I went along with it all. Pretty frightening, but luckily nobody from the Uni. moved in on me. The programs seemed to grow and change. It was hard keeping track of each one. They developed lives of their own. Quite chaotic from the outside, but participants seemed to know what they were doing.

Getting in fees was a problem, but we worked on that one too, and there are now programs with funding support from different government departments and agencies. Even the local squattocracy's chipped in for a couple. And some courses *are* supported by fees, but rather irregularly in terms of who pays how much.

And that's sort of where I am now. It's not easy getting facilitators for the programs, especially from the Uni., because academics are inclined to think they have the answers: either for how to do things, or for what should be taught. I really need leaders who think they know nothing. The academics are good, though, in helping out with specific tasks and problems, and I do use them a fair bit in that way.

The Ambiguity of Belief[3]

The case study here is that of Marian, in her role as community development coordinator in a remote but quite substantial mining town (Plumbarton). The town serves as the residential and service center for the mine workers and the service industries. The work force is very mixed, including a high proportion of new immigrants, although they are spread across a range of national and ethnic groups.

Marian is here reflecting on her conducting of the recent policy review, which she undertook in her portfolio of responsibilities. The tension between the realities defined by the singular and plural poles of the tension is articulated by Marian in her analysis of her involvement in the process. The singular pole is represented particularly by the views of the Community Development Council, but also by Marian's initial (naive) view of what a policy document could reasonably provide in this context. The plural pole is represented by Marian's view of the community and the task at hand, and her ultimate view of the utility of a good policy document.

> The problem that we faced before, and which precipitated the policy review, was that our work was always just *reactive* to funding opportunities or program pressures from outside. Our programs may have been fine but were not ours in the sense that they were developed *because* the community wanted them and saw them as a high priority.
>
> Accordingly, we agreed that I should lead a review (and reformulation) of our policy, with a view to our identifying our own community priorities, which we could then use to inform our decisions as to which purposes we should be running with, and what particular slant we should be giving to them, especially those where the crucial impetus comes from the creation of opportunities for outside (funding) support.
>
> The Community Development Council—effectively my advisory group—agreed that the policy review should incorporate and be based on a comprehensive survey and analysis of Plumbarton's development needs. That was fine, except that they had an archaic notion of reaching some sort of *consensus* across the whole community as to our policy priorities in this area. I tried to point out to them that consensus, if authentic, could only be at such a level of generality as to be utterly useless, and that it generally aimed to be more specific, in which case it was inevitably oppressive, patronizing, or colonizing of those perspectives not emerging as dominant within it.
>
> The Council members stuck to their guns, arguing along the lines that we all shared this town together and that its particular development needs were transparently and objectively obvious to anyone who took the trouble to look seriously for them; consensus, therefore, could not be oppressive, patronizing, or colonizing, except to those persons too foolish, lazy, or selfish to open their eyes to the community's needs.
>
> I've worked with this lot for a while now, so I've learned how to handle them. They're all really nice people and committed to what we're doing, but they do have some quaint notions. I

therefore structured my needs assessment and analysis in such a way as to identify and articulate the *differences* between the various groups and interests in the community, as well as the similarities. That meant using different approaches with different groups—asking different questions, in different ways, using different instruments, talking to different sorts of people, even using anonymous suggestion boxes with one group, focus groups with some, document analysis with another, and so on. In terms of standard survey research and needs assessment methodology, it would be seen as an ill-designed shambles. I saw it (and still see it) as the (then) best possible set of procedures by which I could obtain valid pictures of the way the various groups and interests in the community *saw* their community, what they saw as being *important* in it, and therefore what they saw it *needing* in terms of its development.

As I expected, I ended up not with bundles of priorities that could be reconciled and combined in any fair fashion but with quite different images of what the community was and what it needed. These images weren't just different in what they saw as important, they actually *saw* the community quite differently.

Needless to say, my report and draft policy to the Community Development Council was a bit of a shocker to them. They did, though, eventually come around to my view (not, I think, because they were convinced, but more out of respect for all the work that I had done). After some further refining, we endorsed what may best be termed a 'pluralistic' policy—not one set of priorities, procedures, and criteria, but quite a large number, and with overriding acknowledgments that there will be other realities not represented there, and that those articulated there are subject to constant reformulation. The policy therefore includes also overarching principles that leave open the contingent possibility of other and different perspectives being added, or being addressed in spite of their absence from the policy document.

A number of Council members, I am sure, feel that the policy document is an entirely useless mess. I must say, though, that I am quite proud of it. It certainly doesn't tell us our priorities in any straightforward way or, really, in any way at all. It is, though, extremely helpful in sensitizing us to the sorts of considerations, commitments, and concerns that are important to different community groups.

The Determination of Individual Identity[4]

The case study here is that of Helen—a qualified lawyer and adult educator—in her role as a Continuing Professional Education Officer, working for the state body which has licensure (and educational) responsibility over the legal profession in that state. The body involves itself directly with the provision of continuing professional education (CPE) for the legal profession. In the case before us, Helen's office has been charged with the task of addressing what are seen variously as sexist and racist judgments by the state judiciary in recent years. Helen is here reflecting on her approach to this particular task. In terms of the tension, she is working in the fragmented pole, and is contrasting her approach with that in the more traditional holistic pole.

> The judiciary are not too difficult a group to bring together in major centers, for intensive programs of one or a few days. They are largely based in those centers and they have reasonable access to time for CPE, or are circuit judges with generous provision for residential CPE. Our traditional approach, then, to this problem would probably have been to organize a series of short, intensive workshops, with a follow-up session or two, to cover the whole judiciary throughout the state, over a six-month period. Participation would not, I believe, have been an issue, since this particular educational need has been given such a public airing through the mass media in recent years that no judge wants to be exposed to the possibility of public condemnation and ridicule for any apparently racist or sexist remark or judgment.
>
> My concern about that approach, is that it ignores what we know about human nature and does not take cognizance of the poor record of success of such programs in the past. The fact of the matter is that sexism and racism, where they exist in judicial deliberations, are embedded within—are an integral component of—each particular case and judgment; they are part of the way the judges perceive, think about, and act out their judicial responsibilities in each case; they are, in other words, part of the discourse in which each judge unconsciously embeds each case. They are not necessarily closely tied to a judge's conception of his or her ideal as a judge. Neither are

they necessarily a part of a judge's understanding of the law, of how it should operate, even of how it *does* operate. All of those elements, while interrelated, can be operationally quite autonomous and in conflict with each other.

My problem, then, with the traditional approach, was that I felt that all it would do for most judges would be to create or expand yet another compartment in their minds, wherein would be housed all of this good knowledge about the meaning and impact of sexist and racist judgments and comments, and how to avoid them—having no impact on those other components, wherein the practical discourses of their actual practice as judges are housed.

What I considered to be necessary here was an approach to CPE that directly presented the day-to-day practice of each judge *as* a judge. We therefore set up a national network of acknowledged experts in such matters, and connected them via e-mail with all of the cooperating judges (initially not all of them; now after six months, we have all but two in the state enrolled).

The experts agree to provide, over periods of time (which they routinely e-mail to us), a critical response to any material sent to them by any of the judges. They agree also to be available then, on-line at a negotiated time for any follow-up exchange. The judges, for their part, are encouraged to take every opportunity in cases which might be contentious, to defer judgment and to e-mail to us their draft deliberations, judgments, and any other pertinent thoughts. We then identify one, two, or three experts (depending on our assessment of the case) to whom we forward that material for critical comment. We then monitor each exchange, and facilitate as necessary, but mostly they run satisfactorily themselves.

We also—with the agreement of those involved, and as anonymously as possible (which possibility is limited)—send out to all network judges and the expert panel a weekly bulletin of exchanges from that week: each presented as a brief case study, including initial and final articulation, and any necessary contextual information. This is a very important part of the process, because we recognize that we are trying to change the *culture*, the discourse, of judicial judgments. We can only change individual action in the long run if we do it *through* that discourse.

There was, of course, quite a bit of work to do in setting up the system. We had to run initial workshops to develop some sensitivity in identifying the sorts of cases that might best be handled in this way. We also had a lot of work to do in getting some of the judges to use e-mail. Some of them still don't, but they have secretarial or other staff doing it for them.

Our monitoring and process evaluation of the program indicates that it is being used well—admittedly much more by some judges than others, but that is not necessarily a problem, given that some judges *need* assistance much more than others. The match between need in this regard and utilization we have yet to assess. There also appears to be valuable feedback coming through from the experts—critical, perceptive, and incisive—and in some cases, robust exchanges are following. However, we have yet to undertake an evaluation of the actual *impact* of the program on judgments, although we are planning an initial study after the first full year of program operation.

I must say, I'm rather proud of the program: it uses contemporary communications technology; it embeds CPE for judges in their individual workplaces; it utilizes the best available expertise throughout the country; it gives educational intervention just *when* and *where* it is needed, precisely focused *on* what is needed, and as it is requested *by* the learner; and it takes into account what we know today about human nature or identity, and its impact on adult learning.

The Control of Identity[5]

You will recognize that the immediately foregoing case study strongly addressed the points in this tension as well as those of the determination tension. Nevertheless, I here offer another case study, more specifically addressing the control of identity tension. It is that of Bruce, in his role as an Education Officer in an Australian institute of technical and further education (TAFE). In that role, Bruce has particular responsibility for the coordination and management of criteria and procedures for the recognition of prior learning (RPL) in the diverse vocational education and training (VET) programs taught by the institute. The institute itself is an amalgamation of a number of previously separate local TAFE colleges in a geographical area. Here Bruce reflects on his work in setting up and running the RPL program. In that reflection, the autonomous pole of the tension emerges in the realities of what Bruce presents as the traditional view, and the embedded pole in the realities that he is seeking to create and enhance.

> Right. What we are doing here is responding to the current demand for RPL in all areas. It goes with the competency movement,[6] but is much wider than that. On the one hand, it seeks to make VET more efficient—to give recognition for skills and knowledge already learned, so as not to waste resources on unnecessarily teaching them to students who already have them. On the other hand, it seeks to respond to demands for the recognition of anything at all in an individual's personal experience that may be pertinent to the educational task at hand.
>
> None of this really happened previously, except to a limited extent, namely, when we gave advanced standing or credit on the basis of formal studies undertaken elsewhere. And that was pretty limited because most of our students didn't have much in the way of formal educational achievements, and we took a pretty narrow view of what was to count. Students were seen as progressing logically through their careers and their lives. Anything they did was judged in terms of how it contributed to that linear path. Any apparent deviations from the path were seen as transgressions and were discounted. Any uncertainty about the direction of the path was seen as a weakness, even as a pathological failing. Failure to achieve was your own responsibility and a personal shame. Conversely, success was yours to relish, to profit from and to provide a personal security blanket. You were a plumber, a fitter and turner, an electrician, or whatever. That meant certain formal study and appropriate practical experience. The experience you got on the job; the study we provided in TAFE. Working out what credit or advanced standing to award was easy—we just looked at the relevant courses passed. So the job was just part of the normal course management. My job didn't even exist.
>
> Now it's all different. Nobody seems to expect the students to be responsible for anything. If they fail, it's because they're victims of their upbringing or personal circumstances. If they succeed, we've got the training thing right. They may be totally aimless, and all over the place, but we judge them equally. Whatever course they want to do, we have to take on

board anything from their experience that looks as though it might stand instead of some of the course.

I'll tell you—it's an interesting job, if it's nothing else. The things that some students come up with—you'd be amazed.

But that's one side of the story. The other is that TAFE sees itself as having a *duty* to the students (and to society) to *encourage* them to optimize their RPL. And that's interesting too, because many of them are just not tuned in to the way things are. They are still stuck in the old ways: going around with loads of guilt about their past failures and confusions; feeling like abject failures because they don't have it all together and aren't personally empowered like everyone was supposed to be. They feel like they've nothing to bring to the course but themselves and their failings.

So we have to persuade them to look differently at what they've done and who they are; to see their failures (and their successes) as functions of where they were at the time, not as their personal doing; to look positively at what they got out of those experiences, at how that learning might help them now and might be counted toward the course.

All of that means running a pretty full-on publicity program. We hit them hard, right from when they first make contact with the Institute. We have eye-catching posters everywhere. In fact, they're so outrageous that people keep nicking them as collectors' pieces, and we've had a flood of complaints from namby-pambies; but it's all good publicity, and that's what we need. We reckon that we have to saturate TAFE student life—especially around enrollment times—with the belief that RPL is where it's at. It's what Bagnall and his fellow air-heads would call something like 'embedding it in the student discourse, because that is what defines who the students are, how they see themselves, and what they do.' Right on. See! I have learnt something from your 'rabbitings.'

The Homogeneity of Sociality[7]

The case study here is that of Ian, who, as a self-directed learner, has been going about the task of designing his own educational program. Ian worked for a number of years in his Church as an instructor in liturgy for lay preachers. He was then offered a new position by the Church, adapting an overseas distance-based program for use in parishes across Australia, and designing and setting up management and tutor support systems for the program. He felt that the demands of the new position went far beyond his knowledge and capabilities, especially in the areas of program design and management, and distance-based education. He responded to that assessment by setting up his own educational program. Here he recounts aspects of that process. In terms of the homogeneity tension, his experience underlines the extent to which he is located in the realities of the dedifferentiated pole, whereas the traditional educational providers are still rather firmly in the old differentiated realities.

> I started off by approaching my old Alma Mater, to see what they (or should I say, 'she'?) had to offer in the areas that I wanted. What I was looking for were resources that I could use in my own time and in my own way to learn in this area; not fully structured and programmed resources, but with sufficient structure to serve as a guide to where I was going, and with negotiable access to private tutoring assistance when I wanted it. I thought that communications should be undertaken in the first instance on-line with desk-top computers, not that I knew anything about it, but I did know that that was where distance education was rapidly heading and that I should therefore learn about the technology by using it in my own studies.
>
> My University was very keen to help. They sent me brochures on the continuing education courses available this year in my areas. I read through the materials, noting the unalloyed quality of what was on offer, but also its apparent rigidity: scheduled evening classes, enrollment dates, starting times, fixed length, predetermined content, and so on. I got back to them, pointing out that my needs were different; that I was a busy person, with particular learning needs—needs that I wanted to address in my own time and way. They politely indicated that they were doing things in the way that their (considerable) experience had found was the most effective, and that if I wanted distance education, then I should go to an open learning agency. They put me on to a couple: one university, the other TAFE.
>
> I followed those up and certainly got a good response with respect to study location and the use of contemporary communications technology. But they were both thoroughly locked into rigid course structures: time-lines, content, assignments, tutorial assistance, and so on. I told them that it was

insane in this day and age that that was all they could do. I pointed out that their failure to serve the needs of learners such as myself was not only disrespectful of their clients' needs, but was also suicidal for them, since de-regulation of their privileged provider status under pressure from thoroughly dissatisfied consumers such as I would leave them without work. They indicated in response that, while competition was tough, they were nevertheless doing quite nicely, thank you.

I thought it best not to take things any further in that direction. Reluctantly giving up on the educational institutions, I took my needs to some of the commercial companies involved in developing and marketing computer software, a private VET consultant, and to the local Institute of Management. At last I had found some people who were willing to assist *me*, instead of just running their old traditional educational agendas. I got just what I wanted: a choice of different sorts of resources; expert guidance in making selections; attractively presented materials; Internet communication with negotiated private tutorial assistance; even resources were available through the Internet, and I could connect up when I wanted with other learners and experts in my area around the world. It was not cheap, but the actual cost to me was under my control—I paid only for what I chose from the menu of options. As my start-up study grant for the new job was running out, I found that I was in a position increasingly to assume control of my own learning, calling less on tutorial assistance. I was also increasingly able to optimize the use of expert guidance; again, it was expensive, but I could make the best use of it by putting only key and well-informed questions, or suggestions for response.

Reflecting on it afterwards, I was amazed at the atavistic attitude of the traditional educational providers, including those that presented themselves as being at the forefront of educational innovation. What they all seemed to be ignoring is that the world no longer sees education (or anything else for that matter) as the exclusive domain of properly qualified, initiated, and enculturated experts. Education is anybody's and everybody's business—as both providers and learners. If you can make it work, and if you can sell it, then it's probably meeting someone's learning needs. Certainly, that was my experience and it gave me a really firm foundation on which to

> move into the new job. Had I stuck with the traditional educational providers, I believe that I would still be studying courses in educational management and distance education, and wondering how to do my job.

The Temporality of Sociality[8]

The final case study is that of Lucy, in her role as a private provider of vocational education and training (VET). She has a rapidly growing enterprise focusing not only on the provision of VET courses, but also on their development for sale to other providers. In the present case study she was taking the initial step into the development of training modules for VET practitioners: a developmental process that she likes to see based on the learning assessment. Here she reflects, somewhat ruefully and ironically, on that experience. In terms of the temporality tension, her curriculum developer is firmly located in the realities of the developmentalist pole, while she is in those of the presentist.

> My approach to curriculum design has a number of key elements. Most importantly here, I insist on hiring the best expertise available, and I insist that the curriculum be assessment-driven. With the Training Reform Agenda,[9] the establishment of the ANTA[10] and the development of competency standards[11] for VET practitioners, I saw a need for better quality and more relevant training programs than those that were generally available. I was looking at the development of a package of modules but, as is my normal practice, I moved to develop just one initially, so that I could get a feel for the area and the key players involved in it.
>
> What I did, then, was to contract this leading academic in the field (whom you would know well) to develop what he saw as an appropriate foundational skills module. I gave him a pretty free hand, with just a few parameters, like its magnitude, its clientele base, its use of competency standards, its assessment-driven nature, and its appropriateness for flexible mode delivery.
>
> Well, you should have seen what he came up with—straight out of Noah's Ark, I told him. It had all this stuff on the history, sociology, and philosophy of VET in Australia. It related present Government thinking to historical developments and to the economic, political, and social changes occurring at the moment. It even included some basic

psychological theory and showed how that was being used to inform teaching-learning practice. The assessment that he designed was all analytical, essay-based, to test student understanding of the picture of the field that he had painted. It was all good stuff; no doubt about it. But what could I *do* with it?

I told him—'Where are the competency standards?' I said to him—'Look, you and I both know that the standards are pretty shaky and of doubtful value, but the fact is, I have to use them. My registration as a VET provider depends on my doing so and I haven't a snow-flake's-chance-in-hell of selling my modules unless they *are* based on the standards.' I also asked him—'What gives with the assessment? It's supposed to be, *has* to be, competency-based?'

Needless to say, he got rather defensive—arguing that practitioners would be much better placed to respond to future contingencies if they saw them and their work in a broad historical context; if they understood what social progress amounted to and how others had contributed to it, and what needed to be done (with their help) to further progress it.

You can imagine—my jaw dropped so heavily, it nearly hit the floor. I said to him—'Get real, for heaven's sake. Not to put too fine a point on it, history is seen these days as just a fetish, or as something you play with to create your own realities. Who knows what 'progress' is? How do *you* know what 'progress' is? What right have you to impose that view on others? Why should they be interested? What they want to learn is how to *manage* the contingencies that arise. They don't know the future. You don't know the future. None of us knows the future. Let's give our future VET practitioners the basic skills to work with whatever arises and to be free to create whatever they can to further their interests.'

I then explained to him (again!) that what I wanted was a curriculum that did just that: skills-based, assessment-driven, and the development of understanding only to the extent that it was *necessary* to apply the skills.

He was getting really agitated by then, and starting to pick holes in my arguments. I just told him that it didn't matter. That that is the way the contemporary world is. Beautiful as they are, I told him, we don't need educational dinosaurs like his curriculum (or *him* for that matter), except in museums of antiquity. He thought that that was a bit over the top, with which I had to agree—in social relations at least; but substantively it's *true*!

We came to a mutually agreeable understanding about his fee, and I have since moved forward with the development of a good set of modules, using *other* experts. I still have his curriculum in a file marked 'VET Anachronisms.' I wouldn't publicly admit to owning it though. Nobody would want to buy it anyway.

Progress?

With that, we close my attempt to present some of the implications of postmodernity for adult education practice—"in-the-raw," so to speak—through dialogues in Chapter 6 and the case studies of the present chapter. The next chapter seeks to draw together the common threads that interweave those dialogues and case studies. In so doing, it moves the analysis back to a more theoretical level. It is to be hoped, though, that the grounding of events presented in these two chapters will make the more formal exposition of the next chapter both understandable and informative.

Before doing so, however, let me say a few words about the title and subtitle of the present chapter. A "boundary rider" in European colonial history was a horseback rider who patrolled the lengthy—often only poorly fenced and demarcated—borders or boundaries of the vast cattle stations in drier parts of Australia and other such countries. It was a lonely and often dangerous job—with the constant threat of attack from dispossessed indigenous peoples, cattle rustlers, inclement weather, and disrespectful wildlife. The title follows from the subtitle. Its literal meaning pertains to the horsehair that was used to pack the saddles. Its metaphorical meaning here is seen as pertaining to the modernist inheritance with which our adult education boundary rider must ride. Metaphorically, the subtitle may be taken as capturing important elements of the work of contemporary adult educators: caught, as they so often are, riding a thin line between hostile attack from competing interests and impoverishment through neglect from an unsympathetic market.

Chapter 8

Odors in the Ether: Tendencies in Postmodern Adult Education

In this chapter I return to an earlier attempt to identify a number of formal tendencies that may be seen as characterizing postmodern adult education events (Bagnall, 1994d). Those tendencies are identified singularly from the "postmodern" ends of the tensions introduced in Chapter 5 (and used illustratively in the following two chapters). Nevertheless, the tendencies are variously evidenced in those dialogues and case studies, and are here illustratively grounded in them. The tendencies have been derived analytically from the qualities of postmodernity articulated in Chapters 3 and 4. They represent an alternative view of postmodern adult education from that identified through the tensions.

In considering these tendencies, it should be kept in mind that they do not include those more modernist realities incorporated in and problematized by postmodernity, and which constitute the "modernist" poles of the tensions introduced in Chapter 5. The picture of postmodern adult education that they represent is therefore strongly lopsided in its artificial purity and simplicity.

It should also be kept in mind that the recognition of this particular set of tendencies is substantially an arbitrary matter. By that I mean that the way in which the nature and diversity of postmodern adult education are clustered into particular qualities (the "tendencies" here) is not something that derives from the nature of the field itself or from its postmodern nature. In using the set of eight tendencies here noted, I have attempted to focus attention on those contrasts with modernist adult education practice that strike me—experientially, as an adult education practitioner and scholar of adult education practice—as being notable. Their recognition, therefore, is a function of the particular realities and understandings that I bring to the task. An infinity of alternative ways of cutting the cake undoubtedly may be recognized, each no doubt better suited to the interests and perspectives of some readers than is the one here provided. The tendencies here noted should therefore be seen not as definitive of postmodern realities in adult education but rather as indicative of the qualities embedded in those realities.

Each tendency is given a label descriptive of its central quality. That label is used here as a section heading in which the tendency is articulated: first, by describing the quality that the tendency is seen as capturing; second, by grounding it analytically in postmodern culture; third, by illustrating it with reference to the dialogues and case studies of the preceding two chapters; and, finally, by commenting upon its broader consequences for the field.

Heterodoxy

By heterodoxy is meant the tendency toward the creation of educational events that are intentionally different from the traditional or the orthodox: from those events which are seen as exemplifying or giving expression to historical or contemporary modes, patterns, or norms of educational provision and engagement. There is thus perceived a tendency for educational action to be directed centrifugally or divergently away from the conventional, the traditional, the orthodox.

Such a tendency is seen as arising directly from the postmodern celebration of difference and spontaneity, in the context of freedom from cultural constraint and restraint: educational freedom in this case. In part, difference is not only a quality which arises contingently from the self-reflexive pluriformity of social contexts; it is also something which is valued in itself. It is a quality which may be actively sought—experimentally, spontaneously, impulsively—as an expression of the postmodern cultivation of desire. In the context of decentered responsibility, and an embracing of emotive, nonrational, unconscious impulses to human action, the drive to heterodoxy becomes an alluring freedom in itself—minimally constrained by convention, responsibility for consequences, the demands of rationality, or common sense.

Heterodoxy emerges in the dialogues and case studies presented in the previous two chapters, but not strongly so. Perhaps the best illustration of this tendency is in the case study of Bruce, the Education Officer in an institute of technical and further education, where he has responsibility for that institute's recognition of prior learning (RPL) program. In his marketing of the RPL program, Bruce sought to create difference (and dissonance) as a way of increasing the profile of RPL opportunities among the student population. In other situations—such as the case study of Roger, in his establishing an adult education program with Unicom, and the dialogue with Alex, in which the value of a singular classification system is questioned—heterodoxy may be seen as implied, but not specifically alluded to.

In consequence of this tendency, there is a heightening of the variability of postmodern adult education. This is expressed both temporally, as changeability over time, and contemporaneously, as concurrent diversity or heterogeneity. Forms of adult education engagement thus tend to be ephemeral, and to be individual, even unique.

Expressiveness

By expressiveness is meant the tendency toward adult education that is spontaneously responsive to and reflective of the noncognitive, emotive interests, inclinations, and preferences of its participants. In this regard, it is contrasted to the cognitive, rational, intellectual approach to the planned systematization of educational events that was so prized in modernist adult education. In the latter, programs were variously based on or responsive to theoretical, ideological, institutional, philosophical, moral, or structural concerns: such as the curriculum or educational activities that are seen as being appropriate within a particular educational philosophy, or by a particular educational institution. The contrast may also be drawn with "needs-based" programming, in which educational needs are seen as being educational outcomes desired of others, in the grandly progressive educational models of high modernity (such as that of Kaufman, 1972).

Postmodern expressivism is seen as arising partly from the underdetermination of all human action, and its consequential unpredictability and ambiguity. It also, and more importantly, derives from the perceived importance of the subconscious in guiding human action; from the importance therein of feelings, emotions, and unrationalized inclinations; from the privileging of oral expression over the written; and from the importance of the aesthetic in postmodern realities.

This tendency emerges in a number of the foregoing dialogues and case studies. The case study of Roger, developing his program for Unicom, of Marian, in her development of the policy document for the Plumbarton Community Development Council, and of Bruce, in his marketing of the RPL program, are all strong examples. In the dialogue between Rowan and me over the value of cognitive psychology in informing adult education practice, I am arguing for (among other things) the value of expressiveness, in downplaying the value of learning theory.

In consequence of this tendency in postmodern adult education, there is a diminution in the importance of theoretical (descriptive or propositional) knowledge, and a heightening in that of aesthetic knowledge (knowledge of beauty, rhythm, and harmony) and of existential knowledge (knowledge of self and one's relationships to other realities). With a downgrading of the curricular and procedural value of rationality and systematization, there is an upgrading of the value of the nonrational, the spontaneous, and the *ad hoc*, both in curriculum and in the form of the educational engagement itself. There is also the embracing of a much richer diversity of criteria for the evaluation, justification, and appraisal of adult education: not just or not primarily commodity and cognitive value, but also, and importantly, forms of value such as the aesthetic, spiritual, affective, and experiential.

Reflexive Contextualization

By reflexive contextualization is meant the tendency toward adult education that is self-consciously and critically immersed within and responsive to the subject and cultural context of its discourse. In other words, the goals, curriculum, procedures, and other programmatic features are, self-consciously, both determined (constrained) by and determining of the cultural situation in which they are formulated and realized. This reflexive dependency applies not only to structural, temporal, and procedural aspects of the educational event and its context, but also, and more fundamentally, to their informing theoretical, normative, and aesthetic beliefs. However, the dependency is seen as being only partial: an educational event is both underdetermined by its cultural context and is reciprocally underdetermining of that context. Accordingly, no educational event is seen as being fully specifiable or predictable from its context; nor is any context seen as being fully specifiable or predictable on the basis of its emergent educational events. Postmodern action, similarly, is seen as being an underdetermined phenomenon: rejecting both the actuality of and the search for such synthesizing theories of motivation for engagement as that of Boshier (1973). Educational action and events tend to be interpreted retrospectively from the perspective of one's contemporaneous framework of meaning and identity: taking a reinterpretivist, revisionist, or deconstructivist view of the past (of history) in the light of contingently meaningful and interesting frameworks, rather than through the objective, timeless pictures developed in traditional (modernist) historiography.

This tendency is seen as arising from the postmodern denial of privileged discourses—of privileged paths to the true, the good, the authentic, and the beautiful—and from the culturally embedded, historicist contingency of belief. The lack of constraint from grand, overarching, or underpinning syntheses, theories, philosophies, or narratives—including not only those of a traditional liberal, humanist, progressive, or socialist nature, but also those of a more radical, revolutionary, or reformist bent—is seen as opening the structuring of adult education to the contextual influences of each particular educational event.

Probably each of the dialogues and case studies of the previous two chapters illustrates this tendency in one way or another. The case study of Helen, as a Continuing Professional Education Officer developing a program for judges, focuses most singularly on the tendency. Helen's approach is framed strongly by her recognition of the need both to ground the education program in the work context within which the learning need arises (the framing of judicial judgments) and to embed the learning in that context, in order (reflexively) to change the actions constituting the context. The same may be said for the case study of Ian, in his self-directed program of learning to enhance his capabilities in the development and management of distance education programs, and for the case study of Lucy, in her attempt to develop a foundation training module for vocational education and training (VET) practitioners.

Other case studies—especially those of Roger and Marian—expose the educational diversity that is associated with this tendency, as does the dialogue with Rowan. The dialogue with Alex shows me arguing against singular classification systems and for the contextualization of guiding perceptual frameworks. In the dialogue with Lindsay, I am arguing against a wholesale commitment to humanism, referring to the reflexive contextuality of individual identity, and hence of the need for appropriately sensitive adult education. The same may be said of the dialogue with Chris, in my argument in favor of reverse discrimination in postmodern adult education contexts. Finally, here, the dialogue with Lee, cautioning against a problem-based approach to the formation and professional development of adult educators, may be seen as drawing upon this tendency in questioning the validity of contemporary contexts for the framing of future educational events.

From the reflexive contextualization of adult education there may be seen a flourishing of diversity in the field: diversity in all programmatic aspects (goals, curriculum, processes, participants, and so on). There is a move away from the modernist privileging of theoretical knowledge, toward the embracing of a much greater diversity of knowledge types, including also the ethical (normative or moral knowledge of what should be or should be done), the technical (manipulative or procedural knowledge, both manual and intellectual), the existential, and the aesthetic.

In the resulting heterogeneity, postmodern adult education is open to the formative influences of cultural interests that have been suppressed or marginalized in modernity. It is also importantly unpredictable in nature: underdetermined by its context and hence futuristically opaque. There is a general antipathy to transcontextual and transcultural (e.g., national) constraints and restraints, through such measures as the standardization of curriculum or procedures. Centralized planning, systematization, outcomes-based education, goal-based evaluation, indeed, preplanning *per se*—all revered features of modernist education—are qualities eschewed in postmodern adult education. The role of the state as regulator and provider of adult education is thus a highly contested and problematic one. In the absence of firm regulatory control, the attractiveness to the state of its providing support for adult education is itself diminished: threatening the pragmatic basis of any general state involvement in the field. The tendency toward reflexive contextualization also highlights the importance both of approaches to program development that are endemic to cultural entities and of contract-based programming, whereby an interest group "outsources" the task of program development, while exercising control over the form of the educational engagement.

This tendency may also be seen as encouraging a relatively constricted or short-term perspective of the planned future. The programmatic focus is thus very much on the present and immediately foreseeable realities. Given the provisional, contingent, and contradictory nature of that knowledge which informs action (since, indeed, all knowledge is taken as being of this form), and given the ambivalence, spontaneity, and uncertainty of action itself, there can be no reasonable basis upon which action may be directed to the long-term or indefinite future.

Education, in this quality, is strongly *experiential* in nature—the quality which Edwards (1994), with Usher (Usher and Edwards, 1994), and also Wildemeersch and Jansen (1992) and their co-workers, recognize as a pivotal feature of postmodern educational engagement. Education through experiential learning argues for due recognition of that learning—hence the consequential importance of schemes for the "recognition of prior learning" (RPL) and related notions—a feature of postmodern adult education that is recognized in the case study of Bruce, in which he is shown as being responsible for a program run specifically to encourage and process applications for the recognition of prior learning.

Revisionism

By revisionism is meant a tendency toward adult education that is based upon a view of knowledge and meaning as being properly open to radical reinterpretation, deconstruction, and revision from any contemporaneously and contextually meaningful cultural perspective. The contextual contingency of postmodern belief (including knowledge) opens that belief to deconstruction and reconstruction from a potential infinity of contingent perspectives. Fueled by a commitment to the provisional nature of all belief, such deconstruction tends to be radical in nature and degree, and to be so from the cultural perspective of the tradition so involved (be that feminist, black, physically handicapped, or whatever). However, as postmodern critique, the effectiveness of any consequential or entailed social or individual action is strictly limited by, on the one hand, the lack of any firm foundation to such action and, on the other, by the fragmentation of individual identity.

Running counter to this tendency is that toward a passive acceptance of the postmodern status quo: a resignation in the face of the plethora of competing systems of belief and action. However, in adult education at least, it may be hoped that the revisionist tendency will prevail.

The tendency toward revisionism derives, in part, from the strong influence of poststructuralism and critical theory on postmodernity. It may also, though, be seen as deriving from the loss of foundational knowledge in postmodern belief itself. If all belief—whether theoretical, moral, technical, existential, or aesthetic—is contingently underdetermined by empirical reality, then all belief is open to deconstruction and reconstruction from both within and beyond the cultural context of its formulation.

Perhaps the strongest illustration of this tendency in the dialogues and case studies of the previous two chapters is the case study of Lucy, in her development of a foundation training module for VET practitioners. Lucy's criticism of the work of her initial curriculum developer underlines her commitment to historical revisionism (if not revisionism with respect to the realities to which she is herself currently committed). The case study of Ian, in his program to learn about the development and management of distance-based educational programs, is a more learner-centered example of the same quality. The case study of Marian, in her development of a community adult education policy document for Plumbarton, reveals how she crafted into that policy an openness to revisionism in the future. In the dialogue with Alex over the value of classification systems, I am arguing against perceptual and methodological canon. Conversely, in the dialogue with Kim over the desirability of a singular focus on skilling for instructional design and delivery, I am cautioning partly from the observation that postmodern social structures are open to radical review and reconstruction.

In consequence of this tendency, there is lacking any tradition, any norm of belief, any canon, that is sequestered from radical criticism. Accordingly, there is no uncontestable, or even consensual, curriculum, procedures, or standards by which the development of adult education may be guided, constrained, or structured. All belief that potentially informs or is constitutive of adult education events is open to deconstruction and reinterpretation. The contextualized nature of all such events is thereby reinforced, educational engagement being optimally responsive to the cultural situation of its generation, conduct, and appraisal.

Indeterminacy

By indeterminacy is meant the tendency toward uncertainty, indefinability, and unpredictability in the location of authority over and responsibility for educational decisions. The location and specification of educational authority and responsibility are features of central import in modernist educational frameworks, wherein the individual learner, the state or its agencies, providing institutions, and the adult educator have particular spheres of authority and responsibility with respect to the educational engagement—albeit variably so among competing frameworks. That clarity, such as it is, and the value of its pursuit, is lost in postmodern adult education, wherein decision-making authority and responsibility are seen as being dispersed, decentered from those traditional modernist loci, to the shifting plethora and confusion of intersecting and interacting cultural traditions that determine, yet underdetermine, and partially constitute the individual, social, and institutional identity of humanity.

This tendency is seen as arising particularly from the fragmentation of individual identity and the postmodern perception of the importance of nonrational influences upon human action. A clear consequence of these features is the decentering of authority and responsibility away from the (modernist) individual: a consequence reinforced and extended to the whole postmodern sociality by the contingent, changeable, uncertain pluriformity which constitutes that sociality.

The dialogues and case studies of the previous chapters include a number of illustrations of the uncertainties arising in postmodernity with the indeterminacy of power relationships and responsibility. In several of the case studies there is exposed the problematization of traditional institutional and expert power, based in the legitimation of (educational) knowledge. This is evident especially in the case studies of Roger (in his programming for the University), Marian (in her policy formulation for community development in Plumbarton), Ian (in his search for learning support) and Lucy (in her search for curriculum development expertise). The dialogue with Kim over the uncertainties of the future shows me arguing, *inter alia*, that state support for technical and further education (TAFE) is by no means certain in the face of the postmodern indeterminacy of responsibility for that area of educational provision.

Through this tendency, educational authority and responsibility are highly dispersed, and their actual location is rendered both problematic and contestable. The attribution of responsibility for educational actions is correspondingly problematic. Marginalized individuals, and members of minority groups lacking the resources or inclination to address their own educational interests, may thus find those interests to be overlooked by others. The attribution of authority to the state, and the public acceptance of any state assumption of authority, are similarly contestable and problematic. There is a consequential reluctance on the part of the state to assume responsibility for adult education in all but relatively clear-cut cases (if there be any). Fiscal support for adult education from the state tends to be correspondingly minimal.

Privatization

By privatization is meant the tendency toward events in which educational involvement and control are devolved to the participants. In other words, following my earlier analysis of participation (Bagnall, 1989d), there is seen to be a tendency toward participation both as involvement (wherein participants are actively engaged with important elements of or processes in the event) and as control (wherein the actions of the participants are formative in determining the nature of the event—its goals, curriculum, processes, and so on). It is what Bauman (1995) sees as the "privatization" of social responsibility. It favors and reinforces learner independence from the educational institution with respect to the identification of educational interests, the selection of educational goals, and the selection of educational activities.

The tendency may be seen as arising from the loss of the constraining effects of the grand social theories of modernity. The consequential contextualization of educational action—the devolution of educational engagement or involvement and control to particular, local contexts—brings that action and the choices which it presupposes to the level of the particular and the local. Educational participants are denied the structuring certainties of traditional social theory. They are denied the option of passivity within the certainty of those constraints and restraints. Educational choices can no longer be made within the framework of tradition; they are starkly and unavoidably left to the participants to make—either singly or cooperatively—in the light of their contemporaneous inclinations and beliefs. In so making those educational choices, the participants necessarily become both actively involved and active in exercising control over the event.

A number of dialogues and case studies of the previous two chapters focus attention on the privatization of postmodern adult education. The case studies of Bruce (RPL), Ian (self-directed learning), and Lucy (VET training module development) each build upon the privatization of educational responsibility: both in its provision (Lucy) and in responsibility for its form and attainment (Bruce and Ian). The dialogue with Kim over the future possibilities of trade training highlights the existential uncertainty and isolation that flow from the tendency to the privatization of educational responsibility.

This tendency, then, may be seen as giving expression to the educational value of participative involvement and control (for which see, e.g.: Dean and Dowling, 1987; B.L. Hall, 1981; Kindervatter, 1979). It does, though, leave little or no room for non-engagement: for the choice to participate without the existential burden of active involvement in and contributory control over the educational event. Perhaps complete withdrawal from participation is the only alternative, but even that is a choice from which the subject cannot escape.

Phenomenalism

By phenomenalism is meant the tendency toward adult education that gives expression to the value of the engagement in itself—to the intrinsic value of the event—rather than to the attainment of the extrinsic ends to which it is directed. In this tendency, postmodern adult education may be seen as contrasting strongly with the contemporary modernist educational emphasis on utilitarian and pragmatic instrumentalism. In instrumentalism, an educational event is valued for the positive effect that it has on the attainment of desired outcomes extrinsic to the event itself: educational outcomes such as enhanced levels of skill or socially desirable attitudes, and educational consequences such as the enhanced probability of gaining employment with those skills, or of abstaining from antisocial actions with those attitudes. In contrast, under phenomenalism an educational event is valued for the quality of the learning experience, whatever that be: the joy of new understanding, the elation of transformative change to one's perspective, the satisfaction of successfully mastering a skill, the exhilaration of a new aesthetic appreciation, and so on. Such education is, in other words, an end in itself: an "autotelic" engagement.

In this regard, interestingly, there may be observed a convergence between postmodern education and the idealist strand in high modernist liberal education. In that strand—exemplified in the works of educationists such as Hutchins (1970), O'Hear (1981), and Paterson (1979)—educational goals are seen as being necessarily noninstrumental, and educational outcomes as being sufficiently so. While that thesis should not be seen as appropriate to postmodernity, it does, nevertheless, lead to a parallel tendency to value the intrinsic, rather than the extrinsic, qualities of educational engagement. However, in postmodern education, but not in educational liberalism, that tendency is a contingent, rather than an ideological, matter, and it is therefore contextually grounded, as I have advocated elsewhere (Bagnall, 1990b) in a critique of the liberal thesis of noninstrumentalism.

In postmodernity, educational phenomenalism is seen as arising particularly from the postmodern loss of progressive social human vision, and from the value that is placed upon the quality of the immediate experience of engagement. In the context of the profound unpredictability, changeability, uncertainty, and ambiguity of postmodernity, there can be little encouragement to engage rationally in the planning, management, and evaluation of adult education on the basis of the extent to which it addresses extrinsic outcomes.

None of the dialogues or case studies in the previous two chapters focuses strongly on the tendency to phenomenalism. That situation is more a reflection of the professional context from which the examples were taken—the formation and professional development of adult educators—than it is a reflection of the unimportance of the tendency.

Such a context involves strongly goal-oriented, and hence outcomes-driven, educational involvement. Both the dialogues and the case studies reflect the corresponding paucity of phenomenalism. Undoubtedly, embedded within the activities touched upon in a number of the case studies would be phenomenalist educational activity, but it has not emerged as central to the case studies themselves. Here I would particularly identify the community development policy crafted by Marian, and also possibly the program developed by Roger for the University's company Unicom, although the commercial nature of the company may militate against strongly phenomenalist activity in the latter case. In the case study of Bruce, the marketing of the RPL program also draws upon appeal to phenomenalist inclinations, although the campaign itself is extrinsically directed (to encouraging engagement in RPL assessment).

This tendency toward phenomenalism runs counter to the contemporary emphasis on both credentialism and outcomes-driven adult education: including competency-based education and training (Bagnall, 1994e). The credentialing of educational attainment is premised largely on its instrumental value in the subsequent attainment of extrinsically valued states of affairs (such as employment or social standing). Outcomes-driven education—as has been argued by, for example, Ashworth and Saxton (1990), Bagnall (1994a), and Pope (1983)—is, by its nature, strictly nonphenomenal, instrumental, extrinsically valuing, and modernist. Competency-based education and training, as a form of outcomes-driven education, is no less so.

Dedifferentiation

Finally, by dedifferentiated is meant a tendency for adult education to be perceived as continuous with other related fields of human activity (such as research, social work, political activism, and recreation) and within itself. It is therein seen both as being immersed in and invaded by contingently related discourses, and as lacking differentiation into distinct structural or functional categories. In its contextual aspect, dedifferentiation may be seen as taking the form of both the immersion of adult education in related activities (e.g., the reformulation of employment contexts as educative environments) and the invasion of adult education by those activities (e.g., the use of adult education for recruitment to higher degree programs). It may be seen as occurring in all aspects of the field: its functions or purposes; responsibility for provision; the organizational structures with which it is involved; and the processes and content with which it is concerned. Postmodern adult education may be seen, then, as being both everywhere and nowhere: diffused throughout the institutions of society, yet difficult to isolate as an entity in its own right.

This tendency is seen as arising directly from the impermanence, the ephemerality, the changeability of all concepts and conceptual boundaries in postmodernity. That conceptual uncertainty both follows from and contributes to the prevailing postmodern flexibility of all social (including institutional) categories and boundaries. Within postmodernity, all categories and boundaries are seen as contingent artifacts, open to reformulation in response to changed circumstances.

Both internal and contextual dedifferentiation are touched upon in the dialogues and case studies of the previous two chapters. The dialogue with Alex over the value of classification systems shows me arguing for the reality of the postmodern internal dedifferentiation of adult education as a field of practice. Similarly, the case study of Roger in his university program development alludes strongly to the dedifferentiation of roles, between himself as the programmer on the one hand, and the learners or clients with whom he is working on the other. The dialogue with Kim focuses more on contextual dedifferentiation, where the blurring and shifting of traditional roles and responsibilities for trade training render future structures and roles highly unpredictable. Similarly, the case study of Ian evidences contextual dedifferentiation in the shifting of responsibility for adult education from traditional educational providers to commercial companies and consultants.

Contextual dedifferentiation entails, also, a deprofessionalization of the field. That is to say, on the one hand, responsibility for adult education provision becomes even more diffused throughout postmodern culture than it was in modernist culture: becoming a feature of many other institutions and roles. On the other hand, and following from this, the personal backgrounds and training for adult education practice, and the codes governing that practice, are even more diverse than they were in modernity. Practitioner identification with the field is correspondingly diverse: ranging from a failure to recognize it as such to seeing it as central to one's professional identity. Unless the state is persuaded to regulate the expectations or requirements of persons who act as adult educators, the profession may thereby be seen as losing whatever distinctiveness it had in modernity.

Intrinsic dedifferentiation may be seen as reinforcing the already-noted antisystems nature of postmodern adult education. It suggests a responsiveness to educational events that is contextualized and ad hoc, each event being seen as reflexively and complexly related to its cultural contexts. The plurality of those contexts suggests a tendency for adult education engagement, curricula, and goals to be opaque, multilayered or diffuse, and resistant to deterministic analysis, criticism, and understanding.

Onward

So much for the formal tendencies of adult education engagement. They represent a field so suffused with change, uncertainty, difference, irony, unpredictability, and contradiction, that their identification itself may best be seen as a supreme folly—as an attempt to define the indefinable. The latter may well be true, but the folly was indulged in the hope that the fruits may serve to inform the reader's understanding of the field, to at least some degree.

The folly is continued and compounded in the next chapter, where the tendencies here articulated are drawn together into two nodal categories of programmatic responses on the part of adult educators to the postmodern context.

Chapter 9

Fashioning Educative Difference: Nodal Forms of Engagement

In this chapter, our attention shifts from the general properties of adult education events to the question of how adult-education-providing agencies may best respond programmatically to the post-modern cultural context. The focus is on the nature of the interaction between the learner and the adult educator—on the characteristics of the interface between the educational consumer and the educational provider—through examining the ways in which adult education programmers may best respond, in their program development, to the postmodern cultural context.

The analysis is based on a recently published paper (Bagnall, 1994c). The material from that paper, though, is here grounded illustratively in the case studies outlined in Chapter 7. The assumed notion of the "adult education programmer" is that of a person, office or agency working in the public domain (such as through a university, college, or community-based organization) for the purpose of planning, providing, and appraising adult education activities for public participation or engagement.

The two broad types ("nodal forms") of programmatic response to postmodernity here identified are not, in themselves, new or exclusive to the postmodern context. Neither is it the case that other traditional, more ideologically driven forms of program development (such as those driven by liberal, radical, or progressive social philosophies) are not evident in a postmodern world. It is merely being suggested that these latter forms are much diminished in importance.

The two nodal forms should be seen as ideal types, in the Weberian sense of theoretically pure types, the utility of which is in their focusing of analytical and critical attention (Weber, 1947, pp. 10-11). However, their realization in actual, situationally responsive programming events may be much less pure and clear-cut. They are termed "nodal" in that sense: that of ideal types distilled from anticipated and perceived realities which are characterized more by events that are hybrid forms between these two and beyond them with other more traditional forms of adult education engagement.

The two nodal forms are here examined separately: each is described; it is grounded in the case studies of Chapter 7; its important strengths and weaknesses are noted; and it is related to the tendencies identified in the previous chapter. In discussion of the two nodal forms, there are articulated a number of educational consequences of working within these two approaches to programming.

In their ideal form, the categories have been recognized on the basis of two key concepts, encapsulating—consistent with the postmodern context—the locus of control of the programmatic discourse: (1) the distribution of controlling *authority* over the major, defining, program components (aims, access, format, scheduling, content, assessment, funding); and (2) the locus of *responsibility* for the provision of the program that incorporates those components. Using the concepts of authority and responsibility in this way, the two identified categories of importance from the programmer's perspective are: (1) the *contractualist,* wherein authority is shared between the learners, or their representative(s) or spokesperson(s), and others who serve as educationists, while the responsibility is with the educationists; and (2) the *open marketeering,* wherein authority and responsibility are both located with the educationists. In other words, the locus of control over decisions about programmatic aspects, in contractualist programming, is shared between the learners and the external educationists; whereas, in open marketeering it lies with the external educationists.

Contractualism

The contractualist response to postmodernity is to work *with* identified groups of learners or their representatives (or even, possibly, an individual learner acting on his or her own behalf) in *negotiating* the form of a program. The programmer or agency thereby becomes immersed within—an integral part of—the shifting pluriformity of postmodern interests, or at least of selected sectors of that pluriformity. The decision-making authority over the form of the program is shared, although the educational provider assumes responsibility for the preparation and conduct of the agreed program. The contract itself may be either formal or informal to a greater or lesser extent.

Contractualism emerges within the majority, if not all, of the case studies introduced in Chapter 7. This is true, perhaps most singularly, in the programmatic approach that Roger developed in the first case study after his initial failure in programming for the University company Unicom. The actual *concept* of RPL (the recognition of prior learning) underpinning the fourth case study—that of Bruce marketing the TAFE institute RPL program—is also essentially contractualist. From the perspective of the learner, rather than the educator, the fifth case study may be seen as Ian searching for an adult education provider with whom he may successfully negotiate a program of professional education through what is here identified as a contractualist approach. In the remaining case studies—for example, that of Helen, in her development of the CPE program for the judiciary—contractualism is implicit in the activity described, rather than being a substantive focus of the case study itself.

The process of program negotiation that is central to contractualism requires of the client groups not only that they are aware of their learning interests, but also that they articulate those interests. The same applies to the programmers, to the extent that they seek to introduce constraints and restraints (such as principles of good programming practice) to the programmatic activities and outcomes. The opportunity to so negotiate into a program one's interests as a programmer is, indeed, one of the strengths of contractualism.

Other strengths of contractualism[1] derive from its tendency to be outcomes-driven and objectives-based (Bagnall, 1992a, 1992b)—that is, to be directed toward the attainment of prespecified (contractually agreed) outcomes, through activity structured to achieve the enabling educational goals or objectives. The explicit articulation of the desired outcomes encourages attention to be focused on their desirability: enhancing the likelihood of producing programs that are functionally relevant and meaningful to the contracting parties. Similarly, the more or less rational structuring of educational activities to achieve the desired outcomes encourages both educational effectiveness (the maximization of desired educational outcomes) and educational efficiency (the optimization of educational outcomes relative to educational costs). The process is also inherently respectful of the individual freedom and self-determination of the contracting parties. It is empowering to those persons who are directly engaged in the process.

The limitations of contractualism, particularly within a postmodern cultural context, also derive from its tendency to be outcomes-driven and objectives-based, and from the practical constraints imposed by its essential nature as a process of negotiation.[2] It may be seen as favoring group or organizational interests over those of individuals—as a function of the negotiation process. Accordingly, the relevance of contractualist curricula may be expected to be similarly biased. Similarly, to the extent that it is empowering to the contracting parties, it is empowering to a small, elite group or, at best, representatives of groups of learners. For the majority, the negotiations would be undertaken by others. The cost of high efficiency and effectiveness is also likely to be a tendency to curricular simplification, orthodoxy, fragmentation, and inflexibility. Contractualism is based on the assumption that the learners are the best judges of what is in their own educational interests: both in terms of goals and content and in terms of procedures. Any limitation to the learner's self-knowledge and knowledge of relevant educational opportunities and alternatives would thus tend to make the resulting education both more orthodox and more straightforward than it might otherwise be. The contractualist inclination to enhance efficiency and effectiveness by precisely specifying intended outcomes or consequences would also have a simplifying, perhaps a trivializing, effect on the curriculum. The educational enterprise may be invaded by tokenism—a tendency to replace the attainment of educational outcomes with tokens of attainment, which become detached from actual substantive learning—involving tokens such as enrollment, engagement, the provision of materials, certification, and activism (Bagnall, 1994a).

Contractualism tends further to encourage inflexibility in the course of a program: contractual obligations serving as a restraint to educational responsiveness to changed circumstances. The demands of contractualism for the prior specification of intended outcomes tend also to fragment adult learning into discrete and isolated bits. Any coherence that may result is more likely to be an expression of individual or social development than of those articulated organizational or group wants and interests that emerge in and survive the restraints and constraints of the negotiating process. In its largely private nature, contractualism is also likely to enhance inequality in educational outcomes. Those persons who have the self-confidence, the aptitude and skill, and the external resources to negotiate education on their own behalf are likely to be, overwhelmingly, the already better educated. The instrumental tendency in contractualism would tend to heighten socioeconomic advantage as a consequence of those very educational advantages. The biasing of contractualist curricula in favor of organizational or group interests would also, of course, tend to exclude outsiders from the ensuing educational engagement.

Contractualism also exposes the tensions and contradictions inherent in postmodern adult education practice. As I have argued elsewhere (Bagnall, 1992b), contractualism encompasses a number of conservative tendencies that are in opposition to those of postmodernity. These oppositions may be viewed within the framework of tendencies identified in the previous chapter. They emerge, then, between the already articulated postmodern tendencies and the more conservative tendencies of contractualism:

1. the postmodern tendency toward curricular and procedural heterodoxy (education that is intentionally different from the

traditional or the orthodox), and a contrary tendency in contractualism toward orthodoxy;
2. the postmodern tendency toward expressiveness (education that is spontaneously responsive to and reflective of the noncognitive, emotive interests of its participants), and the contrary tendency in contractualism toward rationality;
3. the postmodern tendency of reflexive contextualization to encourage a diversity of knowledge forms (including theoretical, ethical, technical, existential, and aesthetic) and criteria for the evaluation and justification of education, and the contrary tendency in contractualism toward a central focus on technical knowledge and the commodification of education (i.e., its valuation on the basis of its market value);
4. the postmodern tendency toward revisionism (wherein knowledge and meaning are seen as being open to radical reinterpretation, deconstruction, and revision), and the contrary tendency in contractualism toward a pragmatic view of knowledge and meaning (in the sense of their being rationally and objectively derivable from empirical perception);
5. the postmodern tendency toward phenomenalism (the valuing of the educational engagement in itself), and the contrary tendency in contractualism toward educational instrumentalism (the valuing of education on the basis of the extent to which it is seen as meeting ends extrinsic to the educational event); and
6. the postmodern tendency of dedifferentiation to generate educational complexity (in which educational engagement, curriculum, and goals are seen as opaque, multilayered, and resistant to determinative analysis and criticism), and the contrary contractualist tendency toward simplicity.

Contractualism also highlights the tension between the postmodern tendency toward indeterminacy on the one hand (in the sense of unpredictability and uncertainty as to the location of educational authority and responsibility) and privatization on the other (which may be interpreted as the locating of educational authority and responsibility in that sector of society which most immediately benefits from it).

A straightforwardly modernist response to these contradictory tendencies would be to argue *against* the use of contractualism as a programmatic response to postmodernity. Such a response, however, is inappropriate within a postmodern cultural context, wherein all human action is characterized by its inherent oppositions and contradictions, and by the tensions and conflicts that those oppositions and conflicts create.

Open Marketeering

The open marketeering response to postmodernity is the public marketing of programs or program components (such as study guides and other educational resources) for subscription and engagement by those persons who are attracted and are able to so subscribe and engage. It includes what Jarvis (1989, p. 27) terms the "free-market demand model" of adult education provision. Program development is fundamentally undertaken *by* the educational provider *for* the interested public. While being essentially public and open in its mode of presentation, the attractiveness of and opportunity for engagement in it would commonly be manipulated through pricing, content, timing, location, selective publicity, and the specification of prior learning expectations and requirements for related experience.

Open marketeering may be, to varying degrees, either *reactive* or *manipulative*. To the extent that it is reactive, it is responsive to perceived educational interests in the consumer market—identified through appropriate surveys of one sort or another. To the extent that it is manipulative, it is directed seductively to molding the educational interests of potential consumers to seek the educational programs that the providing agency is marketing.

The use of the mass media in public education campaigns—especially by the state and powerful private interests—may be of considerable importance in the management of social reproduction through the consumer market. In this form of open marketeering, the persuasive stimulation or seduction of that market is, in itself, the primary educational act, albeit one which is standardly instrumental to the achievement of other ends—such as reducing the incidence of smoking, motor vehicle accidents, births, violent crime, or whatever. In those cases where the state is seen as the primary beneficiary of public education programs of the open marketeering variety, it generally bears the costs (although private sponsorship is sometimes also involved).

Open marketeering emerges explicitly within several of the case studies introduced in Chapter 7. Bruce's publicizing of RPL opportunities in the TAFE Institute is a clear example of manipulative open marketeering. Bruce may be seen there as using every available, affordable, and efficacious means of "massaging" his market—to the end of persuading the students to avail themselves of the opportunities for RPL. In the final case study, Lucy's approach to the provision of curriculum modules would appear to be centrally one of reactive open marketeering. She may be seen as identifying an emerging educational demand through market research, and of responding to it with the development of educational resources that are finely tuned to the identified characteristics of the demand. In all respects she appears to be creating educational opportunities that are directly responsive to the market. As was noted for contractualism, open marketeering is more implied in the other case studies than it is the focus of substantive attention. The two nodal forms also emerge in combination. The case of Ian, for example, in his search for appropriately tailored or responsive educational provision to meet his distance education and educational management learning needs, may be interpreted as including both reactive open marketeering and contractualism on the part of the educational providers. More transparently, Bruce combines manipulative open marketeering in publicizing the RPL program, with contractualism in negotiating the RPL itself.

As a response to the consumerist, changeable, and fickle postmodern sociality, open marketeering appears to be highly congruent with its cultural context. Its perceived benefits are, in all important respects, the same as those for contractualism: the likelihood of there being produced educational programs that are functionally relevant and meaningful to the learners; its inherent respect for individual freedom of educational choice and responsibility; its consequential empowerment of learners; and the efficiency and effectiveness of its operation. In open marketeering, the qualities of relevance, respect for individual freedom, and empowerment, insofar as they *are* evidenced, may be even more fully distributed to the learners than is the case with contractualist programming. Indeed, open marketeering, within the consumer market, is a fundamentally public, open form of programming.

However, like contractualism, open marketeering has a number of intrinsic limitations which relate closely to those of "needs-based" programming, where "needs" are perceived as individual wants, desires, or preferences (see, e.g.: Griffin, 1983, Chapter 3; James, 1956; Lawson, 1979, Chapter 5; Monette, 1979). These limitations arise in the context of the educational free market, which is integral to this approach (Bagnall, 1994a, 1994d). The commodification and privatization (in terms of cost) of adult education limit its availability to those who are attracted by and able to afford such a commodity. Programs are thus increasingly available only to meet the interests of that particular sector of the adult population. The educational interests of minority, marginalized groups of adults tend to be put aside as uneconomic. The packaging and commodification of openly marketed postmodern adult education also result in a highly fragmented provision, and one which is unlikely to progress significantly beyond the relatively trivial and superficial. Innovative forms of educational engagement do, indeed, emerge in a competitive situation, although the innovations tend to be directed to market sectors that are already successfully consumerist. Open marketeering thus also tends to be highly and covertly manipulative and, to that extent, not respectful of individual or group autonomy. In its selective targeting of persons who not only value adult education, but also who are able and willing to engage in it, open marketeering may therefore be seen as providing education disproportionately for the already better-educated sectors of the adult population. To that extent, it thereby contributes further to educational and any consequential inequality. It tends, also, to be a high risk strategy for the educational provider.

The tensions and contradictions inherent in postmodern adult education must be a part of an open marketeering approach to programming, just as they are of a contractualist approach. They may, however, be more readily sidelined in the case of open marketeering. An exception to that generalization may be the evident tension between the postmodern tendency toward privatization and the consequential learner independence from the educational institution (with respect to the identification of educational interests, goals, and activities), and the tendency in open marketeering toward learner dependence on the providing agency in these respects.

Discussion

Postmodernity, as it has here been articulated, presents adult education programmers and providing agencies working in the public domain with a highly uncertain task. Its problematization of the grand constraining educational frameworks of modernity undermines any practical certainty as to the proper nature and purposes of one's work as a programmer. In that uncertainty, postmodernity offers no vision of for what and in what ways adult education programming should be undertaken. The lack of any consensus on the constitution of a center or the limits of adult education, and its general de-differentiation—both internal and external—leave a normative void.

Contractualism, as an essentially cooperative approach through which providing agencies negotiate the form of adult education programs with identified groups in the postmodern pluriformity, appears superficially to provide a satisfactory response to this void.

However, it has a number of intrinsic weaknesses, and it foregrounds contradictory tendencies inherent to the postmodern context in which it operates.

Open marketeering appears to be the programmatic approach which is most congruent with a postmodern sociality. Nevertheless, it too has a number of inherent weaknesses and may similarly highlight certain contradictory features of postmodernity.

Whatever programmatic approach or combination of approaches is adopted in a postmodern cultural context, the resulting educational activities will, unavoidably, take on the characteristics of that context. Those characteristics have been outlined in the foregoing chapters. In drawing this part of the analysis to a conclusion, four additional, more strongly evaluative, features of postmodern adult education should be noted: its cognitively diminished, nonself-sustaining, conceptually situational, and procedurally indefinable nature.

By cognitively diminished is meant the postmodern shifting of emphasis away from cognitive understanding, theory, and discursive or linguistic usage, in favor of the iconic or figural, the image, and the aural. This is a major element in what Lash (1990) terms the "dedifferentiation" of postmodernity. It may be seen as arising from: the populist inclinations of postmodernity; the invasion of all culture by the aesthetic realm and its values; the cultural dominance of the mass media, especially television; the downgrading of theory consequent upon acceptance of the contingency of belief and being (including the recognition that meaning is to be found only within particular discourses); and the importance of the subconscious as a constraint and restraint to individual belief and action. In consequence of such cognitive downgrading, there is a favoring of simple, expressive language over the complex and analytic, and a favoring of nonlinguistic communication over the linguistic.

By nonselfsustaining is meant the failure of postmodern adult education to foster the values necessary for the humane maintenance of the postmodern social context. With the downgrading of the grand constraining narratives of social theory to the status of particular contingent discourses, it may not be possible to sustain those values—such as respect, empathy, moderation, honesty, altruism, and benevolence—upon which the survival of the postmodern sociality in recognizably humane form is dependent. Even the value of tolerance is not evidently derivable from postmodernity, although Bauman (1991b) seems to believe otherwise. In any event, the insufficiency of tolerance is a point which Bauman recognizes clearly. The principal practical implication of this feature of postmodernity is that an appropriate set of values—of at least a procedural nature—must be brought to it, if it is to be self-sustaining.

By conceptual situationalism is meant the contingent grounding of conceptual boundaries and terms in what is perceived to be most important and meaningful in any particular situation. The importance of consistency and tradition are correspondingly diminished. Conceptual categories and terms thus become open across contexts and over time. Conceptual situationalism is a clear function of the postmodern commitment to the contingency of all belief, and to the emphasis on instrumentalism. Among other things, it results in a general blurring of conceptual distinctions between fields of human activity, such as those between: education and research, teaching and learning, and learning and its application to social or individual problems. As has been argued elsewhere (Bagnall, 1990a; Lawson, 1982), with any such loss of discriminability there is a corresponding loss of the intellectual and practical power which it otherwise affords.

Finally, here, by procedural indefinability is meant the refusal of postmodern theory to provide any guidance as to which courses of action are more or less desirable or undesirable. This is straightforwardly a function of the postmodern commitment to pluralism and contingency. Viewed positively, procedural indefinability has the virtue of leaving all curricular decisions to the parties involved, working within whatever cultural traditions they bring to the situation. Viewed negatively, in its lack of restraint and constraint it may sanction any action in the name of education—even action of a thoroughly inhumane nature. The need for outside values emerges here, as it does with the nonselfsustainability of postmodern program development.

Postmodernity, then, leaves adult education programmatic activity in a characteristically paradoxical state. Seemingly unlimited opportunities and freedoms are opened to contractualist negotiation and open marketeering by postmodernity's lack of universal, formal, and procedural constraint and restraint. However, the continued existence of such opportunities and freedoms is threatened by the very same lack of universal, formal, and procedural constraint and restraint.

Chapter 10

Fanning the Flames: Research in Postmodern Adult Education

In this chapter, attention is turned to the implications of the postmodern cultural context for the nature of *research* in adult education. By "research" here is meant activities that are directed to the generation and dissemination of public knowledge that either illuminates or informs a category of phenomena or actions: practice in the field of adult education in this case. In other words, research in the field is here being seen as activity that is undertaken self-consciously within and reflexively for the broader field of practice.

Most centrally, the nature of research in adult education is seen here as a matter of knowledge or, more correctly, belief. Three broad considerations, then, may be posited:

1. the sort of *belief* that is generated in the process of research; that is, what is to count as an acceptable research outcome;
2. the sort of *criteria* that are used to evaluate or judge research activity that is directed toward the generation of that belief; in other words, the criteria that are used to determine what is to count as acceptable research; and
3. the sort of *procedures* that are used to generate the belief; that is, the research methods or techniques that are seen as contributing to the generation of the research outcomes.

Those three considerations are clearly closely interrelated, and are used as such in what follows.

While incorporating the foregoing considerations, the analysis is structured here with reference to the three primary qualities that are built into the already articulated conception of postmodern belief: its *indeterminate, contextualized,* and *fragmented* nature. To each of these qualities is related a broad property of adult education research in postmodernity: to the indeterminate nature of belief, the *authorial* nature of research; to the contextualized nature of belief, the *interpretive* nature of research; and to the fragmented nature of belief, the *project-based* nature of research. Within each of these categories, the more particular dimensions and implications of the general qualities are teased out and related to modernist research practice.

Before drawing the chapter to a conclusion, attention is turned briefly to postmodern adult education research as a *profession* or a vocation. Here the qualities of the postmodern sociality are most strictly relevant and are, accordingly, used to tease out some pertinent implications.

Research as Authorial

All belief in postmodernity, you may recall, is seen as being *indeterminate:* underdetermined by any other realities to which it relates, and therefore tentative, uncertain, and subject to contestation. This quality of belief may be seen as deriving from the contingency of all belief on the perceptual frameworks through which it is mediated. The standing of a belief—its truth, utility, authenticity, form, or formulaic conformity, as the case may be—is thus dependent upon its informing framework of understanding: the view of the world in which it is embedded. In other words, the indeterminate nature of belief derives from the interpretative nature of perception (in which all belief is ultimately grounded). Belief, then, must be underdetermined by any objective reality to which it refers, to the extent that it does so refer.

Related to the indeterminate quality of belief, research in postmodernity may be seen as "authorial" in nature. By this is meant that it is located *within* particular discourses or intersubjective frameworks of language and meaning. The indeterminate nature of belief grounds that belief not in universal verities or other transcendental qualities but rather in the "language games" (following Wittgenstein, 1963) in which the belief is embedded. That is not, of course, to deny material reality, nor to deny that some beliefs about material reality are better or more useful than others. What is being denied here is, rather, that we can *judge* which interpretations are better or more useful than others outside the discourses (language games, frameworks of meaning) through which the interpretations are formulated.

"Authorial" is being used here, then, not in the sense of the individual subject as author, but rather in the sense of the *discourse* as author. What is being said about research, in this regard, is that it makes sense only *as* a part of the discourse in which it is embedded and that researchers therefore have an obligation to be clear and open about the nature of that discourse. Research is thus perceived as *inter*subjective. Which is not to say that it cannot be (nor that it is not) undertaken by individuals, but rather that the individuals undertaking it are doing so as *part of* the tradition of that discourse; they are working through and giving expression to currents in the discourse; what they think and do are implicated by those currents.

Importantly, then, postmodern research is undertaken from *within* discourses, rather than transcendentally across them. In this sense, traditional ethnographic research—to the extent that the meanings that it generates are crafted (critically) from the perspectives of the participants—provides some sort of a model of research in postmodernity. Such research seeks to acknowledge and respect the cultural embeddedness of belief.[1]

Criticism of beliefs is thus importantly a discourse-dependent matter. Which is not to say that it is not, or should not be, across discourses in the sense of being from one and of another. Rather, it is to say that such criticism should be *sensitive* to the realities of the discourse which is its object: that it should respect the discourse-dependent nature of those realities and of the different and possibly incommensurable beliefs constituting the discourse from which the criticism is being crafted. The authorial nature of postmodern research thus encourages a degree of *humility* about the standing of one's own beliefs, perspectives, commitments, and situation.

This quality of postmodern research acknowledges the value-laden nature of all belief. It therefore acknowledges the irremediably *political* nature of research.[2] Research may foreground, expose, explain, and contest the political dimensions of educational practice, or it may merely accept those realities. But what it cannot do is to put them aside, to extract politically neutral (value free) meaning from its educational context without impoverishing that meaning.

Belief that is generated through postmodern research thus tends to be highly tentative and self-conscious. It is light on claims to generalizability, universality, and imaginings of the progressive advance of human understanding. It seeks to be seen more *beside* other interpretations, than to displace them. It tends to be self-consciously reflective, rather than proudly assertive. It is avowedly—explicitly and implicitly—located within a particular discourse, whether its object be that discourse or some other. It is thus intersubjective, rather than either objective or subjective. Rather than aspiring to neutrality, it is embracing of the political realities in which educational practice and belief are embedded.

The sort of criteria, then, that are applied to the evaluation of postmodern research—in its design, undertaking, and reporting—include those of: the extent to which the research clearly and openly acknowledges the nature of its own discourse and its political dimensions; the extent to which it acknowledges and articulates realities of its object discourse (its "referentiality"); the extent to which it evidences sensitivity to those realities; and the extent to which it reveals a self-awareness of its own indeterminacy and fragility.

Procedurally, the authorial nature of research, in giving expression to those sorts of criteria, encourages research that is participative rather than spectatorial. By this is meant not that research is collaborative rather than individual (it may be either), but rather that it tends to be undertaken from the perspective of an *insider*—one who is participatively engaged in the discourse that is the object of the research—rather than from the perspective of the outsider, the spectator, the non-engaged, dispassionate observer. Participative involvement is seen here as encouraging empathic identification with the discourse that is the object of the research, and therefore as encouraging the qualities of referentiality, sensitivity, and so on, that are important to the interpretations that the research seeks to generate. The research also tends to be philosophical, not in the sense of being purely philosophical, *sense stricto*, but more in the sense of being philosophically reflective and critical of its own constructs, assumptions, and meanings—philosophical as *a* quality of its design, undertaking, and reporting, but not *the* defining quality of it.

In respect of this quality, postmodern research tends also to utilize *qualitative*, rather than quantitative procedures and technologies (Bagnall, 1994f, Chapter 12; Briton, 1996; Usher, Bryant, and Johnston, 1997).[3] A more qualitative approach is indicated clearly by the greater facility with which such an approach may give expression to the particular qualities of the discourses involved. Quantification necessarily—by its very nature—diminishes the rich variability that characterizes all discourse. There is, correspondingly, a strong tendency in postmodern research to respect that diversity through giving individual expression to its particularities.

Research as Interpretation

Postmodern belief, you may further recall from Chapter 3, is not just indeterminate, but also *contextualized*. By this latter term is meant that beliefs have meaning only within cultural contexts: the meaning of any given belief is dependent upon the cultural context in which it is being used. A given statement of belief (a given "signifier")—a "fact," "description," "analysis," "critique," "exhortation," "utterance," "theory," or whatever—may therefore be given quite different meanings in different cultural contexts. Any given context has its own (ever-changing) contributing discourses, its contributing conventions of language use, conceptual meanings, interests, priorities, expectations, power relationships, value commitments, and beliefs about the world. Together with the subjective experience of each individual who interprets any particular statement of belief, each of these cultural phenomena contributes to the (context-specific) meaning given to that statement.

Postmodern research, then—in being directed to the generation of belief—must be responsive to its contextualized nature, and it is so particularly through the general quality of being *interpretive* in nature. By this is meant, following Bauman (1987), that research is essentially directed to interpreting or explaining and critically reflecting upon patterns of belief and action in adult education practice, and to articulating those patterns in the public domain. This is an activity, though, that is importantly *reflexive*, in that, in interpreting a context of adult education practice, it does not *de*scribe that context, so much as *in*scribe an interpretation onto it (Fuente, 1993; Hassard, 1993; Kemmis, 1991; Usher and Edwards, 1994; Wildemeersch, 1992). It is an activity which, thereby, actually (reflexively) reconfigures the context that is the object of its attention—the referent of the interpretation. It is thus formative of, not neutral with respect to, the objects of research. It reflexively *generates* meanings—cultural realities—and, in so doing, it impacts on the identities of the individuals who are involved (as subjects) or become involved with those realities. Consistent with the postmodern condition, such action is undertaken *self-consciously*—with an awareness of its contextually reflexive nature and therefore of its formative impact on educational practice.

In these features, interpretive research is commonly contrasted with that which is "empirical-analytic" in the late-modernist tradition of strongly and positivistically empiricist research (see, e.g.: Achinstein, 1968; Ayer, 1959; Carnap, 1962; Hempel, 1965; Merriam, 1991). In that tradition, the researcher is seen as objectively discovering, and reflecting in the research outcomes, the truth that is immanent to the objects of the research: as mirroring in the research outcomes, the empirical realities of educational practice. It is a strong tradition in educational research, and one which its apologists—such as Gage (1989)—naturally seek to maintain.

Interpretive research in education is thus, self-consciously, directed to interpreting, critically reflecting upon, forming, and articulating the nature of educational belief in its contextually grounded richness. It seeks to acknowledge, through working within, the situational or contextual nature of educational belief. It seeks to acknowledge the interrelationships between all types of belief—theoretical, ethical, technical, existential, and aesthetic.[4] And it seeks to acknowledge the interdependence of belief, intention, and action: what Lyotard (1979/1984a) recognizes as the "performative" nature of postmodern knowledge. This interrelationship recognizes the inseparability of meaning from the commitments and intentional activities that characterize the cultural contexts in which meaning is grounded.

Educational research in postmodernity is thus directed more at the elucidation of *meanings* and is in that sense hermeneutic in nature (Gadamer, 1977; Geertz, 1979). It is directed less at predicting and controlling events or, as Bauman (1987) terms it, at "legislating" the nature of (future) events. It tends, therefore, to be *historicist*, rather than universalist, in the sense that its focus is on the meanings attributed to events by those who participate in them, rather than on any posited underlying or overarching causes of those meanings or of other educational realities. There is a corresponding blurring of the distinction between the researchers undertaking the research and the subjects of the research. There is a tendency, indeed, for these two entities to be one and the same.

Interpretive research is directed more to giving expression to the complexity of educational phenomena, than it is to simplifying that complexity. It thus tends to be situationally grounded in the phenomena that are its object, rather than being paradigmatic or theory-driven. Insofar as it is an autonomous exercise, its autonomy is of the situation or the phenomenon, rather than being of any (grand) theory. In other words, it tends to craft its own explanatory constructs and to draw eclectically on others in the service of interpreting the (situated) objects of its concern, rather than to bring coherent theory to those objects as a means of explaining them.

Interpretive research certainly accepts that some interpretations are better or more useful than others, and it may be "progressive" in that sense. It therein accepts that interpretations may properly be contested and rejected or reformulated in the face of competing interpretations. However, any such rejection or re-formulation is seen as a situationally specific, not a universal and general, decision. It is, in other words, more a putting aside than a moving beyond—and it is a putting aside to which one may return on another occasion, when that belief may yet again be found to serve a valuable purpose in a different context. Any notion of research as a continuous forward or upward progression (whether linear, spiral, or whatever) is therefore rejected. Progress is, rather, short-lived—specific to contemporary commitments, interests, and projects. Nothing necessarily carries forward to any other or future commitments, interests, or projects. Between contexts—whether contemporary or temporal in their relational distribution—the notions of progress or regress are themselves highly problematic, because they are highly dependent on the values immanent to the respective contexts.

The belief that is generated through interpretive research tends, therefore, to be reflective of the commitments, interests, concerns, and problems of the contexts which it seeks to interpret. It tends to be richly interpretive of the diversity of realities constituting the contexts. It may be so, though, in a critically reflective (and reflexive) manner, in the sense of its turning the contextually grounded constructs back onto the context, to identify and expose commonalities and differences, consistencies and inconsistencies, concordances and discordances, justices and injustices, and so on. Interpretive research will, therefore, tend to be tied closely to articulated contexts of educational practice, rather than to transcendent educational questions, concerns, or issues of educational import. It tends to be integrated with actions that contribute to that practice, as much as it is integrated with the ideas (beliefs) that frame it.

The sort of criteria, then, that are used in the evaluation of interpretive research, assess the extent to which the foregoing qualities are realized in the design, undertaking, and reporting of the research. Those criteria include notions such as: the extent to which the research does acknowledge the commitments, interests, concerns, problems, and beliefs of the contexts which it seeks to interpret (its referentiality); the extent to which it does interpretive justice, in a situationally sensitive manner, to the diversity of realities constituting its focus; the extent to which it is critically reflective; and the extent to which it integrates interpretation, critical reflection, and action in a participative fashion. Rejected are (modernist) notions such as the simplicity or parsimony of explanation ('Occam's razor'),[5] the power that it gives in prediction and control, its generalizability, its contribution to universal or transcendent theory, its freedom from the values and interests of the researcher and the subjects of the research, and the objectivity with which the researchers engage in the research process.

The sort of research procedures appropriate to the interpretive nature of postmodern research, then, are those that satisfy the criteria applied to its evaluation. They tend to be driven by, grounded in, the research context, rather than by theoretical frameworks drawn from the discipline of education or from related disciplines (such as psychology or sociology). They tend, therefore, to draw eclectically on techniques from any range of disciplinary sources that may best address the research interests that emerge from the given context. Those interests may be quite diverse and incoherent, and the research techniques selected to address them may be no less so. As an epistemic activity that is grounded in educational practice, the research, in its interests and techniques, may be expected to change (possibly radically) in the course of the research project. In remaining sensitive to the diversity of beliefs that constitute any imaginable context of educational research, interpretive research also tends to be more qualitative than quantitative in nature, although quantitative elements are not infrequently built on more qualitative components in addressing specific questions.

Research as Project-Based

Referring back to Chapter 3, you may further recall that postmodern belief is not just indeterminate and contextualized, but also *fragmented* among those contexts. In other words, belief is not just derived from and meaningful within particular contexts, but is also potentially incommensurable across them. So presented, this quality of postmodern belief is derivable directly from its contextualized nature (given the premise of a pluriformity of cultural contexts). Nevertheless, it is recognized here as a separate quality to give recognition to its epistemic importance and to that of its implications for the generation of belief through research.

Those implications are here drawn together into the *project-based* nature of postmodern educational research. By this notion is meant the tendency for research to be constructed into discrete entities, in all of its qualities: the policy that governs it; the funding that supports it; the purposes to which it is directed; the methods by which it is undertaken; its impact; and its evaluation. Those entities may be of varying magnitude: from quick-fire surveys of opinion to major reviews extending over a number of years. They may also range over quite isolated projects, connected only with a practical context, to quite complex, nested series of subprojects, serving a hierarchy of increasingly more inclusive projects. What is not strongly in evidence, however, is the (modernist) conception of research activity structured according to the progressive advance of knowledge along certain (universal) lines—such as the progressive refinement of our understanding of skills learning, of measuring intelligence, of the optimization of feedback in teaching, and so on. The universals have been discredited and sidelined. They may be used in an *historicist* fashion to give meaning and coherence to individual and organizational life-passages and missions, and to draw otherwise disparate fragments of knowledge together into meaningful reviews of knowledge, but they have been therein pushed from the generative center-stage of educational (and more broadly, social) research to the post-hoc margins. They are used to sweep up the fragmentary products of research, rather than to define the very purpose, direction, and nature of research—as had been their traditional role in modernity.

Except, then, through such post-hoc rationalizations, postmodern educational research tends to be fragmented among the projects defining the focus of its concern. Any one project is framed by the contingent cultural interests and concerns that led to its formation: each a complex and unique interplay of political, educational, institutional, organizational, and individual considerations, interwoven by the changing policies, practices, and beliefs informing these various dimensions. Each project, then, unless deliberately crafted as a component of a larger one, emerges as more individual and isolated than it is a part of any coherent program or plan of disciplinary or professional advance.

A feature of such project-based research is that it is relatively unconstrained by formal theory. In other words, it is epistemically free to draw upon constructs from any disciplinary or scholarly source—bringing those constructs together in potentially unique ways to focus on the issues being addressed in the project. This contrasts strongly with the more modernist approach to research, which was strongly constrained in its theoretical constructs by the paradigmatic dictates of the discipline within which it was framed.

Another feature of such project-based research is that it tends strongly to presentism, that is, to a concentration on interests, concerns, issues, and problems of the moment, rather than on the timeless concerns and predicaments of humankind, which were seen (idealistically at least) as driving modernist research.

Project-based research also tends to be "surfacized"—to focus on the immediate, superficial, spur-of-the-moment interests or fetishes impacting on or emanating from the field. Therein, surveys of opinion about issues, concerns, and interests with respect to educational policy, approaches, and outcomes become commonplace features of educational research. There is generated a fetish for the collection of data on collective opinion about education and aggregated commitments to it. Educational research acquires an importantly *impulsive* quality—simultaneously opening it up to diverse interests and concerns and exposing it to the trivial, the ill-informed, and the partisan. The tendency to surfacization has been characterized by Wexler (1989, 1993) as the "social and institutional emptying" of education (and, indeed, of other aspects of social life). It should, though, be noted here that such surfacization and fetishization of belief—while a feature of some (perhaps much) postmodern project-based research—is not necessarily a feature of it *per se* (M. Peters, 1992, 1995b).

The project-based nature of postmodern educational research means that it is essentially ideographic (particular, contextualized) in its focus. The important contrast here is with traditional (modernist) educational research which was characterized (however idealistically) as "nomothetic" or theory-driven—directed to illuminating, through the recognition of universal laws, the great burning educational issues facing humankind.

The project-based nature of research, then, identifies the sort of belief that it produces as being not just situated but also situationally isolated. Research-based belief becomes ideographic. It loses its grandeur, its transcendent qualities. It informs not so much the academically ethereal and the socially visionary as the commonplace and happenstance messiness of individual aspirations, failings, successes, inhibitions, dislikes, loves, hates, and so on. The *value* of research-based belief is grounded in its utility, and that presentism drives the research enterprise in all of its aspects: its goals, informing theory, scope, reasoning, activity, and impact. In that grounding, it is simultaneously freed from the modernist constraints of disciplinarity and imprisoned by the constraints of immediacy.

The sorts of criteria by which project-based research is evaluated correspond to its strongly contextualized, ideographic, presentist, and commonly surfacist nature. They embrace such features as: the extent to which the scope of the research project is clearly articulated; the extent to which the outcomes address the purposes (in other words, the extent to which temporary—strictly temporary—epistemic closure is achieved); the extent to which the procedures fit the purposes and scope; and the extent to which the focus and scope of future indicated projects are clearly identified and articulated. In this last quality, project-based research is revealed as being not unconnected with other research projects, but it is so not in any fundamentally developmental and epistemically transcendental sense but rather in the fashion of contrived connectivities—links constructed for the sake of satisfying a desire for connection, rather than being expressions of an ongoing program of (modernist) epistemic generativity.

In terms of research procedures, the project-based nature of educational research indicates, most importantly, a release from the methodological constraint of modernist disciplinary enquiry. Associated with the release is the problematization and erosion of the hierarchy of status that characterized modernist approaches to research. The formerly clear superiority of more formally, theoretically derived and quantitative approaches to research over the less so, has essentially gone, and in its place is a more or less egalitarian acceptance of any mélange of methodological hybrids that can sensibly be crafted to suit a given project. So, not only is there methodological pluriformity, novelty, and pastiche, but there is methodological generativity as well. While some of that freedom is used to draw strongly on available supporting procedures, other expressions of it run to the impulsive and the superficial, with quick-fix surveys of opinions, feelings, attitudes, and so on, on any exciting issues of the moment.

Here, then, is generated an interesting contradiction between the contextually probing and self-reflective approaches indicated by the foregoing two qualities of postmodern research, and the superficial, contextually insensitive tendency that emerges from the fragmented and project-based nature of postmodern research. This contradiction is well illustrated in the contrastive views of postmodern research that are evidenced in the critical pedagogy of authors such as Giroux[6] and the resignation, passive populism, and superficiality of the educational realities and educational research articulated by them as oppositional.

What postmodern adult education research is not, or at least is *not necessarily*, is what Melser (1994, p. 55) has incorrectly argued to be "post modern research methods such as cooperative inquiry and hermeneutic dialogue." It may, at best contingently, include such qualities, but they are not definitive features of postmodernity. Neither is postmodern adult education research necessarily any sort of "action research," as Jennings (1995), Westwood (1991b), and others would like to believe, or at least to hope that it were. Jennifer Gore (1991) is, indeed, quite correct in her analysis of "emancipatory action research" as essentially modernist—with which Stephen Kemmis (1991) is in agreement, in spite of his commitment to such research in education, if humanity is to experience anything approaching a civil society in the future.

Adult Education Research as a Profession

The focus of this chapter thus far has been on the qualities of postmodern *belief*, which has directed analytical attention to the nature of the research activity *per se*. If we were, however, to focus attention on the broader postmodern cultural context, we might expose some of the features of postmodern educational research from the perspective of the professional researcher or academic. Revealed, then, would be a field that is strongly dedifferentiated—experiencing a loss of identity, of exclusivity, of recognition as an entity in its own right. Adult education research in postmodernity emerges as a field that is both integrated with and simultaneously interpretive of other social realities, most particularly those of adult education practice and related fields of social practice—such as counseling and postcompulsory education more generally. Adult education research as a distinctive field, and hence vocation, is thus largely denied. The generation of belief is either grounded in practice or integrated into broader skill-based programs of opinion surveying, data collection, and analysis, or programmatic research and evaluation.

However, for those practitioners or scholars who do, however contrarily, identify with the generation of belief in the field, there is presented a relatively open acceptance of intellectual backgrounds and approaches—both theoretically and methodologically. The criteria have shifted from the modernist formality of initiation through the academic rigors of the academic disciplines, to the postmodern informality of open competition for space in which to be heard as an interpreter and articulator of contextualized realities. Academic rigor within the framework of an academic discipline has given way to a situational sensitivity to cultural differences. The "legislation" (Bauman, 1987) of scholarly and practical standards has given way to the "interpretation" of contexts of practice and educational commitment.

The field of postmodern adult education research as a whole has shifted from the predictable (modernist) formalism and disciplinary compartmentalism in which change was gradual (if uneven), evolutionary, and progressive, to a field of unpredictable pluriformity, radical eclecticism, changeability, informality, and atheoretical responsiveness to the particularities of contingent realities in educational practice.

Modernistically, the project is both supremely successful—as measured by the level of activity and the diversity of that engagement—and a failure: as measured in terms of the loss of commitment to the traditional standards of disciplinary enquiry. But adult education research in postmodernity should not be measured in those terms; it stands firmly in postmodernity, not modernity: uncertain, pluriform, without clear foundation, lacking in any clarity of future vision, grounded only in immediately contingent interests, concerns, and fetishes, and both championed and diminished by the strengths and the limitations of that contingency.

Chapter 11

The Situationally Sensitive Wayfarer: Being an Adult Educator in the Age of the Chameleon

The task in this, the final chapter is to tease out the implications of postmodern adult education practice for the nature of the adult educator *as* an adult educator. In other words, it is to identify (or, more correctly, to speculate upon) the professional qualities of adult educators working within a postmodern cultural context. Building on my earlier articulation of situational sensitivity (Bagnall, 1995a), the picture here painted of the postmodern adult educator is that of the *situationally sensitive wayfarer*—one whose professional engagements are characterized by: reflexive awareness; individual and organizational responsibility; tolerance of and respect for difference; sympathetic understanding of and responsiveness to the particularities of lived events, across the range of knowledge types (technical, ethical, theoretical, existential, and aesthetic); respect for persons and their cultural realities; and the capability, understanding, and disposition to negotiate the recognition of discriminative realities and the alleviation of discriminative injustice. Those qualities and the sort of individual knowledge that they presuppose are here examined, with a concluding pass at identifying the implications of such a conception for the formation and professional development of adult educators.

The Situationally Sensitive Wayfarer

The notion of the postmodern adult educator as a situationally sensitive wayfarer is tackled here by examining what are seen as the six (clusters of) qualities that characterize the adult education engagements of such a practitioner. The qualities are seen as *descriptive* of the actions that adult educators who are adapted to the postmodern cultural context are likely to evidence in their work. They are not presented here as an ideological blueprint of the "good," the "true," or the "authentic" postmodern adult educator, since any such characterization is contrary to the nature of postmodernity itself. Each of the qualities is also grounded briefly in the case studies introduced in Chapter 7.

The order in which the first four qualities are here presented has no particular significance. However, those four are seen as coming together in the fifth quality, and the sixth is seen as an articulation of the sorts of knowledge that underpins the exercise of the preceding qualities. These relationships should become clear as the chapter unfolds. It should also become apparent that none of the qualities is discrete—that as a whole, they constitute an interlocking, overlapping, and intermelding set.

1. Reflexive Awareness

Reconstructing Mezirow (1981, 1991) and following Usher and Edwards (1994), the concept of reflexive awareness is that of action taken with an understanding of the assumptions underpinning the action, of the culturally constructed nature of those assumptions, of the limitations to human action that the assumptions impose, of their potentially contestable nature, and of the extent to which they are (reflexively) asserted, reinforced (even if redefined) by our complicity in their adoption and use. The assumptions here may be with respect to any informing aspect of the engagement: its proper form; the nature of identity, humanity, or learning; the qualities of justice; the rights and duties of educators and learners; the nature of knowledge; and so on.

Such an understanding of the assumptions underpinning one's actions is seen as encouraging a *humility* with respect to the importance of one's own framework of beliefs, and a corresponding reluctance to impose it upon, or to expect it of, others. This quality thus foregrounds a tension in postmodern adult education between, on the one hand, the sort of jingoistic hubris that the quality of critical self-awareness denies and, on the other hand, a state of catatonic inactivity and ineffectuality generated by the self-awareness of self-doubt and self-denial in the face of profound epistemic uncertainty. The hubris that is denied by reflexive awareness is that which is seen—from a postmodern perspective—as characterizing the projects of modernity: projects driven by a certainty about the unidirectionality and universality of progress. The spectre of catatonic self-doubt and self-denial that is raised by postmodernity is, perhaps, no less to be avoided.

Postmodernity certainly embraces the modernist ideological frameworks of commitment to social change—incorporating but skeptically problematizing them. In so doing, it embraces individual and collective commitment to any such modernist ideological frameworks. What it does *not* do is to embrace any such commitment as *the* postmodern approach to social change or education. Here Giroux and his fellow apologists[1] for a reconstructed neo-Marxist form of critical pedagogy are shown to be entirely mischievous to the extent that they purvey that critical pedagogy as postmodern. It may be their *response* to postmodernity, but it is not necessarily any more postmodern than any other revivalist responses, such as those of fundamentalist religions. While embracing such ideologies—to the extent that they are held in a reflexively aware manner—postmodernity eschews ideological characterization itself.[2]

What the concept of reflexive awareness does importantly do in postmodern adult education practice, is to pick up on the notion of individuals in postmodernity as reflexively aware of the beliefs, assumptions, and power relationships that define them (albeit indeterminately) *as* culturally constructed individuals and through which they contribute to the construction of the cultural realities in which they live and which, in turn, define their living. This reflexivity, while always partial or incomplete, crucially decenters and drives the deconstruction of modernist notions of professionalism that are based on the individual as a self-identical, autonomous, integrated monad. As will be noted shortly, some of those modernist notions are here incorporated, but in a reconstructed form.

Reflecting back on the case studies introduced in Chapter 7, there is insufficient detail given there to provide any strong examples of this quality. Nevertheless, Ian may be seen as exemplifying a reflexively aware adult educator to the extent that he was alert to his own learning interests and the frameworks of belief and action in which they arose. Ian, you will recall, was seeking educational support for his self-diagnosed need to develop his knowledge in program design and development through distance education. He shows some evidence of being alert to the assumptions, limitations, and consequences of traditional approaches to education, and also of those he increasingly adopted in a more self-directed manner, but this may be an unjustifiedly generous overinterpretation of the extent to which he was reflexively aware.

Roger, in his programming for Unicom over the University's extensive nonmetropolitan region, may be seen as having become considerably more reflexively aware through the experience of his initial programming failures. From that experience, he developed a greater awareness of the assumptions that he was bringing to the task, of the limitations to those assumptions, and of the validity of an open set of alternatives.

2. Individual and Organizational Responsibility

Supporting the quality of reflexive awareness is the acceptance of responsibility for one's beliefs, actions, and their consequences. Such a notion clearly and significantly is in tension with the provisional and contextualized nature of belief and being in postmodernity, which allow (or even encourage) the abrogation of individual responsibility—a point that has been used vigorously in argument against postmodernity.[3] Its apparently anomalous inclusion here as a quality of adult education engagement in postmodernity is based partly on the *professional* nature of that engagement.

In the relatively open, contestable, market-based, and interest-driven world of postmodern realities, it is argued that, regardless of their inclinations, adult educators may expect respect from a client or market sector only to the extent that they do not abrogate their individual responsibility to the contingent discourses informing their identities and actions. Without such respect, it is hard to imagine an individual being able to maintain sufficient authority to continue *as* a professional in the field—unless, that is, they derive their authority from protective organizational structures. Those latter structures, though, are themselves competing for cultural space in the postmodern marketplace, and are seen here as being thereby subject to similar market pressures favoring responsibility. Responsible organizations may conceivably (and demonstrably do) harbor and protect nonresponsible individuals, just as larger organizations may (and demonstrably do) harbor and protect nonresponsible component organizations. Nevertheless, the extent to which such protection may pervade postmodern organizational and, more broadly, social realities must be strongly limited by the postmodern sociality. This is well illustrated in the more recent cases in which individuals and companies have been vilified, boycotted, or prosecuted over publicly perceived actions of social irresponsibility.

Individual and organizational responsibility may, therefore, be seen also as a more pervasive consequence of the postmodern privatization of decision and action. With that privatization is an individualization of accountability and, more broadly, of responsibility for one's decisions and actions.

Reflecting back on the case studies presented in Chapter 7, an example of this quality—as organizational responsibility—may be seen in the case of Bruce's program to market the opportunities for the recognition of prior learning (RPL) available through the technical and further education institute in which the RPL program is located. The case of Lucy, in her development of a foundational module for the professional development of vocational education and training practitioners presents, perhaps, an extreme example of the individual assuming responsibility for the form and consequences of her actions. In her treatment of her initially contracted curriculum designer, it also highlights the harsher, more brutal side of individual responsibility—a point that also has been used against postmodernity as a normative concept.[4]

3. Tolerance of and Respect for Difference

Arising from, or associated with, the humility of reflexive awareness is a tolerance of and respect for otherness, for difference from one's own commitments and realities. This quality constitutes both an *acceptance* (tolerance) of difference and a *valuing* of (respect for) that difference. So perceived, it is a reformulation of the liberal pluralist argument for the toleration of difference.[5] However, in postmodernity this valuing of what is different may be seen as expanding to a valuing of difference *per se*. It therein embraces a valuing of the contrary, the unorthodox, the heterodox—of difference for the sake of difference (Bauman, 1992; Cascardi, 1992; Hutcheon, 1988; Kanpol, 1992).

Frequently, if not generally, those contrary viewpoints will be, not just different from those to which one is committed, but also in *conflict* with them. Thereby, the quality identified here foregrounds one of the classical dilemmas of pluralism: on the one hand, to the extent that one tolerates and values viewpoints other than one's own, to that extent one diminishes the value of and commitment to one's own; on the other hand, to the extent that one has epistemic and normative commitments (the extent to which one 'stands for anything') one's tolerance of and respect for other commitments is likely to be diminished. Such is the postmodern condition.

Zygmunt Bauman also focuses on the danger of postmodern tolerance becoming an indifference to injustice suffered by others—a tolerance of oppression, repression, and disempowerment, so long as it is someone else's experience—what Bauman (1991b, p. 9) has identified as an "attitude of *indifference-fed callousness*." Certainly, unqualified or unalloyed tolerance of difference is open to this consequence or distortion, and it may be seen as a feature of the postmodern sociality. However, societal expectations of adult education practitioners—articulated here particularly in the last of the qualities of the situationally sensitive wayfarer—are seen as denying (or at least severely limiting) such an expression of tolerance in the professional practice of adult educators.

Further, and more strongly, it may be argued that the tolerance of difference in a pluralistic society must be limited in at least two important ways. First, it must be limited by the extent to which difference is not harmful to the welfare or interests of other individuals or groups (a point to which I shall return in the penultimate quality articulated here—that of respect for persons and their cultural realities). Second, tolerance of difference in a pluralistic society must not be extended to embrace (i.e., to tolerate) an *in*tolerance of difference. In other words, actions that seek inappropriately to limit the freedom of others to be different cannot be tolerated in a postmodern sociality.

This quality emerges in a number of the Chapter 7 case studies. Perhaps most notably, Marian—in the approach that she took to community adult education policy development in Plumbarton—based her approach on a tolerance of and respect for difference in others. She deliberately set out to craft a policy framework that was pluralistic and open. Similarly, although not initially, Roger's programming for Unicom developed to the point where it evidenced this quality. That happened, though, only after he experienced failure with a more traditional, formulaic, ideologically driven approach to programming.

4. Sympathetic Understanding of and Responsiveness to Lived Events

While a tolerance of and respect for difference characterizes postmodern engagements in general, the adult education context demands much more of its professionals. In that regard, I here focus on the quality of sympathetically understanding and responding to the particularities of our clients' lived events.

Tolerance of other realities is not necessarily more than a relatively passive acknowledgment of them—a "live-and-let-live" approach to diversity. Sympathetic understanding, however, requires some identification with the realities concerned: not just an awareness of them, but a knowledge of them and an empathy with persons who are committed to them (Seidler, 1991). It involves an approach to events that does more than (modernistically) categorize them, drawing from that categorization the categorical qualities which should define one's actions. It involves, rather, seeing each event as unique, and as importantly so. Such an approach, such a perceptual frame, embodies a search for what *is* importantly unique about each event, for the players involved in it; and it embodies a search for the most appropriate actions through which to respond sympathetically to the event—actions which strengthen and support those qualities of the event over which one negotiates some determinative involvement as an adult educator.

Although sympathetic, such actions in response to the event must be within the frame of one's own realities as an adult educator. It therefore, importantly and unavoidably, involves the negotiation and redefinition of the event itself. One's intrusion as an adult educator cannot but change the situational realities if it is to have any impact. If it has no impact, it cannot be educative—a point made strongly in an earlier work of mine (Bagnall, 1987c). The negotiation itself implies capabilities to which I shall return in the sixth quality of the situationally sensitive wayfarer. The redefinition may range over any degree of magnitude and may pertain to any feature of the event—the way it is perceived, what is seen as being important in it, the learning outcomes that are derived from it, the way in which those outcomes should be achieved, and so on.

In so negotiating and redefining realities, there is demanded understanding and responsiveness across a wide range of knowledge, to the end of its selective and eclectic utilization in the particular language games of the events concerned. Such knowledge may be seen as spanning the full range of traditional modernist categories of knowledge: theoretical, ethical, technical, existential, and aesthetic.[6] These categories, though, are seen as problematic in postmodernity: knowledge being seen there as emerging in particular events only as profoundly complex patterns of discourse and action, the unravelling of which into types such as these is both reductive and destructive of the realities themselves. Any recognition of such a set of alternatives must be seen, then, not (modernistically) as providing classes or situations for identifying, categorizing, and categorically responding to events. Such a set of alternatives must, rather, be seen as *sensitizing* the adult educator to *possibilities*, as *enlarging the potential* for understanding and action. It should be seen not as increasing the power and efficacy of one's action but as enhancing the *responsiveness* of one's actions to the lived realities of others. It should be seen not as tooling one to solve the problems of others but rather as equipping one to *empathize* with their realities and to contribute to the enhancement of what is agreed to be important in those realities.

This approach to the use of knowledge in *sensitizing*, rather than empowering, applies to the use of all knowledge within a situationally sensitive framework. The professional or practical knowledge generated through and applied from the traditional scholarly disciplines (whether psychology, sociology, politics, ethics, or whatever)—no more and no less than that which is generated through the reflective experience of engagement as adult educator and learner—is knowledge which enlarges the potential for understanding and acting in a situationally sensitive manner. It therein heightens, not certainty, decisiveness, and determination, but rather uncertainty, indecisiveness, and a disinclination to intrude into the worlds of others. These are qualities informed by an understanding of the power of individual action to do both good and harm, and of the uncertainties and ambiguities infusing that power: uncertainty as to the situational particularities of appropriate action; ambiguity suffusing the nature of all belief which informs and evaluates the action and its impact. As Lyotard has observed, in postmodernity, knowledge "refines our sensitivity to differences and reinforces our ability to tolerate the incommensurable" (Lyotard, 1979/1984a, p. xxv).

Situational sensitivity focuses on enhancing sensitivity *to* the diversity of knowledge types, rather than on generating or acquiring knowledge *in* any of them. It constitutes what Toulmin (1990) has termed an "horizon of expectation." It may be thus seen as a matter of *functioning* in an essentially contextual or situationally specific manner. Nevertheless, as an approach to the world or, more specifically, to the task of being an adult educator, it is centered within the individual, and is essentially *trans*contextual in that centering. In the particularity of its expression—in the multifarious realities of its being—it is essentially situational (contextual). But this is a situational specificity which can exist only insofar as the adult educator is characterized by that general (transcendental) approach to the particularities of lived events that is embraced by the notion of the situationally sensitive wayfarer.

It is from within the frame defined by this quality that Benhabib argues for a "post-Enlightenment project of interactive universalism" (Benhabib, 1992, p. 3)—an ethics based on "a moral conversation in which the capacity to reverse perspectives, that is, the willingness to reason from the others' point of view, and the sensitivity to hear their voice is paramount" (Benhabib, 1992, p. 8).

The brevity and superficiality of the case studies in Chapter 7 do not allow this quality to be well articulated in any of the events there described. However, the approach used by Marian in her policy development for community adult education in Plumbarton may be seen as building upon a foundation of sympathetic understanding of the lived realities of the Plumbarton residents. The approach then sought to craft policy that was sensitively responsive to those realities. Contrastively, but nevertheless pertinently, Lucy's heavy-handed approach to the development of curriculum may be seen as showing an astute understanding of and responsiveness to the market sector of vocational educators and trainers, to which she sought to direct the course.

5. Respect for Persons and Their Realities

The foregoing qualities come together in the concept of respect for persons and their cultural realities. This concept is fundamentally a reconstruction of the liberal pluralist notion of respect for persons. That notion has been variously and strongly articulated, *inter alia*, by

R.S. Downie and Elizabeth Telfer (1969) from the perspective of schooling and by Nicolas Haines (1981a, 1981b) in his attempt to craft a practical philosophy particularly for adult education. It may be seen also as underpinning Richard Rorty's (1989) articulation of a social philosophy that is responsive to contemporary postmodern realities.

While the concept of respect for persons and their cultural realities may be, and has been, variously articulated, it identifies centrally the qualities of accepting the different beliefs and cultural realities of other individuals and groups—contesting difference only in those cases and to the extent that it is in conflict with the interests or the well-being of others. In other words, belief and culture are seen as *private* matters, to be shared only voluntarily, unless and to the extent that they are in conflict with the interests of others.

In thus seeking to build upon the modernist notion of respect for persons, we must recognize and put aside its grounding in the liberal humanist conception of the individual as an autonomous monad. In postmodernity, the quality for which I am arguing here has no foundation in the essential unity, goodness, or completeness of the socially located individual. Such a conception sits uncomfortably within the postmodern condition. The quality is, rather, one which is crafted—intersubjectively, reflexively, provisionally, and uncertainly—by each adult educator, within and through the flux of professional and practical discourse in which each is located and by which each is indeterminately constituted.

Richard Rorty picks up the concept of respect for persons in his notion of the "liberal ironist," for whom human solidarity is "a matter of imaginative identification with the details of others' lives" (Rorty, 1989, p. 190). For Nicolas Haines (1981a, 1981b), respect for persons is associated centrally with the practical knowledge of how to negotiate realities with other persons—the concept of "practical knowledge" here embracing, in the classical Greek tradition, both moral knowledge and social skills. For R.S. Downie and Elizabeth Telfer (1969), respect for persons is seen as both: (1) an attitude of active sympathy for other individuals in the exercise of their rational wills in the self-determined pursuit of objects of interest to themselves; and (2) an acceptance that the rules by which they guide their conduct constitute reasons which may apply both to them and to ourselves.

In all of these instantiations, the notion of respect for persons is exposed as inherently tensional and conflictual. Any given framework of belief is necessarily constraining, in the sense that it directs its adherents to see and understand particular realities but not others. In other words, any given framework of belief, just because it *is* a framework of belief, limits the freedom of those persons who hold it. Nevertheless, there is considerable variability in the extent to which frameworks *are* thus constraining. The dilemma arises, then—and serves as a source of irresolvable difference and conflict—as to the extent to which, the circumstances under which, and the ways in which individuals, groups, or the state may properly intervene to free individuals from the (undue) constraints of frameworks to which they are committed. A traditional response to this dilemma is largely to limit state intervention to children and adolescents, leaving adults to live within the constraints of their constructs. However, this is too simple a picture when one considers such realities as the numerous public education programs supported by the state—such as campaigns to discourage tobacco smoking, to encourage the wearing of seat-belts in cars, and to address a host of other personal health and safety issues. By its very nature, such education is an attempt by the state to intervene—through public education—in the lives of individual adults in such a way as to disabuse them of existing (adjudged, personally harmful) frameworks of belief. Certainly there is always an element of *public* interest in such campaigns (through savings in public health expenditure and such like), but there is also and importantly an attempt in these sorts of campaigns to *liberate* individuals from beliefs that are personally harmful to them.

Respect for persons also leaves open and unaddressed the intercultural tensions and conflicts that are created by differences in beliefs about what is essentially good and right in human nature and action. Straightforwardly, difference and conflict arise here from a commitment to respect for persons since, on the one hand, the concept calls for intervention to protect the welfare of others who are unduly constrained by their belief yet, on the other hand, it calls for tolerance of those beliefs.

Respect for persons in postmodern sociality, ultimately, calls for the negotiation of the *meaning* of the concept itself, and the *procedures* by which that negotiation and the reconciliation of differences are to be resolved. Assumed in the confrontation of any difference is the right to intrude into the realities of others—in this case, of those with whom one differs. In itself, such intrusion may be seen as evidencing a *lack* of respect for persons. So again, the notion of respect for persons is seen as inherently conflictual: to uphold it in the face of opposition is to work against it; not to uphold it in the face of opposition is to abandon it to that opposition.

Returning to the case studies in Chapter 7, Roger—in his program development work with the University's center, Unicom—may be seen as moving toward an acceptance of respect for persons in his mature programming efforts. There he was seeking to be accepting of and sensitively responsive to the beliefs defining the different communities of interest in the region for which he had been given responsibility. Similarly, in her approach to policy development in Plumbarton, Marian may be seen as giving expression to the concept of respect for the persons for whom the policy was being formulated.

6. Negotiation of Discriminative Realities and Alleviation of Discriminative Injustice

Fundamental, then, to professional development as a situationally sensitive wayfarer is the act of *negotiating*. So acting involves not just necessary skills or (more broadly) *capabilities*, but also *understandings* of different sorts and *dispositions* to negotiate with others.

The *capabilities* must include those of communication—through contemporary communications media, as well as in face-to-face situations. They include, then, what are probably the most complex capabilities possessed by humankind: those of interpreting or giving meaning to communications from imperfectly known others; of anticipating the ways in which those others are likely to respond to particular communications from oneself; of crafting the adjudged most appropriate responses; of interpreting the feedback from one's interlocutors; and of adjusting one's next moves accordingly. Jürgen Habermas (1987) presents his version of an ideal late modernist society as one characterized by "communicative action," in which these various communicative acts are seen as being subject to perfection in the ongoing project of modernity. Jack Mezirow (1991) has picked up Habermas's lead by incorporating into his evolving theory of adult teaching and learning the notion of communicative expertise.

The capabilities also include those of contesting realities without that contestation leading to violence or closure—that is, the capabilities involved in exposing oppressive and unjust realities in such a way that their oppressive and unjust nature is undermined. This involves the decentering of those realities through the skilled use of irony, parody, metaphor, humor, and such like.

The *understandings* involved in the negotiation of realities in postmodernity must include those of the communicative processes themselves, in all of their contemporarily rich diversity. That diversity encompasses not only different modes (aural, visual, and so forth) and media (including print, electronic, direct, and multiple), but also different communicative intentions, approaches, responses, progressions, patterns, and such like—the substance of strong contemporary courses in communication. The understandings must also include, though, the sort of understandings that were noted in the foregoing five qualities of the situationally sensitive wayfarer: a reflexive understanding of oneself in the postmodern world; of what it means to assume responsibility for one's actions and to tolerate and respect difference; of what it means to understand and respond sympathetically to the particularities of lived events; and of what it means to respect others and their cultural realities.

The *dispositions* involved in the negotiation of realities in postmodernity may be seen as paralleling and enacting those of the capabilities and the understandings. Central is the disposition *to* negotiate with others. That disposition, though, builds upon and brings together the dispositions involved in the foregoing five characteristics of the situationally sensitive wayfarer: the (lifelong) disposition to act in a reflexively aware fashion, to act responsibly, to tolerate and respect difference, to act with sympathetic understanding and responsiveness to the particularities of lived events, and to respect others and their cultural realities.

The capabilities, understandings, and dispositions to so act are seen as directed to two general purposes: on the one hand, to the *recognition* of discriminative realities and, on the other hand, to the *alleviation* of discriminative injustice. Negotiating the recognition of discriminative realities involves the negotiation of the way in which realities are constructed or envisioned: what is assumed, what is foregrounded, what is diminished or marginalized, what is idealized, and so on. It also involves the recognition of discriminative injustice: what is to be accepted as unjust; the different types of injustice; the genesis, consequences, and import of those different types; and the interrelationships between them.

Finally here, then, negotiating the alleviation of discriminative injustice involves the negotiation of *actions* to be taken in alleviating identified discriminative injustice. Such action should, of course, be sensitive to the particularities of each such reality and the events in which it is embedded.

In an important sense, this last quality of the adult educator as a situationally sensitive wayfarer is the apogee of professional involvement and engagement *as* an adult educator. The way in which this quality is enacted draws upon and gives expression to each of the others. The quality may be seen, importantly, as grounded in human capabilities, but as not sufficiently defined by those capabilities, regardless of their depth and breadth. Indeed, it embraces no less a depth and breadth of understanding and of associated disposition to act through those capabilities and with that understanding. The notion of the adult educator as a situationally sensitive wayfarer is thus one that is both grounded in human capability (in that it is nothing without that capability) and transcendent of it (in that it is not sufficiently defined by it).

Such action is situational; and it is an act of understanding and a learning engagement in that situatedness. To the extent that the situated event changes only in and through the interactive engagement of the adult educator, to that extent it may also be seen as touching base with the notion of cycles or spirals of action research, involving adult educators in: understanding a situation, planning a response, acting in accordance with the plan, modifying their understanding from the experience of so acting and its consequences, modifying the action plan accordingly, and so on (Kemmis and McTaggart, 1988, p. 13; Lewin, 1952; Sanford, 1970; Zeichner, 1993). Such a notion, while helpful perhaps in focusing attention on possibilities, is far too simplistic and formulaic to represent satisfactorily the *modus operandi* of the situationally sensitive wayfarer. Events change constantly, as much or more from reasons outside the activities of the adult educators, as from them. A formulaic attention to action research cycles may rapidly lock an adult educator into a frame of situational *in*sensitivity, self-absorbed rigidity, and self-righteousness.

The notion of the situationally sensitive wayfarer is importantly that of adult educators with the capability, understanding, and disposition to move sensitively into radically unknown events. Those events may present *to* the adult educators involved, with little or no effective intervention from them (in contrast to the assumptions underpinning action research), or they may be brought about *by* the adult educators, responding to impulse, interest, or contingent opportunity. In any event, the qualities of the adult educator as a situationally sensitive wayfarer may usefully be seen thus as facilitating the *passage* of the individual into such radically unknown events.

Returning, finally, to the case studies introduced in Chapter 7, the most transparent exemplification of this concept may be seen in Helen's program to address the problem of sexism and racism in judicial judgments. The *nature* of that program builds, and builds strongly, on the capabilities, understandings, and dispositions to negotiate discriminative realities and the alleviation of discriminative injustice. The way in which Ian went about developing his program of learning (in distance education, and program design and management) illustrates this quality in actual *program development*. Ian effectively (if rather crudely) negotiated his way around unsatisfactory programs and into the sort of programs that he was seeking. Roger's later programming engagements for Unicom may, similarly, be seen as utilizing the practical knowledge of negotiation that is identified in this quality.

Learning/Curricular Implications

The capabilities, understandings, and dispositions of the adult educator as a situationally sensitive wayfarer may be seen, then, as encompassing a wide-ranging knowledge of the nature and complexity of the human condition, and of engagement with it. In an important sense, individuals with such knowledge may be seen as *roving diplomats* of the human condition—persons who draw upon their knowledge of the human condition to negotiate their way through it, in the cause of their vocation.

What sort of educational experiences or curriculum may contribute most fruitfully to the formation and professional development of such a person? Most centrally, I suggest, engagement *with* the human condition, across the range of its rich cultural diversity: in literature, art, drama, music, the sciences, and diverse sociopolitical, religious, and ethnic frameworks of belief. In other words, it is through *experiential learning* at its richest and fullest (see, e.g.: Boud and Griffin, 1987; Boud, Keogh, and Walker, 1985; Kolb, 1984, 1993; Usher and Edwards, 1994, pp. 196-206). That experiential engagement may be *direct*, through involvement with the lived events of different frameworks, or it may be simulated or vicarious (Andresen, Boud, and Cohen, 1995). In the case of simulated or vicarious engagement, an event is contrived to locate the learner in a situation which is an authentic interpretation of the situation-as-lived: through, for example, dramatic reconstruction, literature, interactive CD-ROM, film, video, story, theater, and so on.

In this regard, postmodernity problematizes the traditional modernist distinction between vicarious experience on the one hand (exposure to a representation of some other reality, such as through a picture, a story, or a film) and simulated experience on the other (as experience of active and interactive engagement in an event that is contrived as a representation of some other reality). Rather, all understanding is seen as based on active engagement—interaction with and in realities. Whether those realities are text-based, spoken, iconic, electronic, or whatever, the extent to which learners learn through or from them is importantly a function of the extent to which they engage actively and interactively with them.

There is an erosion, too, of the modernist distinction between direct experience and simulated experience. On the one hand, "direct" experience is increasingly mediated electronically; on the other, human experience is increasingly of simulacra—of images lacking direct or simple referents (Baudrillard, 1983). With that erosion there is denied the privileging of any mode of engagement over another. The modernist perception of the spoken word as primary, relative to the written as a pale representation of the spoken is strongly challenged (see especially, Derrida, 1976). Conversely, the modernist privileging of the printed word in formal communication, regulation, and argument (especially through the sciences) is eroded in postmodernity with the acceptance of oral history and cultural artifact as not necessarily any less interpretive than is written text. Indeed, the notion of text as different and separate from other interpretations is problematized. All reality in a sense becomes text, to be understood only through being interpreted or "read" as text. While the mass media appear to privilege images and the spoken word, the Internet actually privileges the written over the spoken word, but that privileging, too, is increasingly eroded with the introduction of imaging. If anything in this regard is privileged in postmodernity it is the value of a *diversity* of modes.

The curriculum of wide-ranging engagement with the complexities of the human condition is not one which lends itself to formulaic or universal circumscription. True to its context, it is open to infinitely multiple expressions. It should, though, be educationally true to the important qualities of its professional context—to the foregoing six qualities of the situationally sensitive wayfarer. What, then, is denied—if anything is denied—is engagement that does not contribute to the individual development of those qualities. But, just what those counter-educational experiences may be, must remain a matter for situationally sensitive negotiation to determine.

Postscript

In the Preface, I traced the academic path that had led me to the writing of this book. The process of crafting the ideas for the book itself I characterized there as an ongoing search for meaning—an exploratory journeying through postmodernity and its implications for adult education practice, research, and the formation and professional development of adult educators—in which the view of the scenery and the route itself are constantly changing, and in which the destination remains both indeterminate and illusory.

That characterization remains essentially true at this point in the journeying—the end of the book. My travels have taken me some distance from the conceptions of postmodernity with which I started, through some rich and varied scenery. The different pictures that I have painted selectively of that scenery in the course of the journeying are not all entirely concordant. I have, nevertheless, endeavored to paint a series of images in which each may certainly stand alone, but in the later images of which there are also crucial reflections back to those earlier in the book.

Each of the pictures should be seen as an expression of my interpretations of the scenery at that point in the journey. It should not be viewed as an attempt to provide a recipe for others to follow in their own travels through postmodernity. Practical morality in adult education practice—as in all areas of human engagement—must be, in any civilized sociality, a matter of individual existential choice and action—insofar as such notions are realizable in individual experience. The extent, then, to which any practitioner is influenced by the images presented in this volume is a matter for that individual. Neither are these images to be taken as attempts to produce a framework for adult education policy, although implications for policy clearly flow from them, insofar as they *do* present meaningful interpretations of the postmodern scenery.

What I do hope that readers have obtained, and that others will obtain, from this volume is the stimulus of different ideas with respect to the nature of postmodernity and its implications for adult education. Those ideas may do no more than trigger seemingly tangential thoughts, or generate opposition in outrage at what has been said or not said. In any event, it is hoped that they may encourage and facilitate, if not direct, readers in their own critical reflection upon their experiences in postmodern culture. The nature of those ideas depends, of course, as much or more on what each reader brings *to* their reading of this work, as it does on the work itself. The impact of the work must, similarly, be no less particular to each individual.

To where, then, does the journeying progress from here? That must remain an open and unanswered question for now. I did, though, posit in the Introduction to this book the fragility and contestability of the postmodern condition—noting that it is only contingently an increasingly contemporary reality. It is, therefore, mistaken to view it as *the* contemporary cultural condition. The postmodern condition is contested by forces of both modernity and premodernity, both of which seek to pull humanity back into frameworks of greater stability, certainty, predictability, and uniformity. To the extent, then, that we value the postmodern, it is a condition that must be actively maintained against those opposing currents. Yet, the very extent to which we *do* value it is by no means clear. The account presented in this volume is largely and on balance one of *hope* in the postmodern condition. That assessment is, however, by no means uncontested. The strength and the volume of argument against postmodernity in recent years amounts to a powerful opposition—one which should be considered and engaged, and which may yet prevail. Alternatively, postmodernity itself may give way to cultural influences not yet envisaged.

Notes

Preface

1. All works cited in this section are included in the Reference List under Bagnall.

Introduction

1. See, for example, the works by Lyotard (1979/1984a) and Foucault (1979) as primary works by major postmodern theorists touching on education.

   The mantle of postmodernity is claimed by many proponents of progressive theory such as "critical pedagogy" and emancipatory action research, for example Aronowitz and Giroux (1991), Cherryholmes (1983, 1985, 1988), Doherty, Graham, and Malek (1992), Giroux (1987, 1990, 1992), Hinkson (1991), Kanpol (1992), Kemmis (1991), Kincheloe (1993, 1995), McLaren (1986 1991a, 1991b), M. Peters and J. Marshall (1996), Szkudlarek (1993), Ulmer (1985), Wexler (1982, 1989), and Zavarzadeh (1991).

   Other general discussions of epistemology, curriculum and pedagogy include Alvarado and Ferguson (1983), Birch (1994), Corbett (1993), Doll (1989), P. Gilbert (1989), R. Gilbert (1992), B. Green (1993), Grossberg (1988), Hargreaves (1994), Kanpol (1992), Kenway, Bigum, and Fitzclarence (1993), Leicester and Taylor (1992), Letiche (1991), Levin and Clowes (1991), A. and C. Luke (1990), A. Luke and C.D. Baker (1989), Mckay (1994), B.K. Marshall (1992), Maxcy (1991), McKenzie (1992), Mehl (1994), Orr (1992), M. Peters (1992), Puhr (1992), Sedgwick (1994), Skeggs (1991), Slaughter (1989), and D. White (1989).

   Explicitly Foucaultian works include Ball (1990), Gore (1991), Hoskin (1990), Hunter (1992, 1994), and J.D. Marshall (1996).

   Particular educational engagements are described in a number of works, including those by D'Cruz (1994) and Middleton (1992).

   Educational technology is the focus of much postmodern theorizing, for example Bigum (1987), Bigum, Fitzclarence, and Kenway (1993), Bowers (1980, 1988), Danaher (1994), Ellsworth and Whatley (1990), Hlynka (1991), Hlynka and Belland (1991), Murphy (1988), and Damarin (1991), who also raises feminist issues, as do Brook (1994), Hooks (1993), Lather (1991), Middleton (1992), and Nicholson (1989, 1995).

   Education policy is discussed in postmodern contexts by D. Alexander (1992), Bates (1991), A. Green (1994), M. Peters and J.

Marshall (1996), and, from a sociological view, by Wexler (1987, 1992, 1993).

Usher and Edwards (1994) provide a sound and well-informed, albeit selective, literature review and articulation of educational implications.

Collected works include those by Gitlin (1994), M. Peters (1995a), and R. Smith and P. Wexler (1995).

2. But see, for example, the works by Bagnall (1994b-g, 1995a,b), Bright (1989), Briton (1996), Briton and Plumb (1992), Edwards (1993a), Finger (1990), Fox (1990), Garrick (1994), Jarvis (1996), Jennings (1995), Johnson-Riordan (1994), Letiche (1990), Mosely (1995), Pietrykowsky (1996), Randell (1993), Rhodes (1996), Stanage (1989, 1990), Usher (1989a), Usher, Bryant, and Johnston (1997), Usher and Edwards (1995), Westwood (1991a), and those in the volume edited by Wildemeersch and Jansen (1992).
3. For which see, for example, Bagnall (1991b) and Joad (1957).
4. For which see Bauman (1987), Docherty (1990), and Toulmin (1990).
5. For which see, for example, Derrida (1976), Eagleton (1983), Eco (1989), King (1993, 1994), and Lyotard (1984b).

Chapter 1: The Modernist Inheritance 1

1. For a start, perhaps, the following: Ahmed (1992), J.C. Alexander and P. Sztompka (1990), Bauman (1992), Beck, (1986/1992), Featherstone (1991), Fekete (1988), Harvey (1989), Jameson (1991), Lash (1990), Lash and Urry (1987), Lyotard (1979/1984a), Poster (1989), Rosenau (1992), Seidman and Wagner (1992), Siebers (1994), Smart (1992), and Vattimo (1988).

   For the more stoic reader the following may be added to the list: R. Appignanesi and C. Garrett (1995), Connor (1989), Crane (1994), Crook, Pakulski, and Waters (1992), Frow (1991), Kariel (1989), Milner (1991, Chapter 6), Naremore and Brantlinger (1991), Pefanis (1991), Puhr (1992), and Tester (1993).

   For those readers who are seeking less sympathetic accounts, the following may be preferred: Almond (1992), Borgmann (1992), Brodribb (1992), Callinicos (1990), Coady and Miller (1993), Cocks (1989), Etzioni-Halevy (1985), Fox (1989), Gellner (1992), Hampshire (1992), Hanson (1990), McKay (1994), Norris (1990, 1992), Phillipson (1989), D. White (1989), R. Williams (1989), Windschuttle (1997), and Wolin (1992).

2. See, for example: Anderson (1984), Bauman (1991a), Berman (1982), Calinescu (1977), Kemmis (1992), Lash (1990), T.W. Luke (1990), Scott (1990a), and Toulmin (1990).
3. The gender identification here is traditional and appropriate.
4. See, for example, Randall (1962) and Toulmin (1990).
5. For example: Bauman (1991a), Giddens (1990), Randall (1962), and Vattimo (1988).
6. For example: de Beauvoir (1958/1989), Doan (1994), Flax (1987), Fraser and Nicholson (1988), Jardine (1985), Moi (1988), M. Morris (1988), Nicolson (1990), Owens (1983), Weedon (1987), Yates (1992), and Young (1990).
7. With the notable exception, of course, of politicians, whose utterances were constrained by other means: the fear of public sanction, rejection by party re-selection committees, and so on.

Chapter 2: The Modernist Inheritance 2

1. See, for example: Elias and Merriam (1980) for an overview; Knowles (1980) and Rogers (1969) for a focus on humanism; Hirst (1983), O'Hear (1981), Paterson (1979), and R.S. Peters (1977) for a more strictly liberal focus; Bergevin (1967), Dewey (1916, 1938), and Lindeman (1961) for progressive pragmatism; Gagné (1977) and Skinner (1968) for behaviorism; and Brameld (1971), Dennis and Eaton (1980), and Freire (1972) for a radical focus.
2. Borrowing the metaphor from Newman (1979).
3. See, for example, the "black book" (Jensen, Liveright, and Hallenbeck, 1964) and the series of *handbooks*, especially those from 1960 (Knowles, 1960), 1970 (R.M. Smith, G.F. Aker, and J.R. Kidd, 1970), and 1980 (Boone, Shearon, White, and Associates, 1980; Boyd, Apps, and Associates, 1980; Charters and Associates, 1981; Grabowski and Associates, 1981; Knox and Associates, 1980; Kreitlow and Associates, 1981; Long, Hiemstra, and Associates, 1980; J.M. Peters and Associates, 1980).
4. For this last point, see, for example: Dave (1976), Faure et al. (1972), Fragnière (1976), Lengrand (1970), Peterson et al. (1982), and the Senate Standing Committee on Employment, Education and Training (1991).

Chapter 3: Postmodernity 1

1. See, for example: Bauman (1992), Jameson (1991), and Lyotard (1984b).

2. This notion permeates the work of Friedrich Nietzsche, but is most strongly developed in his posthumously published (1901), *Der wille zur macht* (Nietzsche, 1901/1974b). It underpins the work of Ortega y Gasset (1940/1962), who coined the term *perspectivism* (Kilgore, 1972). Quine (1985, 1990), Karl Mannhein (1952), Thomas Kuhn (1970), and Paul Feyerabend (1978) have each developed strong epistemological arguments through its articulation.
3. See, for example: Gilligan (1982), Noddings (1984), Seidler (1991), and Walkerdine (1988).
4. The notion of "discourse" here is that of linguistically mediated frameworks of belief, meaning, and value—including their attendant concepts and myths—within which individual identity is created. It is what James Gee (1990, pp. 143-145) refers to as "Discourse" (with an upper-case "D")—thereby separating it conceptually from "discourse" (with a lower-case "d"), identifying the (derivative) structure and form of linguistic exchanges. From the perspective of the individual, Gee summarizes the idea of Discourse as follows:

   > A *Discourse* is a socially accepted association among ways of using language, of thinking, feeling, believing, valuing, and of acting that can be used to identify oneself as a member of a socially meaningful group or 'social network,' or to signal (that one is playing) a socially meaningful 'role.'

5. The point here is not that individuals are in any sense naturally or necessarily evil, but that the modernist notion of individual identity cannot be reconciled with events such as the Holocaust, as George Steiner (1970) has articulated most graphically. Zygmunt Bauman (1989) goes further, in arguing that the horrors of the Holocaust actually epitomized the modernist commitment to human perfectibility and that they may be understood only *as* a part of the modernist project—not as an aberration of modernity, but as its realization.
6. See, for example: Baudrillard (1988), Benhabib (1992), Cascardi (1992), Grossberg (1988), and Lash and Friedman (1992).

Chapter 4: Postmodernity 2

1. For further work on the notion of dedifferentiation, refer especially to the works of Baudrillard (Poster, 1988), Derrida (Kamuf, 1991), Eco (1990), Hawkes (1977), and Saussure (1916/1974).

2. See, for example, Derrida's (1994) deconstruction of Marx's use of the metaphor of spectral haunting.

Chapter 6: Eternal Ambivalence

1. The skeptical reader may, though, like to digress at this point into an exploration of Lyotard's critique of pedagogical dialogue (see Sedgwick, 1994).
2. Verner (1962, 1975).
3. See, for example, Elias and Merriam (1980) and Jarvis (1995).
4. Competency Based Training.

Chapter 7: Horsehair in The Undies

1. The situatedness tension identifies the extent to which belief is particular to the frameworks of preordinate perception and belief in which it is generated. The *transcendent* or modernist pole sees truth, goodness, beauty, authenticity, and so on as qualities of situations, regardless of the frameworks of belief in which they are generated. The *particularized* or postmodern pole recognizes belief as being situated in particular contexts or events. Truth, goodness, beauty, authenticity, and so on are therefore qualities of events, including (and importantly) the frameworks of belief that inform them and the identities of the individuals realizing and articulating the frameworks.
2. Pennington and Green (1976).
3. The ambiguity tension identifies the extent to which there are good grounds for accepting alternative views of what is good, true, beautiful, authentic, and so on. The *singular* or modernist pole accepts the in-principle existence of a single ultimately correct interpretation of every reality. The *plural* or postmodern pole recognizes the potential incommensurability of interpretations across different frameworks of belief, and accepts the existence of a plurality of alternative interpretations of any given reality.
4. The determination tension identifies the extent to which individual identity is determined as a plurality of partial identities. The *holistic* or modernist pole sees individual identity as integrated into a coherent unity, deriving from the individual's inherited potential to be a person of a particular sort. The *fragmented* or postmodern pole sees individual identity as fragmented among a plurality of partial identities, identity

being only provisionally determined and underdetermined, and therefore open to the contingent addition of further partial identities.

5. The control tension identifies the extent to which individual action may be seen as deriving from the discourses in which those actions are embedded. The *autonomous* or modernist pole sees individuals as autonomous monads, empowered by their command over their realities. The *embedded* or postmodern pole sees individual action constrained and restrained by the discourses in which individual (fragmented) identity is embedded.
6. This comment refers to the political push by Australian educational planners in government and unions for a system of vocational education and training (VET) that is competency-based (Chappell, Gonczi, and Hager, 1995; C. Collins, 1993; R. Harris, H. Guthrie, B. Hobart, and D. Lundberg, 1995).
7. The homogeneity tension identifies the extent to which sociality is not strongly structured into discrete or lasting autonomous realms. The *differentiated* or modernist pole sees sociality as divided into distinct and lasting spheres or realms of social practice: domains of discourse, social institutions, social classes, organizations, occupations, and individual life roles. The *dedifferentiated* or postmodern pole sees sociality as an unstable, shifting, and unpredictable miasma of social relationships, with social differentiation constantly open to, and the subject of, challenge and reformulation or elimination.
8. The temporality tension identifies the extent to which individual and collective action in cultural formation and interpretation is focused on the immediate situation, the here-and-now. The *developmentalist* or modernist pole defines a temporal perspective that locates the presentness, the here-and-now, in an historically meaningful, developmental, or evolutionary sequence. The *presentist* or postmodern pole defines a temporal perspective that focuses strictly on the here-and-now: the contingent demands, interests, problems, concerns, or issues of the present, as if they were ahistorical events.
9. The Training Reform Agenda is the generic term given to the Australian Federal Government initiative—in cooperation with the state and territory governments—starting in about 1988, to improve the economic performance of Australian industry through more relevant and appropriate vocational education and training. It embraces the requirement for a competency-based approach to all vocational education and training (Australian

National Training Authority, 1994; Dawkins and Holding, 1987; W. Hall, 1995).

10. ANTA is the Australian National Training Authority, established by the Federal Government in 1992 to oversee the development of vocational education and training through the implementation of the National Training Reform Agenda.
11. Competency standards are developed and periodically reviewed through a formal process for each specific field of vocational practice (such as VET itself). Their use in curriculum design and learning assessment is mandated for registered VET programs teaching into that area of vocational practice.

Chapter 9: Fashioning Educative Difference

1. See, for example: Candy and Harris, 1990; Hager and Gonczi, 1991; R. McL. Harris, G. Barnes, and B. Haines, 1991; Masters and McCurry, 1990; Pope, 1983; Tuxworth, 1989; Wolf, 1989.
2. See, for example: Ashworth and Saxton, 1990; Bull, 1985; Chappell, 1989; Field, 1991; Hyland, 1992; Porter, Rizvi, Knight, and Lingard, 1992; Stenhouse, 1975; Stevenson, 1993.

Chapter 10: Fanning The Flames

1. See, for example: Geertz, 1973; Spindler and Spindler, 1987; Van Manen, 1990.
2. "Political," here, in the previously articulated sense of the intersubjective relationships of power, control, and authority (Gramsci, 1971; Johnson, 1988).
3. For which see, for example: Bogdan and Biklen (1992); Denzin and Lincoln (1994); E. Jacob (1987); Neville, Willis, and Edwards (1994); Patton (1980); S.I. Taylor and R. Bogdan (1984).
4. For which last, see Brown (1977).
5. Rejecting, here, not so much the nominalist aspects of William of Occam's philosophy, as its more limited empiricist aspects (for which see Moody, 1965).
6. See, for example: Aronowitz and Giroux (1991); Best and Kellner (1991); Giroux and Simon (1984); Gitlin (1994); Kellner (1988); Kincheloe (1993); McLaren (1991b); Wexler (1987, 1992).

Chapter 11: The Situationally Sensitive Wayfarer

1. See, for example: Aronowitz and Giroux (1991), Bigum (1987), Giroux (1990), Giroux and McLaren (1987, 1989), Giroux and

Simon (1984), Kanpol (1992), Kellner (1988), Kincheloe (1993), Maxcy (1991), McLaren (1991a, 1991b), and Szkudlarek (1993). Other theorists whose work has close links to that of Giroux include Apple (e.g., 1986) and Wexler (e.g., 1989).

2. 'Ideology' here being used in the sense of a normative commitment to a particular vision of what is right and good (following, e.g.: Leach, 1988, p. 2; Seliger, 1974, pp. 119–120).
3. By, for example: Crook (1991), Norris (1990), and Wellmer (1991).
4. See, for example: Bauman (1991b), Borgmann (1992), and Callinicos (1990).
5. See, for example: Dahl, 1993; Hayek, 1960; Mendus, 1989; Mill, 1859/1929; Popper, 1977; Pring, 1992.
6. These knowledge types being constituted, more or less, as follows: (1) *theoretical*—descriptive and predictive knowledge of realities; propositional knowledge; knowledge "that": the evaluative criterion for which is truth or veracity; (2) *ethical*—normative or moral knowledge of what *should* be, or should be done; part of dispositional knowledge; knowledge "why": the evaluative criteria for which are goodness or rightness; (3) *technical*—manipulative knowledge, both manual (of physical realities) and intellectual (of symbols); procedural or operational knowledge and part of dispositional knowledge; knowledge "how": the criteria for which are (variously) formulaic conformity, problem resolution, or situational change; (4) *existential*—knowledge of self and one's relationships to other realities; knowledge of being and identity: the evaluative criteria for which are authenticity and meaning; and (5) *aesthetic*—knowledge of beauty, rhythm, and harmony: the evaluative criterion for which is form.

Works Cited

Achinstein, P. (1968). *Concepts of science: A philosophical analysis*. Baltimore, MD: Johns Hopkins.

Adler, M.J. (1959). *A general introduction to the great books and to liberal education*. Chicago: Encyclopaedia Britannica.

Adorno, T.W., & Horkheimer, M. (1979). *Dialectic of enlightenment*. London: Verso.

Ahmed, A.S. (1992). *Postmodernism and Islam: Predicament and promise*. London: Routledge.

Alexander, D. (1992). Discussion documents as neonarratives. *Journal of Education Policy*, *7*(1), 71–81.

Alexander, J.C., & Sztompka, P. (Eds.). (1990). *Rethinking progress: Movements, forces and ideas at the end of the twentieth century*. Winchester, MA: Unwin Hyman.

Allen, J. (1992). Fordism and modern industry. In J. Allen, P. Brahm, & P. Lewis (Eds.), *Political and economic forms of modernity* (pp. 229–274). Cambridge, UK: Polity.

Allen, J., Brahm, P., & Lewis, P. (1992). *Political and economic forms of modernity*. Cambridge, UK: Polity.

Almond, B. (1992, October 16). An anchor for the ego. *The Times Higher Education Supplement*, *1041*, 15 & 17.

Alvarado, M., & Ferguson, B. (1983). The curriculum, media and discursivity. *Screen*, *24*(3), 20–34.

Anderson, P. (1984). Modernity and revolution. *New Left Review*, *144*, 96–113.

Andresen, L., Boud, D., & Cohen, R. (1995). Experience-based learning. In G. Foley (Ed.), *Understanding adult education and training* (pp. 207–219). St. Leonards, New South Wales: Allen & Unwin.

Antonio, R. (1989). The normative foundations of emancipatory theory: Evolutionary versus pragmatic perspectives. *American Journal of Sociology*, *94*, 721–748.

Appignanesi, L. (Ed.). (1989). *Postmodernism: ICA documents*. London: Free Association Books.

Appignanesi, R., & Garrett, C. (1995). *Postmodernism for beginners*. Cambridge, UK: Icon.

Apple, M.W. (1986). *Teachers and texts: A political economy of class and gender relations in education*. New York: Routledge & Kegan Paul.

Arac, J. (1987). *Critical genealogies, Historical situations for postmodern literary studies*. New York: Columbia University Press.

Aronowitz, S., & Giroux, H.A. (1991). *Postmodern education: Politics, culture and social criticism*. Minneapolis, MN: University of

Minnesota Press.

Ashworth, P.D., & Saxton, J. (1990). On 'competence'. *Journal of Further and Higher Education, 14*(2), 3–25.

Australian National Training Authority. (1994). *Description of the National Training Reform Agenda.* Brisbane, Queensland: Author.

Ayer, A.J. (Ed.). (1959). *Logical positivism.* Glencoe, IL: Free Press.

Bagnall, R.G. (1975). Study-research groups as a method of teaching the natural sciences. *International Journal of University Adult Education, 14*(2), 21–41.

Bagnall, R.G. (1976). Teaching through research: A new technique of teaching natural science subjects. *Continuing Education in New Zealand, 8*(2), 61–67.

Bagnall, R.G. (1978a). *An experiment in adult instruction: The integration of education and research* (Department of University Extension Monograph in Adult Education No. 2.). Wellington, New Zealand: Victoria University.

Bagnall, R.G. (1978b). University extension in North America: Some patterns and issues with implications for New Zealand practice. *Continuing Education in New Zealand, 10*(2), 19–43.

Bagnall, R.G. (1978c). Principles of adult education in the design and management of instruction. *Australian Journal of Adult Education, 18*(1), 19–27.

Bagnall, R.G. (1979). Adult education in the sciences: An examination of the educational imperative and available instructional processes. *Continuing Education in New Zealand, 11*(1), 33–44.

Bagnall, R.G. (1980). Descriptive concepts in adult education: Could classification split the millstone? *Proceedings of the Twenty-First Annual Adult Education Research Conference* (pp. 11–16). Vancouver, British Columbia: Adult Education Research Conference.

Bagnall, R.G. (1982). Scientific research, design, and evaluation paradigms in the training of adult educators. In N. Haines (Ed.), *Canberra papers in continuing education: New Series 2* (pp. 1–22). Canberra, Australian Capital Territory: The Australian National University Centre for Continuing Education.

Bagnall, R.G. (1983a). An analysis of Verner's classification of educational processes. Part 1: The distinction between methods and techniques. *Studies in Continuing Education, 9*, 88–105.

Bagnall, R.G. (1983b). An analysis of Verner's classification of educational processes. Part 2: Methods. *Studies in Continuing Education, 9*, 106–119.

Bagnall, R.G. (1983c). An analysis of conceptual and terminological confusion in adult education. In R.G. Bagnall (Ed.), *Canberra papers in continuing education: New series 3* (pp. 59–72). Canberra, Australian Capital Territory: The Australian National University Centre for Continuing Education.

Bagnall, R.G. (1983d). The nature of research in adult education and its relationship to practice in Australia. In C. Crane & A. Davies (Eds.), *Adult education: Perspectives and practices* (pp. 49–61). Canberra, Australian Capital Territory: Australian Association of Adult Education.

Bagnall, R.G. (1983e). Adult education research in Australia: The harsh reality. In R.G. Bagnall & R.J. Clark (Eds.), *New England monographs in continuing education: Number 1* (pp. 21–37). Armidale, New South Wales: University of New England Department of Continuing Education.

Bagnall, R.G. (1987a). An examination of 'content' in adult education events. *Australian Journal of Adult Education, 27*(1), 13–16, 24.

Bagnall, R.G. (1987b). Enhancing self-direction in adult education: A possible trap for enthusiasts. *Discourse, 8*(1), 90–100.

Bagnall, R.G. (1987c). Adult education as manipulation: Three bases of authoritative injustice. *New Zealand Journal of Adult Learning, 19*, 51–58.

Bagnall, R.G. (1988a). Reconceptualising and revaluing distance education through the perspective of self-direction. In D. Sewart & J.S. Daniel (Eds.), *Developing distance education* (pp. 93–95). Oslo, Norway: International Council for Distance Education.

Bagnall, R.G. (1988b). Comprehensive surveys of adult education: A recipe for ossifying provision? *Studies in Continuing Education, 10*(1), 59–68.

Bagnall, R.G. (1988c). Participation in adult education: Key categories in programme evaluation. *Indian Journal of Adult Education, 49*(2), 27–34.

Bagnall, R.G. (1989a). Educational distance from the perspective of self-direction: An analysis. *Open Learning, 4*(1), 21–26.

Bagnall, R.G. (1989b). Educating adults and adult self-education. Who does what? *Australian Journal of Adult Education, 29*(1), 22–28.

Bagnall, R.G. (1989c). Participation by adults: Some traps for development educators. *Adult Education and Development, 32*, 23–28.

Bagnall, R.G. (1989d). Researching participation in adult education: A case of quantified distortion. *International Journal of Lifelong Education, 8*, 251–260.

Bagnall, R.G. (1989e). To participate voluntarily in adult education. *Studies in the Education of Adults, 21*(1), 41–56.

Bagnall, R.G. (1989f). Gossamer in the cyclone or pissing into the wind? A critique of Nicolas Haines's philosophy for continuing education. In M. Brändle (Ed.), *Fanning the winds of change: Crisis or opportunity* (pp. 12–28). Canberra, Australian Capital Territory: Australian Association of Adult and Community Education.

Bagnall, R.G. (1990a). Lifelong education: The institutionalisation of an illiberal and regressive ideology? *Educational Philosophy and Theory, 22*(1), 1–7.

Bagnall, R.G. (1990b). The intrinsic nature of educational goals: A critique. *International Journal of Lifelong Education, 9,* 31–48.

Bagnall, R.G. (1990c). Education beyond macro-level needs: A critique of Boshier's model for the future. *International Journal of Lifelong Education, 9,* 317–329.

Bagnall, R.G. (1990d). On the normative aspects of adult education taxonomies. *Adult Education Quarterly, 40,* 229–236.

Bagnall, R.G. (1990e). Skills training for adult educators: Necessary but not sufficient. *International Journal of University Adult Education, 29,* 57–67.

Bagnall, R.G. (1990f). Vocational education for Australian adult educators: An argument for a liberal approach. *Australian Journal of Adult and Community Education, 30*(1), 22–29.

Bagnall, R.G. (1991a). The intrinsic nature of educational goals: A reply to Lawson. *International Journal of Lifelong Education, 10,* 237–238.

Bagnall, R.G. (1991b). Relativism, objectivity, liberal adult education and multiculturalism. *Studies in the Education of Adults, 23*(1), 61–84.

Bagnall, R.G. (1992a). Continuing education in the Australian university: A critique of contract-based curriculum development. *Studies in Continuing Education, 14*(1), 67–89.

Bagnall, R.G. (1992b). Contractualism: The modern alternative to liberal adult education in the Australian university. In C. Duke (Ed.), *Liberal adult education—Perspectives and projects* (pp. 53–66). Warwick, UK: Continuing Education Research Centre, University of Warwick.

Bagnall, R.G. (1992c). The philosophical context of environmental continuing education. Does the content make a difference? In R. Harris & P. Willis (Eds.), *Striking a balance: Adult and community education in Australia towards 2000* (pp. 253–263). Adelaide, South Australia: Centre for Human Resource Studies, University of South Australia and South Australian Branch of the Australian Association of Adult & Community Education.

Bagnall, R.G. (1994a). Performance indicators and outcomes as measures of educational quality: A cautionary critique.

International Journal of Lifelong Education, 13, 19–32.

Bagnall, R.G. (1994b). Continuing education in postmodernity: Four semantic tensions. *International Journal of Lifelong Education, 13,* 265–279.

Bagnall, R.G. (1994c). Responding to the postmodern: Continuing education programming in uncertainty. *Canadian Journal of University Continuing Education, 20*(1), 43–62.

Bagnall, R.G. (1994d). Postmodernity and its implications for adult education practice. *Studies in Continuing Education, 16*(1), 1–18.

Bagnall, R.G. (1994e). Pluralising continuing education and training in a postmodern world: Whither competence? *Australian and New Zealand Journal of Vocational Education Research,* 2(2), 18–39.

Bagnall, R.G. (1994f). *Conceptualising adult education for research and development: Selected critiques.* Brisbane, Queensland: Centre for Skill Formation Research and Development, Griffith University.

Bagnall, R.G. (1994g). Adults and education in a postmodern world: What relevance the family? In *Adults, education, families: Papers from the 34th National Conference of the AAACE* (pp. 7–20). Sydney, New South Wales: New South Wales Branch of the Australian Association of Adult & Community Education.

Bagnall, R.G. (1995a). Discriminative justice and responsibility in postmodernist adult education. *Adult Education Quarterly, 45,* 79–94.

Bagnall, R.G. (1995b). *Issues and implications in the epistemology and ethics of adult education events: Selected critiques.* Brisbane, Queensland: Centre for Skill Formation Research and Development, Griffith University.

Bagnall, R.G. (in press). Moral education in a postmodern world: Continuing professional education. *Journal of Moral Education.*

Ball, S.J. (Ed.). (1990). *Foucault and education: Disciplines and knowledge.* New York: Routledge.

Barthes, R. (1973). *Mythologies.* St. Albans, London: Paladin.

Bates, R. (1991, November). *Schooling the future: An investigation of schools, students and postmodern culture.* Paper presented at the Annual Conference of the Australian Association for Research in Education. Surfers Paradise, Queensland. Hawthorn, Victoria: Australian Council for Educational Research.

Baudrillard, J. (1983). The ecstasy of communication. In H. Foster (Ed.), *The anti-aesthetic: Essays on postmodern culture* (pp. 126–134). Port Townsend, WA: Bay.

Baudrillard, J. (1988). Simulacra and simulations. In M. Poster (Ed.), *Jean Baudrillard: Selected writings* (pp. 166–184). Cambridge, UK:

Polity.

Bauman, Z. (1987). *Legislators and interpreters: On modernity, postmodernity and intellectuals.* Cambridge, UK: Polity.

Bauman, Z. (1989). *Modernity and the holocaust.* Ithaca, NY: Cornell University Press.

Bauman, Z. (1991a). *Modernity and ambivalence.* Cambridge, UK: Polity.

Bauman, Z. (1991b). *Postmodernity: Chance or menace?* Lancaster, UK: Centre for The Study of Cultural Values.

Bauman, Z. (1992). *Intimations of postmodernity.* New York: Routledge.

Bauman, Z. (1993). *Postmodern ethics.* Oxford: Blackwell.

Bauman, Z. (1995). *Life in fragments: Essays in postmodern morality.* Oxford: Blackwell.

Beck, U. (1992). *Risk society: Towards a new modernity* (M. Ritter, Trans.). London: Sage. (Original work published 1986.)

Bell, D. (1979). *The cultural contradictions of capitalism* (2nd ed.). London: Heineman.

Bell, D. (1980). *Sociological journeys: Essays 1960–1980.* London: Heineman.

Benhabib, S. (1992). *Situating the self: Gender, community and postmodernism in contemporary ethics.* Oxford: Polity.

Bennett, T. (1991). Working in the present. *Australian Universities Review, 34*(1), 14–16.

Bergevin, P. (1967). *A philosophy for adult education.* New York: Seabury.

Berman, M. (1982). *All that is solid melts into air: The experience of modernity.* New York: Verso.

Best, S., & Kellner, D. (1991). *Postmodern theory: Critical investigations.* New York: Guilford.

Bigum, C. (1987). *Without walls.* Geelong, Victoria: Deakin University Press.

Bigum, C., Fitzclarence, L., & Kenway, J. (1993). That's edutainment: Restructuring universities and the Open Learning Initiative. *Australian Universities Review, 36*(2), 21–27.

Birch, D. (1994). Editorial: Teaching the postmodern. *Southern Review, 27*(3), 248–251.

Black, J. (1970). *The dominion of man: The search for ecological responsibility.* Edinburgh, Scotland: Edinburgh University Press.

Blid, H. (1990). *Education by the people: Study circles.* Stockholm, Sweden: Arbetarnas Bildnings Forbund.

Bloom, A. (1987). *The closing of the American mind.* New York: Simon & Schuster.

Bloom, H. (1994). *The western canon: The books and school of the ages*. New York: Harcourt Brace.

Boal, A. (1979). *Theater of the oppressed* (A.C. & M.-O.L. McBride, Trans.). London: Pluto.

Bogdan, R., & Biklen, S. (1992). *Qualitative research in education* (2nd ed.). Boston: Allyn & Bacon.

Boje, D.M. (1994). Organisational storytelling: The struggles of pre-modern, modern and postmodern organisational learning discourses. *Management Learning, 25*(3), 433–461.

Boone, E.J. (1970). The Cooperative Extension Service. In R.M. Smith, G.F. Aker, & J.R. Kidd (Eds.), *Handbook of adult education* (pp. 265–281). New York: Macmillan.

Boone, E.J., Shearon, R.W., White, E.E., & Associates. (1980). *Servicing personal and community needs through adult education*. San Francisco: Jossey-Bass.

Borgmann, A. (1992). *Crossing the postmodern divide*. Chicago: University of Chicago Press.

Boshier, R. (1973). Educational participation and dropout: A theoretical model. *Adult Education, 23*, 255–282.

Boshier, R. (1978). Adult education programme planning and instructional design. *Continuing Education in New Zealand, 10*(1), 33–50.

Boud, D., & Griffin, V. (Eds.). (1987). *Appreciating adults learning: From the learners' perspective*. London: Kogan Page.

Boud, D., Keogh, R., & Walker, D. (Eds.). (1985). *Reflection: Turning experience into learning*. London: Kogan Page.

Boughton, B. (1994). In search of the other 'Great Tradition': Communists and socialists in Australian adult education. In *Adults, education, families: Papers from the 34th National Conference of the Australian Association of Adult and Community Education* (pp. 21–32). University of Technology, Sydney, New South Wales: New South Wales Branch of the Australian Association of Adult and Community Education.

Bove, P. (Ed.). (1980). A supplement on irony. *Boundary 2: A Journal of Postmodern Literature and Culture, 9*(1), 1–3.

Bowen, J., & Hobson, P.R. (1987). *Theories of education: Studies of significant innovation in western educational thought*. Brisbane, Queensland: Jacaranda Wiley.

Bowers, C.A. (1980). Ideological continuities in technicism, liberalism, and education. *Teachers College Record, 81*, 293–321.

Bowers, C.A. (1988). *The cultural dimensions of educational computing: Understanding the non-neutrality of technology*. New York: Teachers College Press.

Boyd, R.D., Apps, J.W., & Associates. (1980). *Redefining the discipline of adult education.* San Francisco: Jossey-Bass.

Boyle, J.M., Jr., Grisez, G., & Tollefsen, O. (1976). *Free choice: A self-referential argument.* Notre Dame, IN: University of Notre Dame Press.

Boyne, R., & Rattansi, A. (1990). The theory and politics of postmodernism: By way of an introduction. In R. Boyne & A. Rattansi (Eds.), *Postmodernism and society* (pp. 1–45). London: Macmillan.

Brameld, T. (1971). *Patterns of educational philosophy: Divergence and convergence in culturalogical perspective.* New York: Holt, Rinehart & Winston.

Braverman, H. (1994). The real meaning of Taylorism. In F. Fischer & C. Sirianni (Eds.), *Critical studies in organization and bureaucracy* (rev. ed.) (pp. 55–61). Philadelphia: Temple University Press.

Briggs, A. (Ed.). (1959). *Chartist studies.* London: Macmillan St. Martins.

Bright, B. (1989). *Theory and practice in the study of adult education: The epistemological debate.* London: Routledge.

Briton, D. (1996). *The modern practice of adult education: A postmodern critique.* Albany, NY: State University of New York Press.

Briton, D., & Plumb, D. (1992). Vaclav Havel, postmodernism, and modernity: The implications for adult education in the West. *Proceedings of the 33rd Annual Adult Education Research Conference* (pp. 19–23). Saskatoon: University of Saskatchewan.

Brodribb, S. (1992). *Nothing Mat(t)ers: A feminist critique of postmodernism.* Melbourne, Victoria: Spinifex.

Brook, B. (1994). Speculative feminist fictions: Teaching in postmodernism. *Southern Review, 27,* 276–284.

Brown, R.H. (1977). *A poetic for sociology.* Cambridge, UK: Cambridge University Press.

Bull, H. (1985). The use of behavioural objectives: A moral issue? *Journal of Further and Higher Education, 9*(3), 74–80.

Burbules, N.C. (1986). Radical educational cynicism and radical educational skepticism. In D. Nyberg (Ed.), *Philosophy of education: 1985* (Proceedings of the 41st Annual Meeting of the Philosophy of Education Society, 12–15 April 1985) (pp. 201–205). Normal, IL: Philosophy of Education Society, Illinois State University.

Burgin, V. (1986). *The end of art theory: Criticism and postmodernity.* London: Macmillan.

Calinescu, M. (1977). *Faces of modernity: Avant-garde, decadence, kitsch*. Bloomington, IN: Indiana University Press.

Callinicos, A. (1990). *Against postmodernism*. New York: St. Martins.

Candy, P.C. (1986). The eye of the beholder: Metaphor in adult education research. *International Journal of Lifelong Education, 5*, 87–111.

Candy, P.C. (1991). *Self-direction for lifelong learning: A comprehensive guide to theory and practice*. San Francisco: Jossey-Bass.

Candy, P., & Harris, R.McL. (1990). Implementing competency based vocational education: A view from within. *Journal of Further and Higher Education, 14*(2), 38–58.

Carnap, R. (1962). *Logical foundations of probability*. Chicago: University of Chicago Press.

Cascardi, A.J. (1992). *The subject of modernity*. New York: Cambridge University Press.

Castoriadis, C. (1989). The imaginary: Creation in the social-historical domain. In L. Appignanesi (Ed.), *Postmodernism: ICA documents* (pp. 39–43). London: Free Association Books.

Catley, B., & Rann, M. (1992). Government's role in adult education and training. In R. Harris & P. Willis (Eds.), *Striking a balance: Adult and community education in Australia towards 2000* (pp. 35–45). Adelaide, South Australia: Centre for Human Resource Studies, University of South Australia.

Chappell, C. (1989). Competency issues in TAFE teacher training. *Australian Journal of TAFE Research and Development, 7*(1), 21–28.

Chappell, C., Gonczi, A., & Hager, P. (1995). Competency-based education. In G. Foley (Ed.), *Understanding adult education and training* (pp. 175–187). St. Leonards, New South Wales: Allen & Unwin.

Charters, A.N., & Associates. (1981). *Comparing adult education worldwide*. San Francisco: Jossey-Bass.

Chené, A. (1983). The concept of autonomy in adult education: A philosophical discussion. *Adult Education Quarterly, 34*, 38–47.

Cherryholmes, C. (1983). Knowledge, power and discourse in social studies education. *Boston University Journal of Education, 165*, 341–358.

Cherryholmes, C. (1985). Theory and practice: On the role of empirically based theory for critical practice. *American Journal of Education, 94*(1), 39–70.

Cherryholmes, C. (1988). *Power and criticism: Poststructural investigations in education*. New York: Teachers' College Press.

Chia, R. (1995). From modern to postmodern organisational analysis.

Organization Studies, 16, 579–604.

Clark, B.R. (1958). *The marginality of adult education* (Notes and essays on adult education No. 20). Chicago: Center for the Study of Liberal Education for Adults.

Coady, T., & Miller, S. (1993). The humanities without humans. *Meanjin, 53*, 391–399.

Cocks, J. (1989). *The oppositional imagination: Feminism, critique and political theory*. London: Routledge.

Cohen, B. (1981). *Education and the individual*. London: George Allen & Unwin.

Collins, C. (Ed.). (1993). *Competencies: The competencies debate in Australian education and training*. Canberra, Australian Capital Territory: Australian College of Education.

Collins, M. (1991). *Adult education as vocation: A critical role for the adult educator*. London: Routledge.

Congalton, A.A. (1969). *Status and prestige in Australia*. Melbourne, Victoria: Cheshire.

Connor, S. (1989). *Postmodernist culture: An introduction to theories of the contemporary*. Oxford: Basil Blackwell.

Corbett, J. (1993). Postmodernism and the 'special needs' metaphors. *Oxford Review of Education, 19*, 547–553.

Crane, D. (Ed.). (1994). *The sociology of culture: Emerging theoretical perspectives*. Oxford: Blackwell.

Crook, S. (1991). *Modernist radicalism and its aftermath*. London: Routledge.

Crook, S., Pakulski, J., & Waters, M. (1992). *Postmodernization: Changes in advanced society*. London: Sage.

Dahl, R.A. (1993). Pluralism. In J. Kreiger (Ed.), *Oxford companion to politics of the world* (pp. 704–707). New York: Oxford University Press.

Damarin, S.K. (1991). Feminist unthinking and educational technology. *Educational and Training Technology International, 28*, 111–119.

Danaher, P.A. (1994). Open learning: Problems and potentials. *Social Alternatives, 13* (3/4), 23–26.

Darkenwald, G.G., & Merriam, S.B. (1982). *Adult education: Foundations of practice*. New York: Harper & Row.

Dave, R.H. (Ed.). (1976). *Foundations of lifelong education*. Oxford: Pergamon.

Davis, L.H. (1979). *Theory of action*. Englewood Cliffs, NJ: Prentice-Hall.

Dawkins, J.S., & Holding, A.C. (1987). *Skills formation in Australia*. Canberra, Australian Capital Territory: Australian Government

Publishing Service.

D'Cruz, G. (1994). Representing the serial killer: 'Postmodern' pedagogy in performance studies. *Southern Review, 27*, 323–332.

Dean, G.J., & Dowling, W.D. (1987). Community development: An adult education model. *Adult Education Quarterly, 37*, 78–89.

de Beauvoir, S. (1989). *The second sex* (H.M. Parshley, Trans.). New York: Vintage. (Original work published in translation 1953.)

Dennis, L.J., & Eaton, W.E. (Eds.). (1980). *George S. Counts: Educator for a new age.* Carbondale, IL: Southern Illinois University Press.

Denzin, N.K., & Lincoln, Y.S. (Eds.). (1994). *Handbook of qualitative research.* New York: Sage.

Derrida, J. (1976). *Of grammatology* (G.C. Spivak, Trans.). Baltimore: Johns Hopkins University Press.

Derrida, J. (1994). *The spectres of Marx: The state of the debt, the work of mourning, and the new international* (P. Kamuf, Trans.). New York: Routledge.

Dewey, J. (1916). *Democracy and education.* New York: Macmillan.

Dewey, J. (1938). *Experience and education.* New York: Macmillan.

DiLisi, R. (1980). *Intelligence, intelligence testing and school practices.* Princeton, NJ: ERIC Document Reproduction Service. (No. ED 198 183)

Doan, L. (Ed.). (1994). *The lesbian postmodern* (Series title: 'Between men—between women: Lesbian and gay studies'). New York: Columbia University Press.

Docherty, J. (1990). *After theory: Postmodernism/postmarxism.* London: Routledge.

Doherty, J., Graham, E., & Malek, M., Jr. (1992). Postmodern politics. In J. Doherty, E. Graham, & M. Malek, Jr. (Eds.), *Postmodernism and the social sciences* (pp. 212–220). London: Macmillan.

Doll, W.E., Jr. (1989). Foundations for a postmodern curriculum. *Journal of Curriculum Studies, 21*, 243–253.

Dooley, M. (1995). Murder on Moriah: A paradoxical representation. *Philosophy Today, 39*(1), 67–83.

Downie, R.S., & Telfer, E. (1969). *Respect for persons.* London: George Allen & Unwin.

Dreyfus, H.L., & Rabinow, P. (1992). *Michel Foucault: Beyond structuralism and hermeneutics.* Chicago: University of Chicago Press.

Duderstadt, J.J. (1992). An information highway to the future. *Educom. Review, 27*(5), 36–41.

Dunphy, D., & Stace, D. (1990). *Under new management: Australian organizations in transition.* Sydney, New South Wales: McGraw-Hill.

Dymock, D. (1995). *The sweet use of adversity: The Australian Army Educational Service in World War II and its impact on Australian adult education.* Armidale, New South Wales: University of New England Press.

Eagleton, T. (1983). *Literary theory: An introduction.* Oxford: Basil Blackwell.

Eagleton, T. (1985). Capitalism, modernism and postmodernism. *New Left Review, 152,* 60–73.

Eco, U. (1989). *The open work.* London: Hutchinson Radius.

Eco, U. (1990). *The limits of interpretation.* Bloomington, IN: Indiana University Press.

Edwards, R. (1993a). Changing the subject: Conceptualising adult learning. *Adults Learning,* September: 8–9.

Edwards, R. (1993b). The inevitable future? Post-Fordism in work and learning. In R. Edwards, S. Sieminski, & D. Zeldin (Eds.), *Adult learners, education and training* (pp. 176–186). London: Routledge.

Edwards, R. (1994). 'Are you experienced?': Postmodernity and experiential learning. *International Journal of Lifelong Education, 13,* 423–439.

Elias, J.L., & Merriam, S. (1980). *Philosophical foundations of adult education.* Malabar, FL: Robert E. Krieger.

Eliot, T.S. (1920). *The sacred wood.* London, UK: Methuen.

Ellsworth, E., & Whatley, M.H. (Eds.). (1990). *The ideology of images in educational media: Hidden curriculums in the classroom.* New York: Teachers College Press.

Encel, S. (1984). Working life. In S. Encel, M. Berry, L. Bryson, M. de Lepervanche, T. Rowse, & A. Moran, *Australian society: Introductory essays* (pp. 65–112). Melbourne, Victoria: Longman Cheshire.

Etzioni-Halevy, E. (1985). *The knowledge elite and the failure of prophecy.* London: George Allen & Unwin.

Faure, E., Herrera, F., Kaddoura, A.-R., Lopes, H., Petrovsky, A.V., Rahnema, M., & Ward, F.C. (1972). *Learning to be: The world of education today and tomorrow.* Paris: UNESCO.

Featherstone, M. (1991). *Consumer culture and postmodernism.* London: Sage.

Featherstone, M. (1992). Postmodernism and the aestheticization of everyday life. In S. Lash & J. Friedman (Eds.), *Modernity and identity* (pp. 265–290). Oxford: Blackwell.

Fekete, J. (Ed.). (1988). *Life after postmodernism: Essays on value and culture.* London: Macmillan.

Ferraro, G. (1994). *The cultural dimensions of international business* (2nd ed.). Englewood Cliffs, NJ: Prentice-Hall.

Feyerabend, P. (1978). *Against method: Outline of an anarchistic theory of knowledge.* London: Verso.

Field, J. (1991). Competency and the pedagogy of labour. *Studies in the Education of Adults, 23*(1), 41–52.

Finger, M. (1990). The subject-person of adult education in the crisis of modernity. *Studies in Continuing Education, 12,* 24–30.

Fish, S. (1993). Not for an age but for all time: Canons and postmodernism. *Journal of Legal Education, 43*(1), 11–21.

Flax, J. (1987). Postmodernism and gender relations in feminist theory. *Signs, 12,* 621–643.

Foley, G. (1991). Radical adult education. In M. Tennant (Ed.), *Adult and continuing education in Australia: Issues and practices* (pp. 63–89). London: Routledge.

Foley, G., & Morris, R. (1995). The history and political economy of Australian adult education. In G. Foley (Ed.), *Understanding adult education and training* (pp. 108–120). St. Leonards, New South Wales: Allen & Unwin.

Foster, H. (1983). Postmodernism: A preface. In H. Foster (Ed.), *The anti-aesthetic: Essays on postmodern culture* (pp. ix–xvi). Port Townsend, WA: Bay.

Foucault, M. (1970). *The order of things: An archaeology of the human sciences.* London: Tavistock.

Foucault, M. (1979). *Discipline and punish.* New York: Vintage.

Foucault, M. (1990). An aesthetics of existence. Interview by Alessandro Fontana for the Italian weekly *Panorama* and subsequently in *Le Monde* (A. Sheridan, Trans.). In L.D. Kritzman (Ed.), *Michel Foucault: Politics, philosophy, culture* (pp. 47–53). New York: Routledge.

Fox, S. (1989). The production and distribution of knowledge through open and distance learning. *Educational and Training Technology International, 26,* 269–280.

Fox, S. (1990). Strategic HRM: Post-modern conditioning for the corporate culture. *Management Education and Development, 21,* 192–206.

Fragnière, G. (Ed.). (1976). *Education without frontiers: A study of the future of education from the European cultural foundations plan Europe 2000.* London: Gerald Duckworth.

Frankena, W.K. (1973). *Ethics* (2nd ed.). Englewood Cliffs, NJ: Prentice-Hall.

Fraser, N., & Nicholson, L. (1988). Social criticism without philosophy: An encounter between feminism and postmodernism. *Theory, Culture and Society, 5,* 373–394.

Freeland, J. (1995). Re-conceptualising work, full employment and incomes policies. In J. Inglis (Ed.), *Future of work* (2nd ed.) (pp. 8–44). Leichhardt, New South Wales: Pluto.

Freire, P. (1972). *Pedagogy of the oppressed.* Harmondsworth, UK: Penguin.

Freire, P. (1978). *Pedagogy in process: The letters to Guinea-Bissau* (C. St. John Hunter, Trans.). London: Writers & Readers Publishing Cooperative.

Frow, J. (1991). *What was postmodernism?* Sydney, New South Wales: Local Consumption Press.

Fuente, E. de la. (1993). The last of the modernists: Adorno, Foucault and the modern intellectual. *Meanjin, 52*(1), 87–97.

Gadamer, H.-G. (1977). *Philosophical hermeneutics* (D.E. Linge, Ed. & Trans.). Berkeley, CA: University of California Press.

Gage, N.L. (1989). The paradigm wars and their aftermath: A 'historical' sketch of research in teaching since 1989. *Teachers College Record, 91*, 135–149.

Gagné, R.M. (1977). *The conditions of learning* (3rd ed.). New York: Holt, Rinehart & Winston.

Garrick, J. (1994). Postmodern doubts and 'truths' about training. *Studies in Continuing Education, 16*, 127–142.

Gee, J.P. (1990). *Social linguistics and literacies: Ideology in discourses.* London: Falmer.

Geertz, C. (1973). *The interpretation of cultures.* New York: Basic Books.

Geertz, C. (1979). From the native's point of view: On the nature of anthropological understanding. In P. Rabinow & W.M. Sullivan (Eds.), *Interpretive social science: A reader* (pp. 225–242). Berkeley, CA: University of California Press.

Gellner, E. (1992). *Postmodernism, reason, and religion.* London: Routledge.

Ghirardo, D. (1984/5). Past or post modern in architectural fashion. *Telos, 62*, 187–196.

Gibbins, J.R. (Ed.). (1989). *Contemporary political culture: Politics in a postmodern age.* London: Sage.

Gibbs, B. (1979). Autonomy and authority in education. *Journal of Philosophy of Education, 13*, 119–132.

Giddens, A. (1990). *The consequences of modernity*. Cambridge, UK: Polity.

Gilbert, P. (1989). *Writing, schooling and deconstruction: From voice to text in the classroom.* London: Routledge & Kegan Paul.

Gilbert, R. (1992). Citizenship, education and postmodernism. *British Journal of Sociology of Education, 13*(1), 51–68.

Gilligan, C. (1982). *In a different voice: Psychological theory and women's development*. Cambridge, MA: Harvard University Press.

Giroux, H.A. (1987). Citizenship, public philosophy, and the struggle for democracy. *Education Theory, 37*(2), 103–120.

Giroux, H.A. (1990). *Curriculum discourse as postmodern critical practice*. Geelong, Victoria: Deakin University Press.

Giroux, H. (1992). *Border crossings: Cultural workers and the politics of education*. London: Routledge.

Giroux, H.A., & McLaren, P. (1987). Teacher education as a counter-public sphere: Notes towards a redefinition. In T.S. Popkewitz (Ed.), *Critical studies in teacher education: Its folklore, theory and practice*. (pp. 266–297). London: Falmer.

Giroux, H.A., & McLaren, P. (1989). *Critical pedagogy: The state and cultural struggle*. Albany, NY: State University of New York Press.

Giroux, H.A., & Simon, R. (1984). Curriculum study and cultural politics. *Journal of Education, 166*, 226–238.

Gitlin, A. (Ed.). (1994). *Power and method: Political activism and educational research*. New York: Routledge.

Gordon, P., & White, J. (1979). *Philosophers as educational reformers: The influence of idealism on British educational thought and practice*. London: Routledge.

Gore, J. (1991). On silent regulation: Emancipatory action research and education. *Curriculum Perspectives, 11*(4), 47–50.

Grabowski, S.M., & Associates. (1981). *Preparing educators of adults*. San Francisco: Jossey-Bass.

Graff, H.J. (1987). *The labyrinths of literacy: Reflections on literary past and present*. Philadelphia: Falmer.

Gramsci, A. (1971). *Selections from the Prison Notebooks*. London: Lawrence & Wishart.

Green, A. (1990). *Education and state formation*. London: Macmillan.

Green, A. (1994). Postmodernism and state education. *Journal of Education Policy, 9*(1), 67–83.

Green, B. (Ed.). (1993). *The insistence of the letter: Literacy studies and curriculum theorizing*. London: Falmer.

Green, R. (1994). Lyotard and Mabo: An unprecedented liaison. *Arena Journal, 3*, 149–168.

Griffin, C. (1983). *Curriculum theory in adult and lifelong education*. London: Croom Helm.

Grossberg, L. (1988). Pedagogy in the age of Regan: Politics, postmodernity and the popular. *Curriculum and Teaching, 3*(1&2), 47–62.

Habermas, J. (1983). Modernity: An incomplete project. In H. Foster (Ed.), *The anti-aesthetic: Essays on postmodern culture* (pp. 3–15).

Port Townsend, WA: Bay. (Originally published in 1981 as "Modernity versus postmodernism" in *New German Critique*, 22, 3–14.)

Habermas, J. (1987). *The philosophical discourse of modernity: Twelve lectures* (F. Lawrence, Trans.). Cambridge, UK: Polity.

Habermas, J. (1990). *Moral consciousness and communicative action*. Cambridge, UK: Polity.

Hager, P., & Gonczi, A. (1991). Competency based standards: A boon for continuing professional education? *Studies in Continuing Education, 13*, 24–40.

Haines, N. (1981a). *In respect of persons: A philosophy for continuing education in responsible societies.* Canberra, Australian Capital Territory: The Australian National University Centre for Continuing Education.

Haines, N. (1981b). Progress and provision: Continuing education for responsible society. In N. Haines (Ed.), *Canberra papers in continuing education: New series 1* (pp. 19–31). Canberra, Australian Capital Territory: The Australian National University Centre for Continuing Education.

Halal, W. (1986). *The new capitalism.* New York: Wiley.

Hall, B.L. (1981). Participatory research, popular knowledge and power: A personal reflection. *Convergence, 14*(3), 6–19.

Hall, S., & Jacques, M. (Eds.). (1989). *New Times*. London: Lawrence & Wishart.

Hall, W. (1995). *Getting to grips with the National Training Reform Agenda.* Leabrook, South Australia: National Centre for Vocational Education Research.

Halliday, M.A.K. (1978). *Language as social semiotic.* London: Edward Arnold.

Hampshire, P. (1992). The subtle order from chaos. *The Times Higher Education Supplement, 1043*: 21.

Handy, C. (1990). *The age of unreason.* London: Arrow Books.

Hanson, J. (1990). Beyond postmodernism. Or, is it possible that we need to return to where we started? In A. Blunt (Ed.), *Proceedings of the Annual Conference of the Commission of Professors of Adult Education* (pp. 55–60). Saskatchewan: Commission of Professors of Adult Education.

Hargreaves, A. (1994). *Changing teachers, changing times: Teachers' work and culture in the postmodern age.* London: Cassell.

Harris, K. (1979). *Education and knowledge: The structured misrepresentation of knowledge.* London: Routledge & Kegan Paul.

Harris, R.McL., Barnes, G., & Haines, B. (1991). Competency based programs: A viable alternative in vocational education and training? *Australian Journal of TAFE Research and Development, 6*(2), 1–18.

Harris, R., Guthrie, H., Hobart, B., & Lundberg, D. (1995). *Competency-based education and training: Between a rock and a whirlpool.* Melbourne, Victoria: Macmillan.

Harrison, J.F.C. (1961). *Learning and living, 1790–1960: A study in the history of the English adult education movement.* London: Routledge & Kegan Paul.

Harvey, D. (1989). *The condition of postmodernity: An enquiry into the origins of cultural change.* Cambridge, MA: Blackwell.

Hassan, I. (1971). *The dismemberment of Orpheus: Toward a postmodern literature.* New York: Oxford University Press.

Hassard, J. (1993). Postmodernism and organisational analysis: An overview. In J. Hassard & M. Parker (Eds.), *Postmodernism and organizations* (pp. 1–24). London: Sage.

Haug, W.F. (1987). *Commodity aesthetics, ideology and culture.* New York: International General.

Hawkes, T. (1977). *Structuralism and semiotics.* London: Methuen.

Hawkins, T.H. (1947). *Adult education: The record of the British army.* London: Macmillan.

Hayek, F.A. (1960). *The constitution of liberty*. London: Routledge & Kegan Paul.

Hazard, H.B. (1948). Education for the adult foreign born for citizenship. In M. Ely (Ed.), *Handbook of adult education in the United States* (pp. 52–59). New York: Teachers College, Columbia University.

Heller, A. (1988). *The postmodern political condition.* New York: Columbia University Press.

Hempel, C.G. (1965). *Aspects of scientific explanation.* New York: Free Press.

Hernstein, R.J., & Murray, C. (1994). *The bell curve: The reshaping of American life by differences in intelligence.* New York: Free Press.

Hinkson, J. (1991). *Postmodernity: State and education.* Geelong, Victoria: Deakin University Press.

Hirsch, E.D. (1987). *Cultural literacy: What every American needs to know.* Boston: Houghton Mifflin.

Hirst, P.H. (1974). *Knowledge and the curriculum: A collection of philosophical papers.* London: Routledge & Kegan Paul.

Hirst, P. (1983). Theory of education. In P. Hirst (Ed.), *Educational theory and its foundational disciplines* (pp. 3–29). London: Routledge & Kegan Paul.

Hlynka, D. (1991, June). Postmodern excursions into educational technology. *Educational Technology,* 27–30.

Hlynka, D., & Belland, J.A. (Eds.). (1991). *Paradigms regained: The uses of illuminative, semiotic and post-modern criticism as modes of inquiry in educational technology: A book of readings.* Englewood Cliffs, NJ: Educational Technology Publications.

Hooks, B. (1993). Eros, eroticism and the pedagogical process, *Cultural Studies, 7*(1), 58–63.

Hoskin, K. (1990). Foucault under examination: The crypto-educationalist unmasked. In S.J. Ball (Ed.), *Foucault and education: Disciplines and knowledge* (pp. 29–53). New York: Routledge.

Houle, C.O. (1970). The educators of adults. In R.M. Smith, G.F. Aker, & J.R. Kidd (Eds.), *Handbook of adult education* (pp. 109–119). New York: Macmillan.

Hunt, J.G., & Hunt, L.R. (1987). Here to play: From families to lifestyles. *Journal of Family Issues, 8,* 440–443.

Hunter, I. (1988). *Culture and government: The emergence of literary education.* Houndmills, London: Macmillan.

Hunter, I. (1992). The humanities without humanism. *Meanjn, 51,* 479–490.

Hunter, I. (1994). *Rethinking the school: Subjectivity, bureaucracy, criticism.* St. Leonards, New South Wales: Allen & Unwin.

Hutcheon, L. (1988). *A poetics of postmodernism: History, theory, fiction.* New York: Routledge.

Hutcheon, L. (1994). *Irony's edge: The theory and politics of irony.* London: Routledge.

Hutchins, R.M. (1970). *The learning society.* Harmondsworth, UK: Penguin.

Huyssen, A. (1981). The search for tradition: Avant-garde and postmodernism in the 1970s. *New German Critique, 22,* 23–40.

Hyland, T. (1992). Expertise and competence in further and adult education. *British Journal of Inservice Education, 18*(1), 23–28.

Inbar, D.E. (Ed.). (1990). *Second chance in education: An interdisciplinary and international perspective.* New York: Falmer.

Iragaray, L. (1985). *Speculum of the other woman.* Ithaca, NY: Cornell University Press.

Jacob, E. (1987). Qualitative research traditions: A review. *Review of Educational Research, 57*(1), 1–50.

Jacob, J.R. (1994). The political economy of science in seventeenth century England. In M.C. Jacob (Ed.), *The politics of western science 1840–1990* (pp. 19–46). New Jersey: Humanities.

Jacobs, J.M. (1996). *Edge of empire: Postcolonialism and the city.* New York: Routledge.

James, B.J. (1956). Can 'needs' define educational goals? *Adult Education, 7*, 19–26.

Jameson, F. (1991). *Postmodernism, or, the cultural logic of late capitalism.* London: Verso.

Jardine, A. (1985). *Gynesis: Configurations of woman and modernity.* Ithaca, NY: Cornell University Press.

Jarvis, P. (1989). Content, purpose, and practice. In C.J. Titmus (Ed.), *Lifelong education for adults: An international handbook* (pp. 22–28). Oxford: Pergamon.

Jarvis, P. (1995). *Adult and continuing education: Theory and practice* (2nd ed.). London: Routledge.

Jarvis, P. (1996). Education and training in a late modern society: A question of ethics. *Australian and New Zealand Journal of Vocationatal Education Research*, 4(2), 42–58.

Jarvis, P., & Chadwick, A. (1991). *Training adult educators in Western Europe.* London: Routledge.

Jencks, C. (1987). *Post-modernism: The new classicism in art and architecture.* New York: Rizzoli International Publishing.

Jencks, C. (1989). *What is postmodernism?* New York: St. Martin's.

Jencks, C. (1991). *The language of post-modern architecture* (6th ed.). London: Academy Editions.

Jennings, L.E. (1995). Prisoners of our own perspectives: Recasting action research in modern/postmodern times. *Studies in Continuing Education, 17*, 78–85.

Jensen, G., Liveright, A.A., & Hallenbeck, W. (Eds.). (1964). *Adult Education: Outlines of an emerging field of university study.* Washington, DC: Adult Education Association of the USA.

Joad, C.E.M. (1957). *Guide to philosophy.* New York: Dover.

Johnson, R. (1988). 'Really useful knowledge' 1790–1850: Memories for education in the 1980s. In T. Lovett (Ed.), *Radical approaches to adult education: A reader* (pp. 3–34). London: Routledge.

Johnson-Riordan, L. (1994). In and against the grain of "new times": Discourses of adult education and the challenge of contemporary cultural theory. *Australian Journal of Adult and Community Education, 34*(1), 10–17.

Jones, B. (1990). *Sleepers wake!: Technology and the future of work* (3rd ed.). Melbourne, Victoria: Oxford University Press.

Kamuf, P. (Ed.). (1991). *A Derrida reader: Between the blinds.* Hemel Hempstead, UK: Harvester Wheatsheaf.

Kanpol, B. (1992). Postmodernism in education revisited: Similarities within differences in the democratic imaginary. *Education Theory, 42*, 217–229.

Kant, I. (1934). *Critique of pure reason* (J.M.D. Meiklejohn, Trans.).

London: Dent. (Original work published, in German, 1781.)

Kanter, R.M. (1989). *When giants learn to dance: Mastering the challenges of strategy, management, and careers in the 1990s.* London: Unwin Hyman.

Kariel, H.S. (1989). *The desperate politics of postmodernism.* Amherst, MA: University of Massachusetts Press.

Kaufman, R.A. (1972). *Educational systems planning.* Englewood Cliffs, NJ: Prentice-Hall.

Kellner, D. (1988). Reading images critically: Toward a postmodern pedagogy. *Journal of Education, 170*(3), 31–52.

Kelly, T. (1957). *George Birkbeck, pioneer of adult education.* Liverpool: Liverpool University Press.

Kelly, T. (1970). *A history of adult education in Great Britain.* Liverpool: University of Liverpool Press.

Kemmis, S. (1991). Emancipatory action research and postmodernism. *Curriculum Perspectives, 11*(4), 59–65.

Kemmis, S. (1992, November). *Postmodernism and educational research.* Paper presented at the Joint Conference of the Australian and New Zealand Associations for Research in Education. Geelong, Victoria: Deakin University.

Kemmis, S., & McTaggart, R. (Eds.). (1988). *The action research reader.* Geelong, Victoria: Deakin University Press.

Kenway, J., Bigum, C., & Fitzclarence, L. (1993). Marketing education in the postmodern age. *Journal of Education Policy, 8,* 105–122.

Kerckhove, D. de. (1995). *The skin of culture.* Toronto: Somerville House.

Kilgore, W.J. (1972). Freedom in the perspectivism of Ortega. *Philosophy and Phenomenological Research, 32,* 500–513.

Kincheloe, J.L. (1993). *Toward a critical politics of teacher thinking: Mapping the postmodern.* Westport, CT: Bergin & Garvey.

Kincheloe, J.L. (1995). *Toil and trouble: Good work, smart workers, and the integration of academic and vocational education.* New York: Peter Lang.

Kindervatter, S. (1979). *Non-formal education as an empowering process: With case studies from Indonesia and Thailand.* Amherst, MA: Center for International Education, University of Massachusetts.

King, N. (1993). Occasional doubts: Ian Hunter's genealogy of interpretative depth. *Southern Review, 26*(1), 5–27.

King, N. (1994). My life without Steve: Postmodernism, ficto-criticism and the paraliterary. *Southern Review, 27,* 261–275.

Kitwood, T. (1990). Psychotherapy, postmodernism and morality. *Journal of Moral Education, 19*(1), 3–13.

Knowles, M.S. (Ed.). (1960). *Handbook of adult education in the United States.* Chicago: Adult Education Association of the USA.

Knowles, M.S. (1977). *A history of the adult education movement in the United States* (rev. ed.). New York: Robert E. Krieger.

Knowles, M.S. (1980). *The modern practice of adult education: From pedagogy to andragogy* (rev. ed.). Chicago: Follett.

Knowles, M.S. (1994). *A history of the adult education movement in the United States: Includes adult education institutions through 1976* (rev. ed.). Malabar, FL: Krieger.

Knox, A.B., & Associates. (1980). *Developing, administering, and evaluating adult education.* San Francisco: Jossey-Bass.

Kolb, D.A. (1984). *Experiential learning: Experience as the source of learning and development.* Englewood Cliffs, NJ: Prentice-Hall.

Kolb, D.A. (1993). The process of experiential learning. In M. Thorpe, R. Edwards, & A. Hansen (Eds.), *Culture and processes of adult learning: A reader* (pp. 138–158). London: Routledge.

Kozol, J. (1980). *Prisoners of silence: Breaking the bonds of adult illiteracy in the United States.* New York: Continuum.

Kreitlow, B.W., & Associates. (1981). *Examining controversies in adult education.* San Francisco: Jossey-Bass.

Kroker, A. (1992). *The possessed individual: Technology and the French postmodern.* Montreal: New World Perspectives.

Kuhn, T.S. (970). *The structure of scientific revolutions* (2nd ed.). Chicago: University of Chicago Press.

Kulik, J.A. (1993). An analysis of research on ability grouping: Historical and contemporary perspectives. *National Research Center on the Gifted and Talented Newsletter* (Spring), 8–9.

Kumar, K. (1988). *The rise of modern society: Aspects of the social and political development of the West.* London: Blackwell.

Lacan, J. (1977). *Ecrits: A selection.* London: Tavistock.

Lash, S. (1987). Modernity or modernism? Weber and contemporary social theory. In S. Lash & S. Whimster (Eds.), *Max Weber, rationality and modernity* (pp. 355–377). London: Allen & Unwin.

Lash, S. (1990). *Sociology of postmodernism.* New York: Routledge.

Lash, S. (1994), Reflexivity and its doubles: Structure, aesthetics, community. In U. Beck, A. Giddens, & S. Lash, *Reflexive modernization: Politics, tradition and aesthetics in the modern social order* (pp. 110–173). Cambridge, UK: Polity.

Lash, S., & Friedman, J. (Eds.). (1992). *Modernity and identity.* Oxford: Blackwell.

Lash, S., & Urry, J. (1987). *The end of organised capitalism.* Oxford: Polity.

Lather, P. (1991). *Getting smart: Feminist research and pedagogy with/in the postmodern.* London: Routledge.

Lawson, K.H. (1979). *Philosophical concepts and values in adult education* (rev. ed.). Milton Keynes, UK: Open University Press.

Lawson, K. (1982). Lifelong education: Concept or policy? *International Journal of Lifelong Education, 1*, 97–108.

Leach, R. (1988). *Political ideologies: An Australian introduction.* Melbourne, Victoria: Macmillan.

Leicester, M., & Taylor, M. (Eds.). (1992). *Ethics, ethnicity and education.* London: Kogan Page.

Lengrand, P. (1970). *An introduction to lifelong education.* Paris: UNESCO.

Letiche, H. (1990). Five postmodern aphorisms for trainers. *Management Education and Development, 21*, 229–240.

Letiche, H. (1991). Some postmodern observations on student reflexivity. *Teaching and Teacher Education, 7*, 467–478.

Levin, B.H., & Clowes, D.A. (1991, March). *From positivism to post-modernism: Can education catch up with the paradigm shift?* Paper presented to the Annual Meeting of the Virginia Social Science Association, Christopher Newport College.

Lewin, K. (1952). Group decision and social change. In E.E. Maccoby, T.M. Newcomb, & E.E. Hartley (Eds.), *Readings in social psychology* (3rd ed.) (pp. 197–211). New York: Holt, Rinehart & Winston.

Lewin, K. (1975). *Field theory in social science: Selected theoretical papers.* Westport, CT: Greenwood. (Original work published 1951)

Lindeman, E.C. (1961). *The meaning of adult education.* Montreal: Harvest House. (Original work published 1926.)

Long, H.B., Hiemstra, R., & Associates. (1980). *Changing approaches to studying adult education.* San Francisco: Jossey-Bass.

Lovett, T. (1980). Adult education and community action. In J. Thompson (Ed.), *Adult education for a change* (pp. 115–173). London: Hutchinson.

Lovett, T. (1982). *Adult education, community development and the working class* (2nd ed.). Nottingham, UK: University of Nottingham Department of Adult Education.

Luke, A., & Baker, C.D. (Eds.). (1989). *Towards a critical sociology of reading pedagogy.* Amsterdam, Netherlands: John Benjamin.

Luke, A., & Luke, C. (1990). School knowledge as simulation: Curriculum in postmodern conditions. *Discourse, 10*(2), 75–92.

Luke, T.W. (1990). *Social theory and modernity: Critique, dissent and revolution.* London: Sage.

Lund, R. (1949). *Scandinavian adult education.* Copenhagen, Denmark: Det Danske Forlag.

Lunn, E. (1982). *Marxism and modernism: An historical study of Lukâcs, Brecht, Benjamin, and Adorno.* Berkeley, CA: University of California Press.

Lusterman, S. (1978). Education in industry. In Marquis Academic Media, *Yearbook of adult and continuing education 1978–79* (4th ed.) (pp. 475–479). Chicago, IL: Marquis Academic Media.

Lyotard, J.-F. (1984a). *The postmodern condition: A report on knowledge* (G. Bennington & B. Massumi, Trans.). Manchester, UK: Manchester University Press. (Original work published in France in 1979; same translation also published in Minneapolis: University of Minnesota Press, 1984 & 1989.)

Lyotard, J.-F. (1984b). The sublime and the avant-garde. *Artform, 22,* 36–43.

Mannheim, K. (1952). *Essays on the sociology of knowledge* (P. Kecskemeti, Ed.). London: Routledge & Kegan Paul.

Marshall, B.K. (1992). *Teaching the postmodern.* New York: Routledge.

Marshall, J.D. (1996). *Michel Foucault: Personal autonomy and education.* Dordrecht, The Netherlands: Kluwer.

Marx, K., & Engels, F. (1971). *Capital: A critical analysis of capitalist production. Vol. 1.* London: George Allen & Unwin. (Original work published 1867.)

Maslow, A. (1970). *Motivation and personality.* New York: Harper & Row.

Masters, G., & McCurry, D. (1990). *Competency based assessment in the professions.* Canberra, Australian Capital Territory: Australian Government Publishing Service.

Matthews, J.L. (1960). The Cooperative Extension Service. In M.S. Knowles (Ed.), *Handbook of adult education in the United States* (pp. 218–229). Chicago, IL: Adult Education Association of the USA.

Maxcy, S.J. (1991). *Educational leadership: A critical pragmatic perspective.* Westport, CT: Greenwood.

McHale, B. (1987). *Postmodernist fiction.* New York: Methuen.

McKay, A. (1994). The implications of postmodernism for moral education. *McGill Journal of Education, 29*(1), 31–44.

McKenzie, L. (1992). Education discourse in the postmodern world. *Educational Considerations* (College of Education, Kansas State University), *19*(2), 20–25.

McLaren, P. (1986). Postmodernity and the death of politics: A Brazillian reprieve [Review of P. Freire. 1985. *The politics of education: Culture, power, and liberation.* South Hadley, MA: Bergin & Garvey.] *Educational Theory, 36,* 389–401.

McLaren, P. (1991a). Postmodernism, postcolonialism and pedagogy. *Education and Society, 9*(1), 3–22.

McLaren, P. (1991b). Critical pedagogy: Constructing an arch of social dreaming and a doorway to hope. *Journal of Education, 173*(1), 9–34.

McLuhan, M. (1974). Medium, meaning, message. *Communication, 1*(1), 27–33.

McLuhan, M. (1990). *Meanings of the medium.* New York: Praeger.

McMaster, M., & Randell, S. (1992). Equity and opportunity in adult learning. In R. Harris & P. Willis (Eds.), *Striking a balance: Adult and community education in Australia towards 2000* (pp. 84–91). Adelaide, South Australia: Centre for Human Resource Studies, University of South Australia.

Mehl, J.V. (1994). Historical self-consciousness, postmodernism, and humanities education. *Midwest Quarterly, 35*, 216–228.

Melser, P. (1994). Post modern researching and thesis supervision. In B. Neville, P. Willis, & M. Edwards (Eds.), *Qualitative research in adult education: A colloquium on theory, practice, supervision and assessment* (pp. 51–56). Adelaide, South Australia: Centre for Research in Education and Work, University of South Australia.

Mendus, S. (1989). *Toleration and the limits of liberalism.* Basingstoke, UK: Macmillan.

Mensh, E., & Mensh, H. (1991). *The IQ mythology: Class, race, gender and inequality.* Carbondale, IL: Illinois University Press.

Merriam, S.B. (1991). How research produces knowledge. In J.M. Peters, P. Jarvis, & Associates, *Adult education: Evolution and achievements in a developing field of study* (pp. 42–65). San Francisco: Jossey-Bass.

Mezirow, J. (1981). A critical theory of adult learning and education. *Adult Education, 32*, 3–24.

Mezirow, J. (1991). *Transformative dimensions of adult learning.* San Francisco: Jossey-Bass.

Middleton, S. (1992). A post-modernist pedagogy for the sociology of women's education. In M. Arnot & K. Weiler (Eds.), *Feminism and social justice in Education: International perspectives* (pp. 124–145). London: Falmer.

Mill, J.S. (1929). *On liberty.* London: Watts & Co. (Original work published 1859.)

Milner, A. (1991). *Contemporary cultural theory: An introduction.* Sydney, New South Wales: Allen & Unwin.

Mincer, J. (1962). On-the-job training: Costs, returns, and some implications. *Journal of Political Economics, 70*, 50–79.

Moi, T. (1988). Feminism, postmodernism and style: Recent feminist criticism in the United States. *Cultural Critique, 9,* 3–22.

Monette, M. (1979). Needs assessment: A critique of philosophical assumptions. *Adult Education, 29,* 83–95.

Montroux, P. (1961). *The industrial revolution in the eighteenth century: An outline of the modern factory system in England,* New York: Harper & Row.

Moody, E.A. (1965). *The logic of William Ockham.* New York: Russell & Russell.

Morris, M. (1988). *The pirate's financee: Feminism, reading, postmodernism.* London: Verso.

Morris, R. (1991). Trade union education in Australia. In M. Tennant (Ed.), *Adult and continuing education in Australia: Issues and practices* (pp. 153–174). London: Routledge.

Mosely, D. (1995). Critical theory and postmodernism: Are they relevant to labour market training? *Australian Journal of Adult and Community Education, 35*(1), 61–67.

Murphy, J.W. (1988). Computerization, postmodern epistemology, and reading in the postmodern era. *Educational Theory, 38,* 175–182.

Naremore, J., & Brantlinger, P. (Eds.). (1991). *Modernity and mass culture.* Bloomington, IN: Indiana University Press.

Neville, B., Willis, P., & Edwards, M. (Eds.). (1994). *Qualitative research in adult education: A colloquium on theory, practice, supervision and assessment.* Underdale, South Australia: Centre for Research in Education and Work, University of South Australia.

Newman, M. (1979). *The poor cousin: A study of adult education.* London: Allen & Unwin.

Newman, M. (1994). *Defining the enemy: Adult education in social action.* Sydney, New South Wales: Stewart Victor.

Nicholson, C. (1989). Postmodernism, feminism and education: The need for solidarity. *Educational Theory, 39,* 197–206.

Nicholson, C. (1995). Postmodern feminisms. In M. Peters (Ed.), *Education and the postmodern condition* (pp. 75–85). Westport, CT: Bergin & Garvey.

Nicolson, L.J. (Ed.). (1990). *Feminism/postmodernism.* London: Routledge.

Nielson, K. (1967). Ethics, problems of. In P. Edwards (Ed.), *The encyclopedia of philosophy.* Vol. 3 (pp. 117–134). London: Collier-Macmillan.

Nietzsche, F. (1974a). *The gay science* (W. Kaufmann, Trans.). New York: Vintage. (Original work published, in German, 1887.)

Nietzsche, F. (1974b). *The will to power: An attempted transvaluation of all values* (A.M. Ludivici, Trans.). New York: Gordon Press.

(Original work published, in German, 1901.)

Noddings, N. (1984). *Caring: A feminine approach to ethics and moral education.* Berkeley, CA: University of California Press.

Norris, C. (1990). *What's wrong with postmodernism? Critical theory and the ends of philosophy.* New York: Harvester Wheatsheaf.

Norris, C. (1992). *Uncritical theory: Postmodernism, intellectuals and the Gulf War.* Amherst, MA: University of Massachusetts Press.

Norris, C. (1994). Truth, ideology, and 'local knowledge': Some contexts of postmodern skepticism. *Southern Humanities Review, 28,* 109–142.

Nowell-Smith, P.H. (1954). *Ethics.* Harmondsworth, UK: Penguin.

Oakes, J. (1985). *Keeping track: How schools structure inequality.* New Haven, CT: Yale University Press.

O'Hear, A. (1981). *Education, society and human nature: An introduction to the philosophy of education.* London: Routledge & Kegan Paul.

Orr, D.W. (1992). *Ecological literacy: Education and the transition to a postmodern world.* Albany, NY: State University of New York Press.

Ortega y Gasset, J. (1962). *History as a system and other essays toward a philosophy of history.* New York: W.W. Norton. (Original work published 1940 as *Toward a philosophy of history.*)

O'Sullivan, T., Hartley, J., Saunders, D., & Fiske, J. (1988). *Key concepts in communication.* London: Routledge.

Owens, C. (1983). The discourse of others: Feminism and postmodernism. In H. Foster (Ed.), *The anti-aesthetic: Essays on postmodern culture* (pp. 57–82). Port Townsend, WA: Bay.

Paterson, R.W.K. (1973). Social change as an educational aim. *Adult Education* (NIACE), *45,* 353–359.

Paterson, R.W.K. (1979). *Values, education and the adult.* London: Routledge & Kegan Paul.

Patton, M.Q. (1980). *Qualitative evaluation methods.* Beverly Hills, CA: Sage.

Paulston, R. (1980). *Other dreams, other schools: Folk schools in social and ethnic movements.* Pittsburgh, PA: University of Pittsburgh Press.

Pearse, H. (1992). Beyond paradigms: Art education theory and practice in a postparadigmatic world. *Studies in Art Education, 33,* 244–252.

Pefanis, J. (1991). *Heterology and the postmodern: Bataille, Baudrillard, and Lyotard.* Sydney, New South Wales: Allen & Unwin.

Pennington, F., & Green, J. (1976). Comparative analysis of program development processes in six professions. *Adult Education, 28,* 13–23.

Perez-Martinez, L. (1995). The post-structuralist debate and the new critique of science. *Studies in Symbolic Interaction, 18,* 61–77.

Peters, J.M., & Associates. (1980). *Building an effective adult education enterprise.* San Francisco: Jossey-Bass.

Peters, M. (1989). Techno-science, rationality, and the university: Lyotard on the "postmodern condition." *Educational Theory, 39,* 93–105.

Peters, M. (1992). Performance and accountability in "post-industrial society": The crisis of British universities. *Studies in Higher Education, 17,* 123–139.

Peters, M. (Ed.). (1995a). *Education and the postmodern condition.* Westport, CT: Bergin & Garvey.

Peters, M. (1995b). Legitimation problems: Knowledge and education in the postmodern condition. In M. Peters (Ed.), *Education and the postmodern condition* (pp. 21–40). Westport, CT: Bergin & Garvey.

Peters, M., & Marshall, J. (1996). *Individualism and community: Education and social policy in the postmodern condition.* London: Falmer.

Peters, R.S. (1965). Education as initiation. In R.D. Archambault (Ed.), *Philosophical analysis and education* (pp. 87–111). London: Routledge & Kegan Paul.

Peters, R.S. (1977). *Education and the education of teachers.* London: Routledge & Kegan Paul.

Peterson, R.E., Gaff, S.S., Helmick, J.S., Feldmesser, R.A., Valley, J.R., & Nielsen, H.D. (1982). *Adult education and training industrialized countries.* New York: Praeger.

Phillips, J. (1981). Theory, practice and basic beliefs in adult education. *Adult Education, 31,* 93–106.

Phillipson, M. (1989). *Modernity's wake: The ameruncululus letters.* London: Routledge.

Pietrykowsky, B. (1996). Knowledge and power in adult education: Beyond Freire and Habermas. *Adult Education Quarterly, 46,* 82–97.

Poole, M.E. (Ed.). (1991). *Education and work.* Melbourne, Victoria: Australian Council for Educational Research.

Pope, D. (1983). *The objectives model of curriculum planning and evaluation.* London: Council for Educational Technology.

Popper, C. (1977). *The open society and its enemies.* London: Routledge & Kegan Paul.

Porter, P., Rizvi, F., Knight, J., & Lingard, R. (1992). Competencies for a clever country: Building a house of cards? *Unicorn, 18*(3), 50–58.

Poster, M. (Ed.). (1988). *Jean Baudrillard: Selected writings.* Cambridge, UK: Polity.

Poster, M. (1989). *Critical theory and poststructuralism.* Ithaca, NY: Cornell University Press.

Press, L. (1995). McLuhan meets the net. *Communications of the ACM, 38*(7), 15.

Price, H.H. (1969). *Beliefs.* London: Allen & Unwin.

Pring, R. (1992). Education for a pluralist society. In M. Leicester & M. Taylor (Eds.), *Ethics, ethnicity and education* (pp. 19–30). London: Kogan Page.

Puhr, K.M. (1992). Postmodernism for high school students. *English Journal, 81*(1), 64–66.

Quine, W.O. (1985). *Word and object.* Cambridge, MA: Technology Press, Massachusetts Institute of Technology.

Quine, W.O. (1990). *The roots of reference.* La Salle, IL: Open Court.

Raes, K. (1992). Critical theory in a 'disenchanted world.' In D. Wildemeersch & T. Jansen (Eds.), *Adult education, experiential learning and social change: The postmodern challenge* (pp. 35–50). Belgium: VUGA Gravenhage.

Randall, J.H., Jr. (1962). *The career of philosophy. Volume 1: From the Middle Ages to the Enlightenment.* New York: Columbia University Press.

Randell, S. (1993, November). *Adult education, postmodernity and the future? An Australian experience.* Paper presented at the annual meeting of the American Association for Adult and Continuing Education, Dallas, Texas. (ERIC Document Reproduction Service No. ED 366 756)

Rhodes, C. (1996). Postmodernism and the practice of human resource development in organisations. *Australian and New Zealand Journal of Vocational Education Research,* 4(2), 79–88.

Roberts, L., Schumacher, J.A., Vogel, S., & Rouse, J. (1991). Symposium on the possibilities for a postmodern philosophy of science. *Social Epistemology, 5,* 247–292.

Rogers, C.R. (1969). *Freedom to learn: A view of what education might become.* Columbus, OH: Charles E. Merrill.

Rojek, C. (1993). *Ways of escape: Modern transformations in leisure and travel.* London: Macmillan.

Rorty, R. (1980). *Philosophy and the mirror of nature.* Oxford: Basil Blackwell.

Rorty, R. (1989). *Contingency, irony and solidarity.* Cambridge, UK: Cambridge University Press.

Rose, M.A. (1991). *The post-modern and the post-industrial: A critical analysis.* Cambridge, UK: Cambridge University Press.

Rosen, J. (1990). The message of the medium is the message. *ETC: A Review of General Semantics, 47*(1), 4–51.

Rosenau, P.M. (1992). *Postmodernism and the social sciences: Insights, inroads and intrusions.* Princeton, NJ: Princeton University Press.

Roszak, T. (1972). *Where the wasteland ends: Politics and transcendence in postindustrial society.* London: Faber & Faber.

Rustin, M. (1989). The politics of post-fordism and the trouble with 'New Times'. *New Left Review, 175*, 54–78.

Sanford, N. (1970). Whatever happened to action research? *Journal of Social Issues, 26*, 3–23.

Saussure, F. de. (1974). *Course in general linguistics.* London: Fontana. (Original work published 1916.)

Scheffler, I. (1965). *Conditions of knowledge: An introduction to epistemology and education.* Chicago: University of Chicago Press.

Scott, P. (1990a, August 10). The postmodern challenge I: The many faces of modernism. *The Times Higher Education Supplement, 927*, 32.

Scott, P. (1990b, August 17). The postmodern challenge II: Reinventing a conservative canon. *The Times Higher Education Supplement, 928*, 28.

Sedgwick, P. (1994). Crossing the torrent: Lyotard and the kernel of pedagogy. *Southern Review, 27*, 343–355.

Seguin, E. (1994). A modest reason. *Theory, Culture and Society, 11*(3), 55–75.

Seidler, V.J. (1991). *The moral limits of modernity: Love, inequality and oppression.* London: Macmillan.

Seidman, S. (1994). *The postmodern turn: New perspectives on social theory.* Cambridge, UK: Cambridge University Press.

Seidman, S., & Wagner, D.G. (Eds.). (1992). *Postmodernism and social theory: The debate over general theory.* Cambridge, MA: Blackwell.

Seliger, M. (1974). *Ideology and politics.* London: Allen & Unwin.

Senate Standing Committee on Employment, Education and Training. (1991). *Come in Cinderella: The emergence of adult and community education.* Canberra, Australian Capital Territory: Commonwealth of Australia Senate Publications Unit.

Shuker, R. (1984). *Educating the workers? A history of the Workers' Education Association in New Zealand.* Palmerston North, NZ: Dunmore Press.

Shusterman, R. (1988). Postmodernist aestheticism: A new moral philosophy? *Theory, Culture and Society, 5*, 337–355.

Siebers, T. (Ed.). (1994). *Heterotopia: Postmodern utopia and the body politic.* Ann Arbor, MI: University of Michigan Press.

Skeggs, B. (1991). Postmodernism: What is all the fuss about? *British Journal of the Sociology of Education, 12,* 225–267.

Skinner, B.F. (1968). *The technology of teaching.* New York: Appleton-Century-Crofts.

Slaughter, R. (1989). Cultural reconstruction in the post-modern world. *Journal of Curriculum Studies, 21,* 255–270.

Smart, B. (1992). *Modern conditions, postmodern controversies.* New York: Routledge.

Smith, M. (1991). Adult education at a distance. In M. Tennant (Ed.), *Adult and continuing education in Australia: Issues and practices* (pp. 21–44). London: Routledge.

Smith, M.E.G. (1994). *Invisible Leviathan: The Marxist critique of market despotism beyond postmodernism.* Toronto: University of Toronto Press.

Smith, N. (1992). Geography, difference and the politics of scale. In J. Doherty, E. Graham, & M. Malek (Eds.), *Postmodernism and the social sciences* (pp. 57–79). London: Macmillan.

Smith, R.M., Aker, G.F., & Kidd, J.R. (Eds.). (1970). *Handbook of adult education.* New York: Macmillan.

Smith, R., & Wexler, P. (Eds.). (1995). *After postmodernism: Education, politics and identity.* London: Falmer.

Snow, C.P. (1963). The two cultures. In G. Levine & O. Thomas (Eds.), *The scientist vs. the humanist* (pp. 1–6). New York: Norton. (Original work published in the *New Statesman* (1956, October), 413–414.)

Spindler, G., & Spindler, L. (Eds.). (1987). *Interpretive ethnography of education: At home and abroad.* Hillsdale, NJ: Erlbaum.

Spivak, G.C. (1988). *In other worlds: Essays in cultural politics.* New York: Routledge.

Stanage, S.M. (1989, October). *Lifelong learning: A phenomenology of meaning and value transformation in postmodern adult education.* Paper presented at the annual meeting of the American Association for Adult and Continuing Education, Atlantic City, NJ. (ERIC Document Reproduction Service No. ED 312 391)

Stanage, S.M. (1990). Parlous questions in 'postmodern' adult education: A response to Zacharakis-Jutz. *Adult Education Quarterly, 40,* 237–244.

Steiner, G. (1970). *Language and silence: Essays on language, literature and the inhuman.* New York: Atheneum.

Stenhouse, L. (1975). *An introduction to curriculum research and development.* London: Heineman.

Stevenson, J. (1993). Competency-based training in Australia: An analysis of assumptions. *Australian and New Zealand Journal of Vocational Education Research, 1*(1), 87–104.

Strike, K.A. (1982). *Liberty and learning.* Oxford: Martin Robertson.

Szkudlarek, T. (1993). *The problem of freedom in postmodern education.* Westport, CT: Bergin & Garvey.

Taylor, F. (1972). *Scientific management.* Westport, CT: Greenwood.

Taylor, S.I., & Bogdan, R. (1984). *Qualitative methods: The search for meanings* (2nd ed.). New York: John Wiley.

Tester, K. (1993). *The life and times of postmodernity.* London: Routledge.

Thomas, J.E. (1982). *Radical adult education: Theory and practice.* Nottingham, UK: University of Nottingham Department of Adult Education.

Thompson, A.B. (1945). *Adult education in New Zealand: A critical and historical survey.* Wellington, NZ: New Zealand Council for Educational Research.

Thompson, J. (Ed.). (1980). *Adult education for a change.* London: Hutchinson.

Thompson, J. (1983). *Learning liberation: Women's response to men's education.* London: Croom Helm.

Toulmin, S. (1990). *Cosmopolis: The hidden agenda of modernity.* New York: Free Press.

Tsang, M.C. (1996). Costs of adult education and training. In A.C. Tuijnman (Ed.), *International encyclopedia of adult education and training* (2nd ed.) (pp. 292–300). Oxford: Elsevier Science Ltd.

Turner, R.E. (1934). *James Silk Buckingham 1786–1855: A social biography.* London: Williams & Norgate.

Tuxworth, E. (1989). Competence based education and training: Background and origins. In J. Burke (Ed.), *Competency based education and training* (pp. 10–25). Lewes, East Sussex: Falmer.

Ulmer, G. (1985). Textshop for post(e)pedagogy. In C.D. Atkins & M.L. Johnson (Eds.), *Writing and differently: Deconstruction and the teaching of composition and literature* (pp. 38–64). Lawrence, KS: University Press of Kansas.

Usher, R. (1989a). Deconstructing foundations, reconstructing the pragmatic. In B. Bright (Ed.), *Theory and practice in the study of adult education: The epistemology debate* (pp. 233–241). London: Routledge.

Usher, R. (1989b). Locating experience in language: Towards a poststructuralist theory of experience. *Adult Education Quarterly, 40,* 23–32.

Usher, R., Bryant, I., & Johnston, R. (1997). *Adult education and the postmodern challenge: Learning beyond the limits.* London:

Routledge.

Usher, R., & Edwards, R. (1994). *Postmodernism and education: Different voices, different worlds.* London: Routledge.

Usher, R., & Edwards, R. (1995). Confessing all? A 'postmodern guide' to the guidance and counselling of adult learners. *Studies in the Education of Adults, 27*(1), 9–23.

Van Doren, M. (1943). *Liberal education.* Boston: Beacon.

Van Manen, M. (1990). *Researching lived experience: Human science for an action sensitive pedagogy.* London, Ontario: Althouse Press.

Vattimo, G. (1988). *The end of modernity: Nihilism and hermeneutics in post-modern culture* (J.R. Snyder, Trans.). Cambridge, UK: Polity.

Vattimo, G. (1992). *The transparent society* (D. Webb, Trans.). Cambridge, UK: Polity.

Verner, C. (1962). *Adult education theory and method: A conceptual scheme for the identification and classification of processes for adult education.* Washington, DC: Adult Education Association of the USA.

Verner, C. (1975). *Fundamental concepts in adult education.* In J.H. Knoll (Ed.), *Internationales Jahrbuch für Erwachsenenbildung.* Germany: Bertelsman Universitätsverlag.

Wain, K. (1987). *Philosophy of lifelong education.* London: Croom Helm.

Walkerdine, V. (1988). *The mastery of reason.* London: Routledge.

Ward, S. (1996). *Reconfiguring truth: Postmodernism, science studies, and the search for a new model of knowledge.* London: Rowman & Littlefield.

Weber, M. (1947). *The theory of social and economic organization* (A.R. Henderson & T. Parsons, Trans.). London: William Hodge.

Weeden, C. (1987). *Feminist practice and poststructuralist theory.* Oxford: Basil Blackwell.

Wellmer, A. (1991). *The persistence of modernity: Essays on aesthetics, ethics and postmodernism* (D. Midgley, Trans.). Cambridge, UK: Polity.

Western, M. (1993). Class and stratification. In J.M. Najman & J.S. Western (Eds.), *A sociology of Australian society: Introductory readings* (pp. 54–105). Melbourne, Victoria: Macmillan.

Westwood, S. (1991a). Constructing the future: A postmodern agenda for adult education. In S. Westwood & J.E. Thomas (Eds.), *Radical agendas? The politics of adult education* (pp. 44–56). Leicester, UK: National Institute of Adult Continuing Education.

Westwood, S. (1991b). Power/knowledge: The politics of transformative research. *Convergence, 24*(3), 79–86.

Wexler, P. (1982). Structure, text and subject: A critical sociology of school knowledge. In M. Apple (Ed.), *Cultural and economic reproduction in education* (pp. 275–303). London: Routledge & Kegan Paul.

Wexler, P. (1987). *Social analysis of education: After the new sociology*. New York: Routledge.

Wexler, P. (1989). Curriculum in the closed society. In H.A. Giroux & P. McLaren (Eds.), *Critical pedagogy: The state and cultural struggle* (pp. 92–104). Albany, NY: State University of New York Press.

Wexler, P. (1992). *Becoming somebody: Toward a social psychology of school*. Washington, DC: Falmer.

Wexler, P. (1993, December). *Educational corporatism and its counterposes*. Paper presented at the conference 'After Competence: The Future of Post-Compulsory Education and Training,' Griffith University, Brisbane, Queensland.

White, D. (1989). Theorising the postmodern curriculum. In D. Stockley (Ed.), *Melbourne Studies in Education 1987–88* (pp. 16–22). Bundoora, Victoria: La Trobe University Press.

White, J.P. (1973). *Towards a compulsory curriculum*. London: Routledge & Kegan Paul.

White, R.F., & Jacques, R. (1995). Operationalizing the post modernity construct for efficient organizational change management. *Journal of Organizational Change Management, 8*(2), 45–71.

White, S. (1991). *Political theory and postmodernism*. Cambridge, UK: Cambridge University Press.

Whitelock, D. (1974). *The great tradition: A history of adult education in Australia*. Brisbane, Queensland: University of Queensland Press.

Whitty, G. (1992). Education, economy and national culture. In R. Bocock & K. Thompson (Eds.), *Social and cultural forms of modernity* (pp. 267–320). Cambridge, UK: Polity.

Wildemeersch, D. (1992). Transcending the limits of traditional research: Towards an interpretative approach to development communication and education. *Studies in Continuing Education, 14*, 42–55.

Wildemeersch, D., & Jansen, T. (Eds.). (1992). *Adult education, experiential learning and social change: The postmodern challenge*. Belgium: VUGA Gravenhage.

Williams, B.M. (1978). *Structures and attitudes in New Zealand adult education, 1945–75*. Wellington, NZ: New Zealand Council for Educational Research.

Williams, R. (1988). *Keywords: A vocabulary of culture and society.* London: Fontana.

Williams, R. (1989). *The politics of modernism: Against the new conformists.* London: Verso.

Windschuttle, K. (1997). The ethnic myths of cultural relativism. *Australian Journal of Education, 41*(1), 90–100.

Winsor, D.W. (1992). Talking the post-Fordist talk, but walking the post-industrial walk. *Journal of Organizational Change Management, 5*(2), 61–69.

Wittgenstein, L. (1963). *Philosophical investigations* (G.E.M. Anscombe, Trans.). Oxford: Basil Blackwell.

Wolf, A. (1989). Can competence and knowledge mix? In J. Burke (Ed.), *Competency based education and training* (pp. 39–53). Lewes, East Sussex: Falmer.

Woodhall, M. (1977). Adult education and training: An estimate of the volume and costs. In Organisation for Economic Co-operation and Development, *Learning opportunities for adults. Vol. 4: Participation in adult education* (pp. 317–358). Paris: Organisation for Economic Co-operation and Development.

Woodhall, M. (1989a). Financing adult education. In C.J. Titmus (Ed.), *Lifelong education for adults: An international handbook* (pp. 486–490). Oxford: Pergamon.

Woodhall, M. (1989b). Financing adult education for employment. In C.J. Titmus (Ed.), *Lifelong education for adults: An international handbook* (pp. 490–496). Oxford: Pergamon.

Wolin, R. (1992). *The terms of cultural criticism: The Frankfurt school, existentialism, poststructuralism.* New York: Columbia University Press.

Yates, L. (1992). Postmodernism, feminism and cultural politics: Or, if master narratives have been discredited, what does Giroux think he is doing? *Discourse, 13*(1), 124–133.

Young, I.M. (1990). *Justice and the politics of difference.* Princeton, NJ: Princeton University Press.

Youngman, F. (1986). *Adult education and socialist pedagogy.* London: Croom Helm.

Zavarzadeh, M. (1991). *Theory, (post)modernity, opposition: An 'other' introduction to literary and cultural theory.* Washington, DC: Maisonneuve.

Zeichner, K.M. (1993). Action research: Personal renewal and social reconstruction. *Educational Action Research, 1,* 199–219.

Index

Studies in the Postmodern Theory of Education

General Editors
Joe L. Kincheloe & Shirley R. Steinberg

Counterpoints publishes the most compelling and imaginative books being written in education today. Grounded on the theoretical advances in criticalism, feminism and postmodernism in the last two decades of the twentieth century, Counterpoints engages the meaning of these innovations in various forms of educational expression. Committed to the proposition that theoretical literature should be accessible to a variety of audiences, the series insists that its authors avoid esoteric and jargonistic languages that transform educational scholarship into an elite discourse for the initiated. Scholarly work matters only to the degree it affects consciousness and practice at multiple sites. Counterpoints' editorial policy is based on these principles and the ability of scholars to break new ground, to open new conversations, to go where educators have never gone before.

For additional information about this series or for the submission of manuscripts, please contact:

Joe L. Kincheloe & Shirley R. Steinberg
637 West Foster Avenue
State College, PA 16801